DEFINING MOMENTS
THE VIETNAM WAR

DEFINING MOMENTS
THE VIETNAM WAR

Tom Pendergast

615 Griswold, Detroit MI 48226

Omnigraphics, Inc.

Kevin Hillstrom, *Series Editor*
Cherie D. Abbey, *Managing Editor*

Peter E. Ruffner, *Publisher*
Frederick G. Ruffner, Jr., *Chairman*
Matthew P. Barbour, *Senior Vice President*

Kay Gill, *Vice President – Directories*
Elizabeth Collins, *Research and Permissions Coordinator*
David P. Bianco, *Marketing Director*
Kevin Hayes, *Operations Manager*
Barry Puckett, *Librarian*

Cherry Stockdale, *Permissions Assistant*
Allison A. Beckett, Linda Strand, Mary Butler, *Research Staff*
Shirley Amore, Johnny Lawrence, Martha Johns, Kirk Kauffman, *Administrative Staff*

Library of Congress Cataloging-in-Publication Data

Pendergast, Tom.
 The Vietnam War / Tom Pendergast.
  p. cm. — (Defining moments)
  Summary: "Examines the Vietnam War and its lasting impact on the United States, Vietnam, and the world. Features include narrative overview, biographical profiles, primary source documents, detailed chronology, and annotated sources for further study" — Provided by publisher. Includes bibliographical references and index.
  ISBN 0-7808-0954-8 (hardcover : alk. paper) 1. Vietnam War, 1961-1975.
 I. Title.
  DS558.P45 2006
  959.704'3--dc22
                                                    2006036367

The information in this publication was compiled from the sources cited and from other sources considered reliable. Additional copyright information can be found on the photograph credits page of this book. While every possible effort has been made to ensure reliability, the publisher will not assume liability for damages caused by inaccuracies in the data, and makes no warranty, express or implied, on the accuracy of the information contained herein.

This book is printed on acid-free paper meeting the ANSI Z39.48 Standard. The infinity symbol that appears above indicates that the paper in this book meets that standard.

Printed in the United States

TABLE OF CONTENTS

Preface ix
How to Use This Book xiii

NARRATIVE OVERVIEW

Prologue 3

Chapter One: Vietnam's Long Road to War .5

Chapter Two: Early U.S. Involvement in Vietnam, 1954-1964 19

Chapter Three: Lyndon Johnson's War 33

Chapter Four: Tet: The Turning Point .49

Chapter Five: Vietnamization 59

Chapter Six: The Fall of Saigon 73

Chapter Seven: Patience over Power in Vietnam 85

Chapter Eight: The American Antiwar Movement 99

Chapter Nine: Legacy of the Vietnam War 113

BIOGRAPHIES

George Ball (1909-1994) 129
U.S. Undersecretary of State, 1961-1966

Ho Chi Minh (1890-1969) 133
*Communist Revolutionary and President of North Vietnam
(1945-1969)*

Lyndon B. Johnson (1908-1973) 138
President of the United States, 1963-1968

Henry Kissinger (1923-) 143
American National Security Advisor (1969-1975) and Secretary
of State (1973-1977)

Robert McNamara (1916-) 148
American Secretary of Defense, 1961-67

Ngo Dinh Diem (1901-1963) 154
South Vietnamese president and prime minister, 1954-1963

Richard M. Nixon (1913-1994) 159
President of the United States, 1969-1974

Vo Nguyen Giap (1911-) 165
North Vietnamese senior general (1946-1972) and minister of
national defense (1946-1982)

William C. Westmoreland (1914-2005) 170
U.S. Commander in Vietnam, 1964-1968

PRIMARY SOURCES

Declaration of Independence of the Democratic Republic of Vietnam 177

President Eisenhower Explains the "Domino Theory" 180

Program of the South Vietnam National Liberation Front 182

The 1964 Gulf of Tonkin Resolution 186

America's Policy of Sustained Reprisal in Vietnam 189

Lyndon Johnson Speaks of "Peace Without Conquest" 192

The SNCC Speaks Out on Vietnam 197

A North Vietnamese Soldier Recounts the 1968 Tet Offensive 200

Lyndon Johnson Reacts to Tet 202

American Soldiers Write Home from Vietnam .212

An American Witness to the My Lai Massacre .215

President Nixon Explains Vietnamization 219

The Paris Peace Accords 231

"Facing It": The Vietnam Veterans Memorial 236

Important People, Places, and Terms 239
Chronology 243
Sources for Further Study 253
Bibliography 255
Photos Credits 259
Index 261

PREFACE

Throughout the course of America's existence, its people, culture, and institutions have been periodically challenged—and in many cases transformed—by profound historical events. Some of these momentous events, such as women's suffrage, the civil rights movement, and U.S. involvement in World War II, invigorated the nation and strengthened American confidence and capabilities. Others, such as the McCarthy era, the Vietnam War, and Watergate, have prompted troubled assessments and heated debates about the country's core beliefs and character.

Some of these defining moments in American history were years or even decades in the making. The Harlem Renaissance and the New Deal, for example, unfurled over the span of several years, while the American labor movement and the Cold War evolved over the course of decades. Other defining moments, such as the Cuban missile crisis and the terrorist attacks of September 11, 2001, transpired over a matter of days or weeks.

But although significant differences exist among these events in terms of their duration and their place in the timeline of American history, all share the same basic characteristic: they transformed the United States' political, cultural, and social landscape for future generations of Americans.

Taking heed of this fundamental reality, American citizens, schools, and other institutions are increasingly emphasizing the importance of understanding our nation's history. Omnigraphics' new *Defining Moments* series was created for the express purpose of meeting this growing appetite for authoritative, useful historical resources. This new series, which focuses on the most pivotal events in U.S. history from the 20th century forward, will be of enduring value to anyone interested in learning more about America's past—and in understanding how those historical events continue to reverberate in the 21st century.

Each individual volume of *Defining Moments* provides a valuable resource for readers interested in learning about the most profound events in our nation's history. Each volume is organized into three distinct sections—Narrative Overview, Biographies, and Primary Sources.

- The **Narrative Overview** provides readers with a detailed, factual account of the origins and progression of the "defining moment" being examined. It also explores the event's lasting impact on America's political and cultural landscape.

- The **Biographies** section provides valuable biographical background on leading figures associated with the event in question. Each biography concludes with a list of sources for further information on the profiled individual.

- The **Primary Sources** section collects a wide variety of pertinent primary source materials from the era under discussion, including official documents, papers and resolutions, letters, oral histories, memoirs, editorials, and other important works.

Individually, each of these sections is a rich resource for users. Together, they comprise an authoritative, balanced, and absorbing examination of some of the most significant events in U.S. history.

Other notable features contained within each volume in the series include a glossary of important individuals, places, and terms; a detailed chronology featuring page references to relevant sections of the narrative; an annotated bibliography of sources for further study; an extensive general bibliography that reflects the wide range of historical sources consulted by the author; and a subject index.

Acknowledgements

This series was developed in consultation with a distinguished Advisory Board comprised of public librarians, school librarians, and educators. They evaluated the series as it developed, and their comments and suggestions were invaluable throughout the production process. Any errors in this and other volumes in the series are ours alone. Following is a list of board members who contributed to the *Defining Moments* series:

Gail Beaver, M.A., M.A.L.S.
Adjunct Lecturer, University of Michigan
Ann Arbor, MI

Melissa C. Bergin, L.M.S., NBCT
Library Media Specialist
Niskayuna High School
Niskayuna, NY

Rose Davenport, M.S.L.S., Ed.Specialist
Library Media Specialist
Pershing High School Library
Detroit, MI

Karen Imarisio, A.M.L.S.
Assistant Head of Adult Services
Bloomfield Twp. Public Library
Bloomfield Hills, MI

Nancy Larsen, M.L.S., M.S. Ed.
Library Media Specialist
Clarkston High School
Clarkston, MI

Marilyn Mast, M.I.L.S.
Kingswood Campus Librarian
Cranbrook Kingswood Upper School
Bloomfield Hills, MI

Rosemary Orlando, M.L.I.S.
Library Director
St. Clair Shores Public Library
St. Clair Shores, MI

Comments and Suggestions

We welcome your comments on *Defining Moments: The Vietnam War* and suggestions for other events in U.S. history that warrant treatment in the *Defining Moment* series. Correspondence should be addressed to:

Editor, *Defining Moments*
Omnigraphics, Inc.
615 Griswold
Detroit, MI 48226
E-mail: editorial@omnigraphics.com

HOW TO USE THIS BOOK

Defining Moments: The Vietnam War provides users with a detailed and authoritative overview of this pivotal event in U.S. history. The preparation and arrangement of this volume—and all other books in the *Defining Moments* series—reflect an emphasis on providing a thorough and objective account of events that shaped our nation, presented in an easy-to-use reference work.

Defining Moments: The Vietnam War is divided into three primary sections. The first of these sections, the **Narrative Overview**, provides a detailed, factual account of the Vietnam War. It explores the circumstances that led to the division of Vietnam into northern and southern halves, the political and military considerations that prompted deepening U.S. involvement in Vietnam, the war's deepening toll on soldiers on both sides of the conflict, the impact of the war on Vietnamese communities and landscapes, the American antiwar movement and its cataclysmic impact on U.S. politics and culture, and the events that finally brought the war to a close.

The second section, **Biographies**, provides valuable biographical background on leading figures associated with the Vietnam War, including U.S. presidents Lyndon B. Johnson and Richard Nixon, North Vietnamese leader Ho Chi Minh, U.S. Secretary of Defense Robert McNamara, South Vietnamese President Ngo Dinh Diem, and U.S. Secretary of State Henry Kissinger. Each biography concludes with a list of sources for further information on the profiled individual.

The third section, **Primary Sources**, collects essential and enlightening documents from the Vietnam era, including a 1960 manifesto issued by the newly formed National Liberation Front (the Viet Cong), text of the 1964 Tonkin Gulf Resolution, a 1966 position paper on the war from the Student Nonviolent Coordination Committee (SNCC), Richard Nixon's 1969 speech on "Vietnamization" of the war, and recollections of battlefield experiences from all sides in the conflict. Other primary sources featured in *Defining Moments: The Vietnam War* include excerpts from official documents, papers, letters, and other important works.

Other valuable features in *Defining Moments: The Vietnam War* include the following:

- Attribution and referencing of primary sources and other quoted material to help guide users to other valuable historical research resources.

- Glossary of Important People, Places, and Terms.

- Detailed Chronology of events with a *see reference* feature. Under this arrangement, events listed in the chronology include a reference to page numbers within the Narrative Overview wherein users can find additional information on the event in question.

- Photographs and maps.

- Sources for Further Study, an annotated list of noteworthy Vietnam-related works.

- Extensive bibliography of works consulted in the creation of this book, including books, periodicals, Internet sites, and videotape materials.

- A Subject Index.

NARRATIVE OVERVIEW

PROLOGUE

In the early morning hours of January 31, 1968, American civilians stationed in Saigon, the capital of South Vietnam, awoke to the terrifying sound of gunshots and explosions. These civilians—embassy officials, reporters, wives of officers, and many others—knew they were in a war-torn country, but Saigon had always been a refuge from the conflict. On that fateful morning, however, teams of Viet Cong commandos emerged from underground tunnels and camouflaged vehicles to launch dawn raids on strategic sites throughout the city. Their targets included the American embassy, the presidential palace, the headquarters of both the American and the South Vietnamese army, and the city's leading radio station.

Chaos quickly engulfed the city. Gunfights and explosions erupted in the streets as American and South Vietnamese forces scrambled to meet the threat. The most dramatic of these clashes took place inside the American embassy, where nineteen Viet Cong commandos engaged in a pitched battle with American soldiers before succumbing. Meanwhile, the crackling sound of gunfire issued forth from radios across Saigon as the city's main radio station broadcast live reports of the fighting.

The grim battle for Saigon was echoed all across South Vietnam on that January day—the first day of Tet, the traditional celebration of the Vietnamese New Year. Typically, soldiers laid down their arms during this holiday and returned home to celebrate with their families. But 1968 was not a typical year in Vietnam. For the previous three years, American soldiers had been streaming into the country to help South Vietnam defeat a guerilla army, the Viet Cong, that was armed and aided by Communist North Vietnam.

Tet had its beginnings in the fall of 1967, when Communist strategists planned a bold offensive designed to encourage the South Vietnamese people to rise up against their corrupt government and evict the "imperialistic"

Americans before they gained any more strength. When this sweeping offensive was finally launched by combined Viet Cong and North Vietnamese Army (NVA) troops, it hit 36 out of 44 provincial capitals in South Vietnam, as well as dozens of smaller towns, villages, and military bases.

Early in the offensive the Communists secured several significant victories: they captured the provincial capital of Hue, one of Vietnam's most historic cities, and seized control of many villages. Despite this early success, though, the tide of the fighting soon turned against the Communists. After the initial confusion, South Vietnamese troops fought surprisingly well and American force was applied effectively. Most importantly, South Vietnamese civilians showed no inclination to rise up in revolt and join the Viet Cong cause. Within three weeks, the Tet Offensive had been turned aside. The Communists were expelled not only from the capital of Saigon, but from all the territory they had captured. According to some estimates, the Communist forces suffered over 37,000 dead in the offensive, while only 3,000 American and South Vietnamese soldiers lost their lives.

Military historians have concluded that Tet was a decisive setback for the Communists and a triumph for the Americans and their South Vietnamese allies. But in other ways, Tet was a stunning blow to the United States and the South Vietnamese government. As images from Tet flickered on television sets back in the United States, the American public concluded that it had been deceived by repeated military and administration assurances of imminent victory.

Across the United States, newspaper editors and other opinion leaders turned against the war, joining the thousands of antiwar activists who had long condemned American actions and policies in Vietnam. Perhaps the most influential assessment of the Tet Offensive came from Walter Cronkite, a CBS television news anchorman who was among the most respected men in America. In late February, Cronkite announced on television that Tet proved that the war had essentially turned into a bloody stalemate. "To say that we killed all those people and they didn't kill so many of us misunderstands the whole Vietnam War," explained *Washington Post* reporter H. D. S. Greenway, who was stationed in Hue at the time of the offensive. "[Tet] was a victory for us only in the narrowest sense. It was always a political war. They weren't fighting so much for territory but to win a political war and to mount something as effective as the Tet Offensive showed that all the American ideas of progress were an illusion."

Chapter One

VIETNAM'S
LONG ROAD TO WAR

―◄◀▥ʃ▤►―

Revolution for Westerners is an abrupt reversal in the order of
society, a violent break in history. But the Vietnamese trad-
itionally did not see it that way at all. For them revolution was
a natural and necessary event within the historical cycle.

—Frances FitzGerald, *Fire in the Lake*

To Americans, the Vietnam War was a conflict that lasted more than two
decades, beginning with the first involvement of American military
advisors in the 1950s and ending with the fall of Saigon to North Vietnamese troops in 1975. The most intense period of U.S. involvement in the
war came between 1964 and 1973, when large numbers of American troops
were deployed in South Vietnam to defend that nation against the armies of
North Vietnam and the guerilla army of the Viet Cong.

For the Vietnamese people, however, the Vietnam War was the final
chapter in a protracted, century-long quest to reclaim their national identity.
For the Vietnamese, the Vietnam War did not start in 1964, when U.S. President Lyndon B. Johnson gained Congressional authorization to expand military actions against North Vietnam. It did not start in 1954, when the Geneva
Accords ended long-time French colonial rule over the country—but left the
country divided in two. Nor did it start in 1945, when Communist Viet Minh
forces issued a proclamation of Vietnamese independence patterned after
America's own Declaration of Independence.

For the Vietnamese, the conflict that evolved into the Vietnam War had its
roots in the late nineteenth century, when French colonizers first established
control over the country. The proud Vietnamese people resented being treated as

5

a colony of uncivilized people best suited for growing rice and extracting rubber for their French landlords. But during the first half of the twentieth century, they possessed neither the organization nor the financial means to rise up against the superior military force and economic resources of their French rulers.

Eventually, two powerful forces helped the Vietnamese develop the tools to resist French colonialism. One was nationalism, a desire on the part of a people under foreign control to achieve independence, direct their own affairs, and celebrate their own culture. The other was Communism, a political ideology based on state control over economic activity, natural resource use, and social development as a means of ensuring equal distribution of national resources across society. The forces of nationalism and Communism within Vietnam eventually fostered armed revolt against French rule on a massive scale. This in turn evolved into a long and bloody civil war that killed millions—including more than 58,000 U.S. soldiers who were sent into the conflict.

The Ancient Roots of Vietnamese Culture

The modern state of Vietnam runs along the eastern coast of mainland Southeast Asia, from the southern border of China to the Gulf of Thailand. Shaped roughly like the letter "S," the country is more than 1,000 miles long from north to south, but measures less than 100 miles from east to west along much of its length. It is bordered all along its eastern flank by the South China Sea. Vietnam's western border runs up against Laos and Cambodia. These three nations, along with Thailand, are the nations that comprise the region collectively known as Indochina.

Historians cite the Red River Delta, a region surrounding the present-day city of Hanoi, as the homeland of early ancestors of the modern Vietnamese people. These people gradually joined with scattered peoples located in the nearby mountains to create a modest agriculture-based kingdom called Au Lac. This kingdom was shattered around 208 B.C.E., when Chinese troops invaded the northern half of present-day Vietnam, naming it "Nam Viet," or "land of the southern Viets." The leader of this army, Chinese general Cao T'o (known as Trieu Da in Vietnamese) established an independent kingdom there. This kingdom was in turn conquered by Chinese emperor Wu-ti, who made Nam Viet a province of China in 111 B.C.E.

The Chinese ruled over Nam Viet for the next 8,000 years. During this time the ethnically distinct Vietnamese people slowly absorbed many elements of Chinese culture. The most important of these cultural traditions were the religion known as Confucianism and the hierarchical governmental system known as the mandarinate. Confucianism is an ethical and philosophical system based on the teachings of the Chinese philosopher Confucius (551-479 B.C.). It places great emphasis on social and moral order, reverence for elders and tradition, and worship of ancestors. The mandarinate was a system by which the Chinese maintained administrative control over its territories. Any individual could become a mandarin if he passed a set of examinations, though typically most mandarins came from the wealthier classes.

In 938 C.E., a Vietnamese army led by Ngo Quyen defeated Chinese forces in the decisive naval battle of Bach Dang. This victory ushered in a 1,000-year stretch of independence for the Vietnamese. For much of this time, however, they were threatened by their powerful Chinese neighbor to the north. In addition, they faced challenges from their neighbors in the mountainous regions of present-day Cambodia and Laos, as well as from the aggressive tribes that populated present-day southern Vietnam.

In 1471 the armies of Vietnam began what is known as the "March to the South," a sustained effort to capture the southern coastal regions all the way to the Mekong River delta on the South China Sea. Over the course of 250 years this drive to the south brought all of present-day Vietnam under unified control, but the rugged topography of the countryside ensured a fair amount of local independence. Vietnam's many rivers running to the sea provide rich conditions for the cultivation of rice—long the country's dominant product—but the mountainous ridges between these river valleys made travel difficult. Local villages, not national government, remained the focus of social order, and fiercely independent local authorities and populations sometimes rose up in revolt against the emperors who professed to control the nation.

Despite these challenges, several imperial dynasties controlled Vietnam over the years. The last such dynasty, begun in 1802 by the Emperor Gia Long, was the Nguyen dynasty. This dynasty gave the country the name we use today, Vietnam, but at the end of the nineteenth century it ceded control of the country to France.

France's Colonial Rule

The first Frenchman to arrive in Vietnam was a Jesuit priest named Alexander de Rhodes, who came to the country in 1627. Rhodes's goal was to convert the Vietnamese to Catholicism, and he was enormously successful. Thousands of Vietnamese embraced the Catholic faith in the years following the arrival of Rhodes and other French missionaries. This, in turn, made it easier for France to expand its trade presence in the region. France purchased huge volumes of rice, sold French manufactured goods, and made Vietnam the base for greater French trade throughout Asia.

As France expanded its presence in Vietnam, local rulers expressed alarm about the impact of the French on Vietnamese society. They resented the growing influence of Catholic teachings, which they saw as a threat to the stable Confucian social order. Vietnamese leaders also disapproved of French traders who were aggressive in seeking control over local trade-based economies. In 1858 France explicitly revealed its designs to build a trade empire in Southeast Asia when it sent a naval expedition to the coastal city of Danang and established a large military base there. The pretext for this growing military presence was protection of French missionaries, but exploitation of Vietnam's economic potential was the true motivation.

> *The first Frenchman to arrive in Vietnam was a Jesuit priest named Alexander de Rhodes, who came to the country in 1627. Rhodes's goal was to convert the Vietnamese to Catholicism, and he was enormously successful. Thousands of Vietnamese embraced the Catholic faith in the years following the arrival of Rhodes and other French missionaries.*

Over the course of the late nineteenth century, France gradually assumed complete control over Vietnam. They divided the nation into three administrative provinces: Tonkin, in the north; Annam, in central Vietnam; and Cochin China, in the south. By 1893 they added the mountainous regions of Cambodia and Laos, to the west of Vietnam, to an empire they called the French Indochinese Union, or French Indochina.

The nature of French rule was different depending on the province. In Annam and Tonkin, the French manipulated the existing bureaucracy of the Nguyen dynasty to advance their economic and political goals. In these regions the local leaders, or mandarins, worked with the French and were better able to sustain the distinct characteristics of Vietnamese culture. In Cochin China in the south, however, France sent colonial administrators to govern the region. These bureaucrats established Catholic churches, as well as schools, businesses, laws, and taxes that were distinctly "French" in character. As a result, the culture in Cochin

China—and in directly governed Cambodia and Laos—became a blend of traditional Vietnamese and French elements. These differences in French colonial rule later became important factors in the civil strife that pitted southerners against northerners for control of Vietnam.

The Rise against French Oppression

France's goal in Vietnam was simple: it wanted to extract raw materials (rice, rubber, and coal) that it could sell for a profit, using the Vietnamese population as a captive labor source. It was a model that had been used by the major European powers throughout the nineteenth century in Asia, Africa, and South America. "As was typical of European imperialists of this era," wrote George Donelson Moss in *Vietnam: An American Ordeal*, "the French ruled solely by force, or the imminent threat of force." French rulers, backed by military power, forced many thousands of Vietnamese to labor on rubber plantations. The terrible working conditions drove the death rate at these plantations to four times the national average. The greatest profits in Vietnam, however, came from rice production, so the French dramatically increased the amount of land under cultivation for rice. They imposed high taxes in order to drive peasants from their small plots of land, then forced these same peasants to work on the large rice plantations, which were owned by Frenchmen or by Vietnamese mandarins who had allied themselves with the French.

Many citizens of France and French administrators in colonial Vietnam described their presence in Vietnam as part of a grand *mission civilisatrice* (civilizing mission). They boasted that they were bringing to Vietnam all the benefits of modern culture and lifting the Vietnamese out of a state of barbarism. But in many cases this lofty claim was a cover for selfish and callous behavior. "Many of the French regarded the Vietnamese as an inferior, childlike race, ideally suited for a life of hard work for low wages," according to Moss.

The Vietnamese did not see themselves in these terms. They were proud of their ancient culture and their long history of independence. Moreover, they recognized that under French rule, traditional cornerstones of Vietnamese culture and life were eroding. But when the Vietnamese attempted to resist French rule, as they did periodically throughout the French occupation, they were crushed by the vastly superior firepower of the French armed forces.

Overall, French colonization had a devastating impact on the Vietnamese people. From the 1890s to the 1930s, every measure of national health and prosperity declined. Per capita income fell dramatically as tax rates rose. The national school system, once a source of pride, collapsed; it was replaced by a French-run system that served only 15 percent of the population. Not surprisingly, literacy rates among the Vietnamese population plummeted from 80 percent in pre-colonial days to around 20 percent by 1939.

On a more subtle level, colonialism eroded many of the traditional foundations of Vietnamese culture. It was difficult to maintain Confucian respect for elders and tradition under French rule, and the legitimacy of some local mandarins was cast into doubt when they chose to ally themselves with the French. People began to challenge those rulers who they perceived as puppets or pawns of the French. Moreover, as often happens under authoritarian rule, widespread opposition to the French lessened traditional Vietnamese identification with their village and family clan, and increased identification with Vietnamese people in general. Thus was born the powerful force of Vietnamese nationalism.

French colonization had a devastating impact on the Vietnamese people. From the 1890s to the 1930s, every measure of national health and prosperity declined. Per capita income fell dramatically as tax rates rose. Literacy rates among the Vietnamese population plummeted from 80 percent in pre-colonial days to around 20 percent by 1939.

First Nationalism, Then Communism

As early as the 1880s, anti-French Vietnamese began to organize resistance to colonial rule. These early revolts promoted the return to rule by the Nguyen dynasty, but many Vietnamese no longer trusted the emperors who had given their country away. Early rebellions were weak and primarily local, and they were easily crushed by the French military. French authorities were often aided in this regard by Vietnamese Catholics who identified with the French and acquired wealth and social standing under the colonial system.

After 1900, however, a generation of Vietnamese who had come of age under French rule became better organized. Phan Boi Chau (1867-1940), a well-educated scholar, called for independence from France and the creation of a national constitution. Recognizing the need for widespread support, he spoke to people in larger villages and cities throughout Vietnam and organized mass demonstrations against French rule in 1908. In the years that followed, Chau formed a number of anti-colonialist groups, including the Vietnamese Restoration

10

League in 1912. Chau's resistance tactics against French rule included several bombings, but his influence declined after he was imprisoned in China in 1914 for his attempts to gain support and weapons there. Chau later returned to Vietnam, but in 1925 he was seized by French authorities and placed under house arrest in Hue; he remained there until his death in 1940.

Chau's example encouraged the formation of other nationalist groups. In the 1920s the most successful organization was the Vietnam Quoc Dan Dang (VNQDD, or Vietnamese Nationalist Party). For nearly ten years this group promoted its calls for independence within villages across Vietnam, but the group was destroyed after it mounted a failed military uprising in 1930.

By 1920 Vietnamese nationalist Ho Chi Minh (shown here in France) had become an ardent follower of Communist political ideals.

Watching all these activities from afar was Nguyen Ai Quoc, who later adopted the name Ho Chi Minh (see Ho Chi Minh biography, p. 133). Ho had been a committed nationalist when he left his homeland in 1911. He then traveled around the world for over twenty years. During this time he became convinced that the best tool for achieving Vietnamese independence was the revolutionary ideology known as Communism. Communism promised a nation where the rights of the common workers were protected and where the economic benefits produced by collective effort were shared. To a nation of peasants impoverished by ruthless landowners and foreign capitalists, it was a very attractive ideology.

In the hands of Ho Chi Minh and others, Communism became an effective tool for mobilizing popular opposition to colonial rule. Even before he returned to Vietnam in 1941, Ho helped to organize Vietnamese resistance to the French. He was a founding member of the Indochinese Communist Party (ICP), the first Communist organization in the region, and he actively supported the formation of Communist party cells within Vietnam even while he lived in China and Russia.

The ICP grew in power and influence through the 1930s, attracting harsh reprisals from French colonial authorities. The French convicted Ho of treason in absentia and placed a death sentence on his head—a move that further burnished his growing reputation in Vietnam. French forces also killed thousands of the most militant Vietnamese Communists, and authorities filled Vietnamese prisons with those suspected of supporting the ICP. By the late 1930s, being labeled a Communist in Vietnam was a possible death sentence.

Rise of the Viet Minh

In 1939 France was drawn into World War II. By 1940 German troops occupied most of France. Faced with this turmoil at home, the French grip on power in Vietnam slipped greatly. Japan—which had joined with Germany and Italy against France, the United States, the Soviet Union, and the other Allied powers—moved decisively to advance its interests in Asia. It forced the French administrators in Vietnam and greater Indochina to turn over naval facilities and other resources to the Japanese military. Japan also diverted profits from Vietnamese business operations to Tokyo and other Japanese centers of commerce. By the end of 1941, Japan had assumed a dominant position in Vietnam's affairs.

To Ho and his fellow Vietnamese nationalists and Communists, the unsettled state of affairs in Vietnam presented a great opportunity. Recognizing that not all Vietnamese nationalists were ready to embrace Communism, Ho and others—including Vo Nguyen Giap (see Giap biography, p. 165) and Pham Van Dong—formed a broad-based nationalist organization called Vietnam Doc Lap Dong Minh Hoi (the League for the Independence of Vietnam), better known as the Viet Minh. Emphasizing nationalist themes, the Viet Minh invited people of all social classes to join together to fight for Vietnamese independence.

The Viet Minh were not the only Vietnamese resistance group to take advantage of the tumult of World War II. Two religious sects in the South, the Cao Dai and the Hoa Hao, also sought to build support for Vietnamese independence. But the Viet Minh were the most successful of these nationalist organizations. Returning to Vietnam for the first time in thirty years, Ho proved adept at rallying the Vietnamese people to the Viet Minh cause. "The hour has struck," he declared. "Raise aloft the banner of insurrection and lead the people throughout the country to overthrow the Japanese and the French."

By 1944 the Viet Minh had formed their own army under the command of Vo Nguyen Giap and gained partial control of several provinces in northern Vietnam. At this time the group allied itself with the United States, which wanted to challenge Japanese domination in Asia. Operating through the Office of Strategic Services (OSS), a precursor to the Central Intelligence Agency (CIA), the United States provided the Viet Minh with military training, intelligence, and weapons. By 1945 the United States was bombing Japanese targets in Vietnam as part of its efforts to support the Viet Minh.

The year 1945 brought Vietnam to the brink of independence. In the spring the Japanese turned against the French, seizing full control of the country. The U.S.-backed Viet Minh responded with a new wave of attacks on Japanese forces and facilities. When harsh Japanese policies led to mass starvation in Vietnam during the summer of 1945, popular support for the Viet Minh surged.

In August 1945 Japan withdrew from Vietnam after the United States dropped atomic bombs on the Japanese cities of Hiroshima and Nagasaki. The Japanese government surrendered to Allied forces a few days later. After the Japanese exodus, the Viet Minh seized control of many governmental institutions throughout the country.

On August 29, 1945, the Viet Minh declared the creation of the Democratic Republic of Vietnam (DRV). Four days later, on September 2, Ho Chi Minh addressed half a million Vietnamese in the northern city of Hanoi. He read to them from his country's new Declaration of Independence, which borrowed words directly from the American Declaration of Independence. These events seemed to be the culmination of an eighty-year effort to reclaim Vietnamese independence. But the end of World War II brought the reappearance of an old foe on the horizon.

The Return of the French

In the immediate aftermath of Japan's withdrawal from Vietnam, the United States had signaled tentative support for an independent Vietnam. But that support collapsed when its longtime ally France—desperate to reclaim its dignity and economic standing after the bruising war—announced its intention to reclaim its colonies in Southeast Asia. In northern Vietnam, this declaration had little immediate impact. Ho Chi Minh and the Viet Minh fought off a Chinese attempt to seize power and tightened their grip on power in January

1946 elections, in part because they continued to downplay their Communist ideology in favor of nationalist appeals that resonated with most Vietnamese.

But French troops returned to southern Vietnam in September 1945. Saigon was returned to French hands on September 23 by British administrators who had directed affairs in the region since the end of the war. Over the next few months, the Viet Minh government and the French engaged in negotiations to hammer out a compromise political settlement. Talks broke down, however, and both sides consolidated their military positions. The French regained control over all of the major cities in the southern region they called Cochin China, as well as some northern urban areas. In the Vietnamese countryside, however, the Viet Minh remained in charge.

In December 1946 the escalating tension finally erupted as Viet Minh units attacked French installations in several northern cities. The French recognized that they had become engaged in an all-out war to reclaim "their" Vietnam. Unlike the pre-World War II era, the French now faced a well-organized (though lightly armed) enemy. The Viet Minh were able to field an army of 60,000 troops. They faced a powerful French army of 150,000 troops armed with much greater weaponry. What the Viet Minh lacked in numbers and firepower, however, they made up for in military intelligence. They received vital support from villagers across Vietnam who were willing to report on enemy positions and movements, ferry supplies to soldiers in the field, or pick up a weapon when it became available. This support enabled Giap, who led the Viet Minh military, to avoid large military clashes and wage an effective campaign of guerilla warfare against the French.

Over the course of 1947 and 1948, the war between the Viet Minh and the French ground on inconclusively. In 1949, though, events shifted to favor the Viet Minh. France attempted to boost popular support among the Vietnamese public by declaring that Vietnam, Laos, and Cambodia were independent, "associated" states in the French Union. They also installed a descendant of the Nguyen dynasty named Bao Dai as the head of the French-controlled State of Vietnam. But most Vietnamese saw through the ruse. Noting that the French continued to dominate political and economic affairs, they dismissed Bao Dai as a puppet of the French.

Moreover, the Viet Minh army grew dramatically more powerful during this time. Communists in China had been gaining in strength, and they supplied the Viet Minh with significant amounts of weapons and training. When

14

the Communists seized power in China in 1949, the Viet Minh suddenly had a powerful ally on the northern border of Vietnam. The only downside of this development was that the Vietn Minh were now forced to openly acknowledge their Communist ties.

By the end of 1949 the struggle for Vietnam was increasingly seen by the West as a battle between "free" Vietnam, backed by France, and the Communist Viet Minh, backed by China. It was this characterization that first drew the attention of the United States, for Americans saw Communism as a potentially deadly threat to their own economic and political future. The United States had no interest in direct intervention in Vietnam at this time, but it was happy to supply France with military assistance. Thus, in 1950, the United States sent $10 million to support French efforts against the Viet Minh. This aid package marked the beginning of a quarter-century of deepening U.S. involvement in Vietnam.

Ho Chi Minh at work at a Viet Minh military base in 1950, at the height of the French-Viet Minh war for control of Vietnam.

The Siege of Dien Bien Phu

From 1950 through 1954, French and Viet Minh forces fought a series of pitched battles across North Vietnam. Increasingly, Viet Minh forces proved capable of matching up to the enemy in open battle. As a result, French casualties mounted along with the costs of waging war. The French tried to train a Vietnamese army from the southern provinces that it controlled, but the soldiers in that army had little incentive to fight and proved largely ineffective in battle. Though the French continued to hold major cities throughout the country, the Viet Minh dominated the northern countryside and held significant positions throughout the rural south.

Alarmed by the erosion in its position in Vietnam, the French government assigned General Henri Navarre the job of winning the war in April

A Viet Minh solder waves a flag at Dien Bien Phu, where French forces lost a decisive battle in 1954.

1953. Navarre's plan was to mass French forces in the northwestern village of Dien Bien Phu. From that position he hoped to launch airstrikes against Viet Minh positions and draw the Viet Minh army into a climactic battle that would swing the tide of war to France.

In the meantime, Viet Minh General Vo Nguyen Giap hatched his own plan for military victory. For weeks, Giap prepared Viet Minh forces for a decisive battle at Dien Bien Phu. Thousands of civilians ferried weapons through a network of jungle trails, avoiding French detection. Carrying parts of giant artillery guns piece by piece, the Viet Minh and their civilian supporters massed firepower around the French and allied troops gathered at Dien Bien Phu. By early March 1954, Giap had brought 50,000 soldiers and a similar number of support forces into battle position to face a French garrison that held about 15,000 soldiers.

On March 13, 1954, the battle of Dien Bien Phu began. In a matter of days the base's airfields had been destroyed, cutting the French and allied

Vietnamese forces off from resupply flights. Over the course of seven weeks of intense fighting, the Viet Minh slowly drew a strangling noose around the French units. Though they lost soldiers at an astounding rate, Viet Minh soldiers and civilians dug a network of tunnels under the French positions which they used to carry out surprise attacks. On May 7 a Viet Minh unit made its way into the heart of the French garrison before it was cut down. One day later, the French surrendered. Leaving thousands of French and Vietnamese soldiers on the battlefield in unmarked graves, the Viet Minh then marched nearly 10,000 prisoners to camps hundreds of miles away. Many perished along the way.

At the beginning of their war with the French, Ho Chi Minh had famously proclaimed to the French: "You can kill ten of our men for every one we kill of yours. But even at those odds, you will lose and we will win." Dien Bien Phu seemed to prove Ho's boast, for while the Viet Minh had lost far more men than the French in the siege—as many as 25,000—they had won the battle. This victory did not bring independence, but news of the debacle at Dien Bien Phu shattered already fading French hopes that France and its Vietnamese allies were on the path to victory. With their dreams of restored colonial glory dashed to pieces, the French began looking for a way out of the deepening quagmire in Vietnam.

Chapter Two

EARLY U.S. INVOLVEMENT IN VIETNAM, 1954-1964

What I am concerned about is that Americans will get impatient and say, because they don't like events in Southeast Asia or they don't like the government in Saigon, that we should withdraw. That only makes it easy for the Communists. I think we should stay. We should use our influence in as effective a way as we can, but we should not withdraw.

—President John F. Kennedy, 1963

In the early summer of 1954, delegates from nine interested parties—the Democratic Republic of Vietnam (DRV), the State of Vietnam, Laos, Cambodia, France, China, Russia, Britain, and the United States—gathered in the Swiss city of Geneva. Their goal was to negotiate an end to the war which pitted the Democratic Republic of Vietnam (or the Viet Minh) against France and the French-controlled State of Vietnam. The presence of the world's major superpowers at these negotiations was proof that the eight-year civil war in Vietnam had become a focus of intense international interest.

The United States and Communist China had recently clashed in the Korean War, which ended in the summer of 1953 with Korea divided in two. Both nations were eager to avoid a replay of that costly conflict in Vietnam, but they also recognized that the political stakes in Vietnam were high. China was eager to establish a friendly Communist government in neighboring Vietnam, but the United States was determined to stop the spread of Communism in Southeast Asia. As a result, representatives of both countries became deeply involved in the Geneva negotiations.

The other two major players in Geneva were France and the Viet Minh. Battered and demoralized by the inconclusive struggle in Vietnam (and the

19

still-fresh memories of its occupation by the Nazis during World War II), France wanted to leave the region altogether. It had maintained colonies in Indochina (Vietnam, Cambodia, and Laos) since the middle of the nineteenth century, but its fight against the Viet Minh army had cost millions of French francs, thousands of lives, and political upheaval at home. The Viet Minh and its brilliant revolutionary leader Ho Chi Minh, meanwhile, wanted nothing less than complete Vietnamese independence.

Amidst this swirl of competing interests, negotiators worked for weeks to hammer out a compromise agreement. The final result was the 1954 Geneva Accords, which called for a cease fire and the temporary partition of Vietnam into northern and southern halves along the 17th Parallel. Under this plan, the Viet Minh-controlled Democratic Republic of Vietnam (DRV) received the northern half of the country, the French-backed regime of Emperor Bao Dai was granted control over southern Vietnam, and the French military agreed to a timetable for complete withdrawal from the region.

According to the complicated language of the accords, both Vietnamese sides were to withdraw their military forces into their respective territories. During this same period, any civilians who wished to relocate could do so. Preparations would then begin for national elections to be held in 1956; these elections would reunify the country under a democratically elected government. The plan pleased almost no one, however, and the only parties that signed the accord were France and North Vietnam. "In the end, the Geneva Conference produced no durable solution to the Indochina conflict, only a military truce that awaited a political settlement, which never really happened," wrote military historian Stanley Karnow in *Vietnam: A History.* "So the conference was merely an interlude between two wars—or, rather, a lull in the same war."

For the Viet Minh it certainly was a lull in the same war. Their goal of achieving an independent, unified Vietnam remained unchanged. Meanwhile, supporters of an independent, non-Communist Vietnam were heartened by the United States' clear willingness to fill the vacuum of power left by the withdrawal of the French. As the French departed, the United States positioned itself as the new protector of "free" South Vietnam ("free" was the term the United States used in contrast to the "tyranny" of Communism). Yet the "free" South Vietnam that the United States came to support was itself deeply troubled. These flaws would become all too evident to the United States over the course of the next decade.

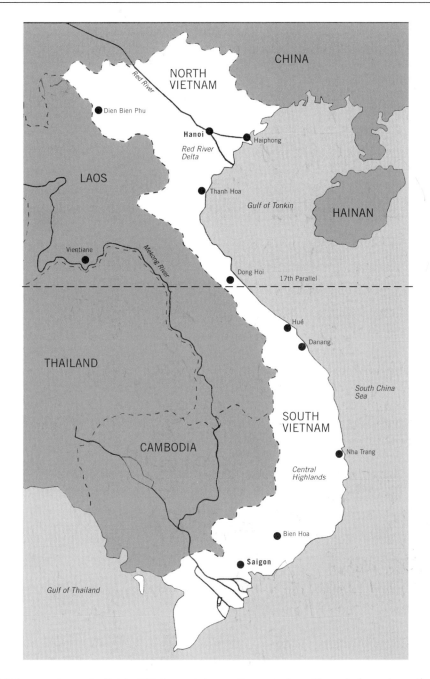

The 1954 Geneva Accords divided Vietnam into northern and southern halves along the 17th parallel.

Political Maneuvering in the North

In the aftermath of the Geneva Accords, military forces, people, and governments in the newly partitioned Vietnam all went through a tumultuous process of regrouping. The Accords called for a "cooling off" period, followed by a planning process leading up to the national elections that would re-unify Vietnam under a single government.

In the north, Ho Chi Minh and his Communist Party, the Lao Dong, fully expected to emerge victorious in the upcoming elections. After all, Ho's leading role in ending French colonial rule had made him a very popular figure across much of Vietnam, including significant swaths of the southern countryside. But the Communists wanted to ensure their success with an overwhelming victory in the North. With this in mind, they focused on placing trained party members at every level of governance, from small villages to provincial capitals to the capital city of Hanoi. These faithful party loyalists worked diligently to carry out the orders issued by the central commanders, or Politburo, of the Lao Dong.

"In the end, the Geneva Conference produced no durable solution to the Indochina conflict, only a military truce that awaited a political settlement, which never really happened," wrote military historian Stanley Karnow. "So the conference was merely an interlude between two wars—or, rather, a lull in the same war."

From 1954 through the end of the decade, the Communist Party relentlessly pushed to reshape the economy of the north along socialist lines. Land redistribution schemes and agricultural collectivization campaigns sparked spasms of unrest among some Vietnamese, but these were brutally suppressed by the Communist leadership. By the late 1950s the Communist grip on power in the north was totally secure. And although the task of governing was complicated by the difficulty of repairing roads, schools, rail lines, and other vital facilities destroyed during the war with the French—a conflict that had been fought mostly in the north—the region benefited from clear and identifiable political leadership and a lofty goal of reunification.

An Unlikely Ally in the South

In the South, however, establishing a stable government proved immensely difficult. One of the greatest problems faced by South Vietnam after the signing of the 1954 Accords was the immense movement of refugees flowing south away from Communist rule. Some 800,000 people crossed the 17th Parallel seeking refuge. Some of these people fled because they had ties to anti-Communist organizations and feared punishment from the Viet Minh government. Others were business owners or landholders who feared that their property would be lost under Communist rule. The majority, however, were Catholics frightened by anti-Communist propaganda that warned of mass executions and labor camps for those who did not join the Party. Catholics sought and received some of the most coveted positions within the Southern government thanks to their strong anti-Communism.

The nominal leader of the government of the State of Vietnam at the time of the accords was Emperor Bao Dai. Though his ties to the imperial dynasties of the former independent Vietnam gave him some historical legitimacy, he was little more than a figurehead from 1949, when the French restored him as emperor, until 1954, when Bao Dai appointed Ngo Dinh Diem (see Diem biography, p. 154) to be his prime minister.

A devout Catholic and an avowed anti-Communist, Diem seemed a good choice because he had a reputation as a longtime foe of French colonial rule. Despite long years of exile, Diem had maintained his ties to the Vietnamese power structure, and he was seen by wealthy landowners, military chiefs, and Catholics as an ideal leader. Their confidence in Diem was further strengthened when he declared that his top priority was to create a government capable of standing up to Ho and his Communist machine.

Diem's path to power was complicated, however, by several other powerful factions in South Vietnam. In the capital city of Saigon, a powerful criminal organization called the Binh Xuyen operated unchecked. It had infiltrated local governments and built a private army that numbered about 25,000. In the countryside, two religious movements—the Cao Dai and the Hoa Hao—fielded their own armed militias. The Cao Dai's private army numbered about 25,000 men, while the Hoa Hao claimed 15,000 soldiers.

All these groups rejected Diem's claims to power. But Diem controlled the national army and he was backed by the United States. Using these assets, Diem moved quickly to consolidate his power. First, he called on loyal generals within the army to attack and defeat the armed opposition. Several thousand Vietnamese, including some innocent civilians, were slain in the ensuing violence, but by mid-1955 Diem had pummeled the Cao Dai and the Hoa Hao into submission. He then called for a public referendum on whether he

The Domino Theory

In the wake of World War II, the United States emerged as the global champion of democracy and free markets—and the sworn enemy of Communism. Immediately following the war, U.S. strategists saw the Communist Soviet Union enhance its power by placing the countries of Eastern Europe behind an "iron curtain" of Communist control. Fears of further Communist expansionism led President Harry S. Truman to announce the so-called "Truman Doctrine" in 1947. This vow to meet any Communist challenge with American force was first applied by Truman to Greece and Turkey, but it eventually became a cornerstone of U.S. foreign policy around the world.

It was President Dwight D. Eisenhower who first articulated the policy that guided U.S. actions in Southeast Asia before and during the Vietnam War. In an April 7, 1954, press conference, Eisenhower was asked to comment on the economic and strategic importance of Indochina, which was then under French control. Eisenhower suggested that America consider the "broader considerations that might follow what you would call the 'falling domino' principle. You have a row of dominoes set up, you knock over the first one, and what will happen to the last one is the certainty that it will go over very quickly. So you could have a beginning of a disintegration that would have the most profound influences." Acknowledging that China had already "fallen" to Communism, Eisenhower explained the costs associated with losing additional countries, and concluded that "the possible consequences of the loss are just incalculable to the free world."

"The domino theory" was decisive in shaping future American actions in Southeast Asia. As a tool for explaining American actions to its own citizens, the domino allegory was effective because it was so easy to understand. The theory was used not only to explain the U.S. desire to prevent South Vietnam from falling to Communism, but was also used by later presidents to justify their policies. President Ronald Reagan, for example, used the domino theory to justify American interventionist policies in Latin America in the 1980s.

U.S. President Dwight Eisenhower greets South Vietnam's President Ngo Dinh Diem in 1957, as U.S. Secretary of State John Foster Dulles (to Eisenhower's left) looks on.

or Bao Dai should be head of state. On October 23, 1955, in a rigged election, Diem won 95 percent of the vote (Bao Dai had gone to live in France and did not even campaign). Three days later, President Diem formally renamed the country the Republic of Vietnam (RVN).

American officials in the administration of President Dwight D. Eisenhower recognized that Diem had limited popular support within Vietnam. But they also judged him to be the man most capable of supporting American interests. They decided, as one reporter later remarked, that the U.S. would "sink or swim with Ngo Dinh Diem." Based on this conviction, the United States directed its Military Assistance Advisory Group (MAAG), which had been formed in

1950 to aid the French, to provide training to the Army of the Republic of Vietnam (ARVN). The U.S. embassy in Saigon also became one of the largest American embassies in the world, and large numbers of Central Intelligence Agency (CIA) operatives were assigned to South Vietnam to advise the Diem government on intelligence operations and strategy. Finally, between 1954 and 1960, the U.S. sent more than $1 billion in financial aid to Vietnam. Much of this assistance was funneled through a program called the Commodity Import Program. This program delivered American consumer goods to a small but politically important group of upper-middle-class merchants who supported Diem.

The Civil War Resumes

Armed with this U.S. support, Diem was able to neutralize political and military challengers within South Vietnam. But both he and his American allies realized that if the 1956 reunification elections mandated by the 1954 Geneva Accords were held, victory would belong to Ho Chi Minh and the Communists. With this in mind, Diem and the Americans refused to make arrangements for reunification elections. Instead, they took steps to firmly establish South Vietnam as a legitimate nation in its own right. This development naturally infuriated Ho Chi Minh and the North Vietnamese government, as well as their Communist allies in the South.

During Diem's first months in office, American analysts remained cautiously optimistic about him. They took note of his apparent progress in eliminating opposition to his rule in the larger villages and cities of South Vietnam, and in 1957 President Eisenhower personally told Diem that "You have brought to your great task of organizing your country the greatest of courage, the greatest of statesmanship."

As time passed, though, Diem's government refused to introduce political or economic reforms that American strategists viewed as essential to building popular support for his regime. Instead, Diem abolished or ignored local governing councils across South Vietnam, keeping all important decision-making power to himself and his inner circle. In a drive to remove any remaining Communists within South Vietnam, Diem's brother, Ngo Dinh Nhu, formed the Can Lao, an armed political machine that served to impose Diem's will. The Can Lao killed or imprisoned anyone suspected of opposing Diem's regime, including local village leaders. The regime then replaced these leaders, most of whom were Buddhist like the people they represented, with Catholics or functionaries

A U.S. military advisor (standing) trains South Vietnamese soldiers in ambush techniques.

loyal to Diem. These heavy-handed tactics further stoked the flames of resentment in peasant villages, where distrust of Diem was already high.

By the late 1950s, armed resistance to Diem's regime had spread across the countryside of South Vietnam. Viet Minh guerillas within South Vietnam attacked or intimidated representatives of Diem's government in village outposts. "By 1960," wrote U.S. diplomat Henry Kissinger in *Ending the Vietnam War*, "some 2,500 South Vietnamese officials were being assassinated every year." Can Lao and ARVN troops crushed the opposition in some villages, only to see the insurgency spring up in other areas. These developments forced the United States to acknowledge that South Vietnam was teetering on the brink of outright civil war.

27

The Emergence of the Viet Cong

After the signing of the Geneva Accords of 1954, the North Vietnamese had focused their attentions on rebuilding their country and training an army. Ho Chi Minh recognized that fighting a direct war against South Vietnam in the late 1950s would be suicidal, given the political and military support that Diem was receiving from the United States. But that did not mean that the Communists could not lend their support to the growing insurgency within South Vietnam in other ways.

Prior to 1960, Communist support for the insurgency in the South was mostly limited to small numbers of Viet Minh agents. These agents entered the South by crossing the Demilitarized Zone (DMZ), a five-mile buffer zone between the two countries, or via an informal trail system that stretched down through the mountains of neighboring Cambodia (this trail system later came to be known as the Ho Chi Minh Trail). These agents served as recruiters for the Communist cause and organizers of anti-Diem activities. But as the insurgency grew in strength, North Vietnam decided to increase its support of the war in the South. At a Communist Party meeting in 1960, the Lao Dong formally declared its intention to liberate South Vietnam from the Diem government and reunify the country.

Taking their lead from the Lao Dong, revolutionaries within the South formed two new organizations. The first, formed in December 1960, was the Mat Tran Dan Toc Giai Phong Mien Nam, or National Liberation Front (NLF), a political group whose stated goal was to drive Diem from power. Two months later, the NLF formed the People's Liberation Armed Force (PLAF), a military force. The NLF was not an openly Communist organization; in fact it portrayed itself as a champion of Vietnamese nationalism and welcomed members who were not Communists. From the beginning, however, the NLF took much of its direction from the North Vietnamese Communists, and many of the generals who led the PLAF came directly from North Vietnam.

Diem and his American advisors recognized the extent of Communist influence in the group and called them the Viet Cong (VC), for Vietnamese Communists. This term became the all-purpose name used by both the South Vietnamese and their American allies to refer to members of both the NLF and the PLAF. In fact, the Viet Cong constituted a 1960s version of the Viet Minh, the Vietnamese guerrillas who had fought against the French back in the 1940s and 1950s.

The Debate Over Diem

During the early 1960s, President Ngo Dinh Diem's leadership of South Vietnam became a subject of intensifying debate in the United States. Some analysts believed that he remained the South Vietnamese leader best equipped to help America keep the Communists at bay. Others had become convinced that the Diem regime was so riddled by corruption and anti-democratic beliefs that it could not be salvaged. Determined to get a fresh perspective on the situation in Saigon, U.S. President John F. Kennedy sent two trusted officials to South Vietnam on a fact-finding mission in September 1963. These representatives were General Victor Krulak of the U.S. Marine Corps and Joseph Mendenhall, who was a Foreign Service Officer (FSO) with the State Department.

According to Kennedy advisor Arthur M. Schlesinger, Jr., the report that Krulak and Mendenhall delivered upon their return symbolized the confusion and uncertainty that surrounded early American efforts in Vietnam. Writing in his memoir *A Thousand Days,* Schlesinger noted that "after a frenzied weekend of inspection and interrogation [in Vietnam], the two men flew back to Washington. They reported immediately to the National Security Council. Krulak told the assembled dignitaries the war was going beautifully, that the regime was beloved by the people and that we need have no undue concern even about Nhu [Diem's brother Ngo Dinh Nhu, who directed the secret police]. Mendenhall told them that South Vietnam was in a desperate state, that the regime was on the edge of collapse and that Nhu had to go. The President listened politely and finally said, 'Were you two gentlemen in the same country?' And so the meetings on Vietnam continued."

Source: Schlesinger, Arthur M., Jr., *A Thousand Days: John F. Kennedy in the White House.* Boston: Houghton Mifflin, 1965.

During the early 1960s, the Viet Cong stepped up the intensity of their attacks across South Vietnam. Backed by popular support in rural villages, the Viet Cong were able to take control of territory in a number of areas to the north, west, and south of Saigon. Within the larger cities (especially Hue and Saigon), NLF members created spy networks that allowed them to track government actions and carry out political activities designed to further destabilize the Diem regime.

The administration of John F. Kennedy, who had been elected president of the United States in 1960, was deeply troubled by the growing Communist threat to South Vietnam. Some of his advisors even suggested that he send American combat troops to Vietnam. Kennedy had no intention of sending American soldiers to fight in a distant Southeast Asian nation that few Americans could find on a map. Yet he could not simply let the nation fall to Communism. This conviction led Kennedy to increase indirect support for Diem's government. By the end of 1962, Kennedy had ordered the creation of a new military assistance operation, called Military Assistance Command, Vietnam (MACV), and increased the number of U.S. military advisors in Vietnam to 9,000. He also increased military aid to the Diem government, including airplanes, helicopters, and armored vehicles. The United States was slowly becoming the backbone of South Vietnam's military, but the ARVN's corruption and morale problems handicapped American efforts to improve its overall performance. American diplomats, meanwhile, urged President Diem to forcefully address the army's problems and introduce democratic reforms that might reverse his plummeting popularity. But Diem and his inner circle continued to resent and ignore this advice.

The Fall of Diem

In 1963 two events proved pivotal in finally bringing down the Diem government. The first of these events took place on January 2, 1963, outside Ap Bac, a village located about forty-five miles southwest of Saigon. On this day, ARVN forces backed by American military advisors launched an attack on Viet Cong forces gathered in the village. But ARVN troops fought poorly as their generals hesitated to press the battle, and the Viet Cong shot down five U.S. helicopters. After the demoralizing defeat at Ap Bac, American military advisors lost all confidence in the existing command of the South Vietnamese army.

Initially, some American and South Vietnamese military officials tried to paint the disaster at Ap Bac as an actual victory. When U.S. journalists learned that these accounts were false, however, they became more skeptical of official accounts of the war. With Ap Bac, wrote Harry G. Summers Jr., in *Historical Atlas of the Vietnam War,* "the credibility gap that would plague the future prosecution of the Vietnam War had begun."

In 1963 the Diem regime was shaken to its core by a series of public ritual suicides carried out by Buddhist monks to protest persecution of Buddhists by the South Vietnamese government.

The second event that doomed Diem occurred on the political front, when he escalated a confrontation with the nation's majority Buddhist population. In the spring of 1963, Buddhists in the city of Hue requested permission to celebrate the birth of the Buddha, the founder of their religion, by flying traditional flags. The South Vietnamese government denied the request, even though Buddhists accounted for about 80 percent of the nation's total population. Then, on May 8, 1963, Diem's troops fired on unarmed Buddhist demonstrators, killing nine. Buddhists took to the streets by the thousands, demanding greater religious and political freedom. Again, Diem cracked down, jailing Buddhist leaders. But instead of silencing his opponents, the repressive tactics sparked a series of new protests against Diem and his corrupt regime.

On June 11, 1963, the unrest reached an explosive new level when an elderly Buddhist monk named Thich Quang Duc sat down in the middle of a busy street in Saigon, doused himself with gasoline, and burned himself to death to protest government repression. Photos of his fiery suicide appeared around the world, drawing attention to the growing resistance to Diem's regime. The Buddhist resistance swelled as several other monks immolated themselves in similar fashion. Buddhist leaders called for Diem to step down and for South Vietnam to reunify with the North. Diem's sister-in-law and top political advisor Madame Nhu made matters worse when she declared that she celebrated each Buddhist "barbecue."

The military failures of the ARVN and the so-called "Buddhist Crisis" ended any hope for the Diem government. Several generals within the ARVN began to plot for Diem's removal from power, and U.S. Ambassador Henry Cabot Lodge advised President Kennedy that perhaps the time had come to end U.S. support for his regime. On November 1, 1963, several generals organized a coup d'etat, capturing and then killing both Diem and his brother, Nhu. The United States had knowledge of the impending coup but did nothing to assist Diem.

Across South Vietnam, people celebrated Diem's demise and expressed hope that the new government might bring about a new era of stability and peace. Those who thought that Diem's removal might usher in a more prosperous and enlightened era were sadly disappointed, however. The generals who took charge of the government were more willing to accept U.S. advice (and money) intended to improve their military capability, but they proved just as inept as Diem at ruling their troubled country. In the months following Diem's fall, the leadership of South Vietnam changed hands several times. During these months, the single greatest stabilizing factor in South Vietnam was the army of U.S. military and political advisors who had been posted in Saigon and other areas of the country (the number of U.S. military advisors in South Vietnam rose from 700 to more than 16,000 during Kennedy's presidency).

In the meantime, the United States also endured a violent change in leadership. President John F. Kennedy was assassinated by a gunman on November 22, 1963, and his vice president, Lyndon B. Johnson, assumed command (see Johnson biography, p. 138). As vice president, Johnson had voiced concerns about growing U.S. involvement in Vietnam; as president, however, he was determined to keep Communism at bay in Vietnam and the rest of Asia. Johnson's belief in the so-called domino theory and his concerns about the political damage that he and his fellow Democrats would suffer if Vietnam was "lost" to Communism convinced him to pour even greater military and economic aid into South Vietnam in the opening months of his presidency.

Chapter Three

LYNDON JOHNSON'S WAR

As one diplomatic initiative after another fizzled, my frustration, disenchantment, and anguish deepened. I could see no good way to win—or end—an increasingly costly and destructive war.

—Robert S. McNamara, *In Retrospect*

After Lyndon B. Johnson took office in November 1963 following the assassination of U.S. President John F. Kennedy, his highest policy priority was to mount an offensive against discrimination and poverty in American society. His ultimate goal was to create a "Great Society" that would provide opportunity and security to every American. "Many Americans live on the outskirts of hope, some because of their poverty and some because of their color, and all too many because of both," he said in his 1964 State of the Union address. "Our task is to help replace their despair with unconditional war on poverty in America."

Many of Johnson's "Great Society" social programs were implemented during the mid-1960s, and several—such as the Civil Rights Act of 1964, the Voting Rights Act of 1965, the Clean Air Act of 1965, and the Medicare and Medicaid legislation of 1965—remain cornerstones of modern American life. Yet the war that defined Johnson's presidency was not his declared "war on poverty," but rather the bloody stalemate that evolved half a world away, in Vietnam.

Looking back on his time in office, Johnson recognized that his presidency was undone by the difficulties of fighting two wars: "I knew from the start that I was bound to be crucified either way I moved. If I left the woman I really loved—the Great Society—in order to get involved with that bitch of a war on the other side of the world, then I would lose everything at home.... But if I left that war and let the Communists take over South Vietnam, then I would be seen as a coward and my nation would be seen as an appeaser and we would both find it impossible to accomplish anything for anybody anywhere on the entire globe." Indeed, despite Johnson's stated desire to leave a legacy of global peace and domestic prosperity, his beliefs about the high stakes involved in Vietnam ultimately led to a deepening spiral of U.S. involvement in that conflict.

Turmoil in South Vietnam

In the political climate of the Cold War, the need to challenge the spread of Communism was virtually unquestioned by American politicians. Their position was widely supported by the American public, which saw Communism as a threat to their way of life and the "domino theory" as a legitimate worry in Southeast Asia, Africa, Latin America, and other regions where Communist movements existed. Lawmakers who dared to question this conventional wisdom ran the risk of being smeared as "Commie sympathizers" and driven out of politics. President Johnson, then, was widely praised in late 1963 when he declared that "I am not going to lose Vietnam. I am not going to be the president who saw Southeast Asia go the way China went."

The South Vietnam that Johnson had pledged to support was in deep trouble, however. Ngo Dinh Diem, its president of nearly eight years, had been assassinated in November 1963 in a coup that was tacitly supported by the United States. The Diem regime was replaced by a rapid succession of governments, some of which lasted only a few weeks before being overthrown. These regimes presided over a South Vietnamese military, the Army of the Republic of Vietnam (ARVN), that was struggling mightily against the Viet Cong insurgency. In fact, much of the countryside in South Vietnam had become Viet Cong territory in the space of a few years, at least during the hours between sunset and sunrise. In addition, a significant proportion of the South Vietnamese population—up to 80 percent according to some estimates—supported reunification with North Vietnam under Communist leader Ho Chi Minh.

A small number of U.S. advisors suggested that, given the chaos that existed within South Vietnam and the evidence that reunification was favored by the majority of Vietnamese, the United States could honorably withdraw and allow the Vietnamese to pursue political self-determination—another of

In 1964-65, President Lyndon B. Johnson (left) and Secretary of Defense Robert McNamara (right) became increasingly alarmed by the political instability afflicting South Vietnam.

America's professed ideals. But most officials did not see this as a realistic alternative, given the perceived importance of halting the spread of Communism in Southeast Asia.

The United States recognized that the Viet Cong had taken great advantage of South Vietnam's political instability in the early 1960s. If the United States was to save South Vietnam, it needed to nurture a strong anti-Communist government willing to accept U.S. guidance. Lawmakers thus joined Pentagon officials in calling for new economic and military aid packages for South Vietnam. Finally, some military advisors in the Pentagon called for aerial bombing of North Vietnam. They believed that a bombing campaign might convince the North to stop its support for the insurrection in the South.

Johnson was troubled by many of these recommendations. He and his closest advisors recognized that South Vietnam's prospects for survival were dim without massive levels of support from the United States. But the president also knew that vast new expenditures in Vietnam would endanger his anti-poverty domestic agenda. Moreover, Johnson was facing an election campaign in the fall of 1964, and he thought his election prospects would be jeopardized if voters thought that he was expanding the war through bombing operations against North Vietnam. But Johnson did approve an expansion of covert operations in Southeast Asia in early 1964. These operations included new aerial surveillance flights, raids on North Vietnamese military installations, and electronic surveillance by U.S. military ships stationed in the Gulf of Tonkin, off the coast of North Vietnam. These covert operations were not disclosed to the American people, who still knew little about the expanding conflict.

The Gulf of Tonkin Resolution

Through the mid-summer of 1964, the Viet Cong further strengthened their presence in the South. Then, in late July 1964, South Vietnamese forces attacked several Communist positions on islands off the coast of North Vietnam. When the American destroyer *Maddox* swept through the area on a surveillance patrol on August 2, North Vietnamese naval boats allegedly opened fire on the *Maddox,* causing minor damage. The *Maddox* retaliated with heavy guns, and planes from a nearby U.S. aircraft carrier, the *Ticonderoga,* offered support. Two nights later, the *Maddox* carried out another patrol in the Gulf of Tonkin, this time accompanied by another American destroyer, the *C. Turner Joy.* Both ships were authorized to approach within eleven miles of the North Vietnamese coastline—one mile inside the twelve-mile territorial zone claimed by the North Vietnamese. That night, both ships reported hostile attacks, citing radar and sonar evidence. The ships responded to these alleged attacks, firing shells into the stormy night skies. Jets from the *Ticonderoga* joined the fray and fired on radar targets.

No further evidence of an enemy presence was found, though, and the guns of the American forces eventually went silent. Military officials later conceded that the August 4 "attacks" may very well have been a phantom non-event triggered by an unfortunate combination of stormy weather and over-eager radar and sonar operators. In later years, after evidence mounted

that the North Vietnamese had probably not launched any attack on the
night of August 4, Johnson admitted
that "for all I know, our navy was
shooting at whales out there."

Nevertheless, when the initial
reports of an August 4 attack on the
U.S. Navy reached Washington, Johnson ordered air strikes against several
North Vietnamese bases and an oil
depot. Declaring that he had evidence
of "open aggression on the high seas"
against U.S. forces, Johnson also spoke
before Congress on August 5, 1964. The
President stated that "the United States
intends no rashness, and seeks no wider
war," but he told Congress that he
wanted authorization to increase U.S.
military involvement in Vietnam. Two
days later, he submitted to Congress a
bill that would authorize him to "take
all necessary measures to repel any
armed attack against the forces of the

In July 1964 alleged Communist attacks on the
USS *Maddox* (seen here) became the justification for passage of the Gulf of Tonkin
Resolution, which broadened U.S. military
involvement in Vietnam.

United States and to prevent further aggression" until such time that the "peace
and security of the area is reasonably assured." This bill—known as the Gulf of
Tonkin Resolution—passed by votes of 416-0 in the U.S. House of Representatives and 88-2 in the U.S. Senate. With the passage of this Resolution, the Johnson administration received the broad authority it wanted to wage war against
North Vietnam and the Viet Cong in whatever manner it desired.

The resolution, which publicly committed the United States to defending
South Vietnam, had immediate political benefits for the president in the 1964
presidential campaign. Combined with Johnson's tough anti-Communist
rhetoric, it helped the president counter the claims of his Republican opponent, Senator Barry Goldwater of Arizona, that he was soft on Communism.
But Johnson knew that most citizens were not interested in sending American
soldiers to fight in a nation they knew little about, and he told audiences on
the campaign trail that "we are not about to send American boys nine or ten

thousand miles away from home to do what Asian boys ought to be doing for themselves." Johnson cruised to victory in the November elections, then began planning for the next stage in America's engagement in Vietnam.

Operation Rolling Thunder

Johnson's critics have charged that he intentionally misled the American people when he claimed that he didn't want to send American boys to Vietnam. In fact, Johnson's fondest hope was that the *threat* of war with the United States would be enough to frighten North Vietnam into backing down from its aggression against South Vietnam. That hope was not realized. Taking advantage of continued political instability in Saigon, the Viet Cong launched a series of attacks on South Vietnamese positions in October 1964. On November 1 an attack on American facilities at an airfield in Bien Hoa killed four Americans and wounded 72 more. These and other attacks prompted the Johnson administration to consider how they might best use the broad war powers granted to them by Congress. The answer, after some debate, was an aerial bombing campaign called Rolling Thunder.

The Joint Chiefs had earlier recommended an intensive campaign of aerial bombing against strategic targets within North Vietnam. Johnson's advisors—especially Secretary of Defense Robert McNamara and National Security Advisor McGeorge Bundy—urged him to adopt such a policy in late 1964 and early 1965 (see McNamara biography, p. 148). Known for their cool, logical approach to solving problems, McNamara and Bundy argued that American bombing policy should reward or punish the Communists, depending on their behavior. If the Viet Cong attacked a village, Americans would bomb a train station; if the Viet Cong attacked a major air base, the Americans would blow up a factory. On the other hand, if Communist incursions eased or if North Vietnam signaled a willingness to come to the negotiating table, American bombing would be curtailed or suspended. Bundy later described this policy as one of "sustained reprisal."

Among Johnson's key advisors, only Undersecretary of State George Ball advised Johnson against an escalation of American military involvement in Vietnam (see Ball biography, p. 129). He was deeply opposed to calls for new bombing campaigns against North Vietnam. In addition, he expressed great concern about sending U.S. ground troops into Vietnam, as a growing number of lawmakers and government officials were urging. Instead, Ball called for America to withdraw from Vietnam before it became more deeply entangled in the conflict. He argued that if U.S. troops were ever sent to Vietnam, they would soon "bog down in the jungles and rice paddies—while we slowly blow the country to pieces." Though Johnson appreciated Ball's advice, he did not follow it.

On February 7, 1965, the Viet Cong attacked an American helicopter base housing U.S. military advisers in the village of Pleiku, killing eight Americans, wounding 137 others, and destroying many U.S. aircraft. American forces struck back, using bombing runs to destroy several army bases within North Vietnam. The Viet Cong next stormed a hotel housing American soldiers, killing 23 and wounding nearly that many. The Americans responded by bombing military sites deeper inside North Vietnam. On February 13 Johnson formally authorized Operation Rolling Thunder, a gradually escalating bombing campaign against targets throughout North Vietnam.

Operation Rolling Thunder lasted for three and a half years with only brief interruptions. It began on March 2, 1965, and lasted until October 31, 1968. Most of these missions were carried out by Air Force units based in Thailand and South Vietnam and pilots from Navy carriers roaming the South China Sea. During the first months of the operation, Rolling Thunder strikes were mostly limited to small military facilities in southern North Vietnam. Over time, however, the bombing area was expanded to sites along Cambodia's Ho Chi Minh trail, larger military bases and supply depots in the north, and finally to Hanoi itself. Air defenses around Hanoi and some other areas were extremely sophisticated, though, and hundreds of aviators involved in Operation Rolling Thunder were shot down and killed or taken prisoner during the course of the war.

Johnson and his inner circle were deeply involved in choosing the timing and targets of bombing operations. For instance, they insisted that American bombers avoid targets in the far north that might draw neighboring China into the conflict. In addition, they often avoided "high-value" targets such as oil refineries, airfields, and power plants, apparently in the hope that North Vietnam would end hostilities in order to save these valuable pieces of infrastructure from destruction.

American Ground Troops Arrive in Vietnam

But American hopes that Rolling Thunder would convince the North Vietnamese and the Viet Cong to suspend hostilities were soon dashed.

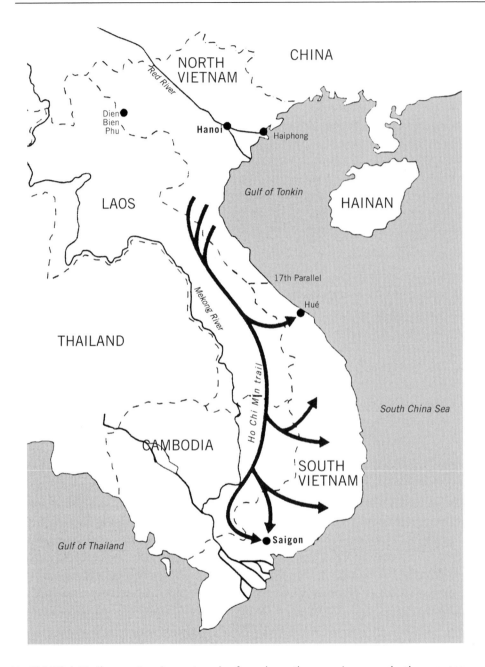

The Ho Chi Minh Trail, an extensive network of roads, pathways, rivers, and other routes running through Cambodia and Laos, was used by North Vietnam to support Viet Cong operations in South Vietnam.

Instead, the flow of supplies and soldiers from North Vietnam down through the Ho Chi Minh Trail and into the battle zones of South Vietnam continued. In fact, the North Vietnamese army (NVA) increased the number of troops it sent south to aid the Viet Cong soon after Rolling Thunder began.

One of the first targets of this new Communist incursion was the American air base in the port city of Danang, near the demilitarized zone that separated the North and South. Fearing that the South Vietnamese troops who guarded the base could be easily overrun by a concentrated Viet Cong/NVA attack, General William Westmoreland, the U.S. commander of military operations in Vietnam, asked the Johnson administration for American ground troops to guard the base (see Westmoreland biography, p. 170). His request was granted, and on March 8, 1965, 3,500 American soldiers landed on the beach in Danang. These were the first armed U.S. combat troops to enter Vietnam.

The insertion of American ground troops into South Vietnam was a crucial moment in the war for several reasons. Up until that time, U.S. strategists had clung to the belief that with training, financial aid, and air support from America, the South Vietnamese military would be able to defend its own country. But the events of 1964 and early 1965 demonstrated that the ARVN simply was not capable of achieving this goal. If the United States wanted to live up to its commitment of keeping South Vietnam from falling to Communism, it was clear that American soldiers would have to shoulder a greater share of that burden.

Thus the United States steadily increased the number of American troops deployed in Vietnam. The 3,500 who landed in Danang in March 1965 were joined by about 25,000 support personnel. In April and May more troops poured in, bringing the total number of U.S. military personnel to 59,900 by June 30, 1965. The numbers jumped from there: to 184,300 by the end of 1965; 385,300 by the end of 1966; 485,600 by the end of 1967; and ultimately reaching a high of 543,400 in the spring of 1969. But the war ground on inconclusively despite this steady escalation, leading some observers to recall President John F. Kennedy's 1961 statement about the perils of committing U.S. ground troops to Vietnam: "The troops will march in, the bands will play, the crowds will cheer, and in four days everyone will have forgotten," he said. "Then we will be told we have to send in more troops. It's like taking a drink. The effect wears off, and you have to take another."

Political Fallout in Vietnam and at Home

The American decision to commit ground troops in Vietnam had significant consequences for the governments of North and South Vietnam. For North Vietnam, the American decision to send in ground troops was a real setback. Ho Chi Minh, General Vo Nguyen Giap, and other Communist leaders knew that they could survive American aerial attacks. But the arrival of U.S. Marines and Army troops on the ground made matters much more difficult for Hanoi. North Vietnamese leaders recognized that they would need to provide more support for Viet Cong war efforts, including deployment of greater numbers of NVA soldiers into the South. With this in mind, they appealed to their Communist allies for more assistance. China and Russia responded by dramatically increasing the amount of war supplies they sent to North Vietnam.

In South Vietnam, the growing presence of American fighting forces further divided the country. Those who wanted independence and reunification were alarmed by the steady growth in American visibility and influence. But two military strongmen who were avowed enemies of Communism took the reins of government in 1965, and strong American support enabled them to give the South Vietnamese government a greater semblance of stability than it had had since the fall of the Diem regime in 1963.

Nguyen Van Thieu and Nguyen Cao Ky began their ascent to power during the brief post-Diem military regimes of Duong Van ("Big") Minh, Nguyen Khanh, and Tran Van Huong. Both men skillfully maneuvered through the dangerous and unstable political environment that existed in Saigon during these turbulent months, and by June 1965 Thieu had become chief of state and Ky had been installed as prime minister. Over the next several months both men acted ruthlessly to protect their power, while simultaneously urging the Americans to increase the number of U.S. troops in Vietnam. In September 1967 Thieu was elected president and Ky took the vice-presidency in national elections that were marred by widespread fraud and harsh repression of voters who supported other candidates (Thieu remained president of South Vietnam until the fall of Saigon in 1975; Ky left the government in 1971 after a falling out with Thieu).

Thieu and Ky put the ARVN at the service of the United States. This decision ended any pretense that South Vietnam was independently controlling its own military—or the larger war effort against the Viet Cong and North Vietnam.

Prime Minister Nguyen Cao Ky (left) and President Nguyen Van Thieu (right) discuss the war in Vietnam at a 1966 conference with U.S. President Lyndon B. Johnson (with back to camera) and other American officials.

The arrival of large numbers of American troops in South Vietnam changed the political dynamics in the United States as well. No longer could Johnson and his spokesmen assure their countrymen that they were fighting a limited war with little danger to American soldiers. But Johnson delivered several speeches designed to win support for the war effort. Speaking at Johns Hopkins University in April of 1965, he told Americans that "because we fight for values and we fight for principles, rather than territory or colonies, our patience and our determination are unending."

Beginning in 1965, however, the Johnson administration was forced to defend its decisions and priorities against a vocal American antiwar movement that steadily grew in size and influence. These protestors challenged the draft that selected young men for compulsory military service, openly questioned the Johnson administration's reasons for going to war, and criticized

U.S. conduct of the war. When American deaths mounted in Vietnam, the antiwar movement grew even stronger until, by 1967, it became a real threat to Johnson's presidency.

U.S. Strategy in Vietnam

The leadership of America's combat troops in Vietnam from 1964 to 1968 fell to General William Westmoreland, a highly decorated general who had fought in World War II and the Korean War. An avowed anti-Communist, "Westie" (as he was known to his troops) argued forcefully for more U.S. troops in Vietnam. His requests were usually granted, so American troop levels in Vietnam increased steadily during his tenure. He also devised and implemented aggressive strategies to root out the Viet Cong and punish their North Vietnamese supporters. But Westmoreland was not permitted to send troops into North Vietnam.

Such a widening of the war ran counter to the strategy chosen by President Johnson, Secretary of State McNamara, and other administration officials. They did not want to advance into North Vietnam or even destroy its military. Instead, they wanted to make the costs of waging war so high for the Communists that they would voluntarily end the fighting and finally recognize the legitimacy of a non-Communist South Vietnam. With this goal in mind, Westmoreland and the American military pursued a strategy known as attrition, which called for exhausting the enemy through constant pressure. This strategy was based on the assumption that once the Communists saw how many soldiers and resources they were losing to the war, they would give up.

As Westmoreland oversaw the deployment of combat troops in bases throughout South Vietnam, he also honed a military plan designed to bring victory by 1967. Step one in his plan called for using American soldiers to help secure government control over the major population centers of South Vietnam, including Saigon, Hue, and Danang, and to counter the growing Viet Cong presence in the surrounding countryside. Next, the Americans would destroy enemy bases in the South and disrupt the flow of supplies from the North, thus choking off the stream of weapons, soldiers, and other materials vital to the Viet Cong war effort. Finally, American troops, working with the ARVN, would eliminate the last vestiges of Communist opposition in the country.

From the start, however, this plan proved difficult to implement. The enemy practiced a form of guerilla warfare that the United States was ill-pre-

By 1966, when this photograph of U.S. troops on a "search and destroy" patrol in Phuc Tuy Province was taken, American forces had become Saigon's primary defense against the Viet Cong.

pared to counter. Viet Cong fighters would appear suddenly, attack a village or a base, then disappear back into the countryside. When the U.S. forces were able to find a concentrated enemy unit to fight, their superior firepower and technology usually brought victory. But these types of clashes were rare, and the Americans were forced to rely on "search-and-destroy" missions to locate elusive enemy units. These missions sent American units into mountainous jungles, low-lying rice paddies, and populated villages in search of targets. Even after American troops cleared an area of Viet Cong guerrillas, though, the enemy often returned when U.S. forces moved on.

Lacking clear indicators of military victory, American leaders began to assess their progress using "body counts," numerical counts of the number of enemies killed. But even though the Americans could always boast of high kill ratios (the rate of enemies killed to U.S. soldiers lost), they were unable to vanquish the enemy. With each passing month, Communist leader Ho Chi Minh's famous declaration during the French-Viet Minh conflict—"You can kill ten of our men for every one we kill of yours. But even at those odds, you will lose and we will win"—seemed as true as ever.

Faced with what historian Pat Hearden characterized in *The Tragedy of Vietnam* as a "killing contest," the Americans raised the stakes. Areas known to contain high concentrations of enemies were characterized as "free fire zones," where any Vietnamese person was considered to be the enemy. In the meantime, the air war in the South brought immense death and devastation. Under an aerial operation known as Operation Ranch Hand, U.S. forces sprayed huge areas of enemy-controlled territory in South Vietnam with Agent Orange. This defoliant killed all vegetation in an area, making it impossible to hide in the jungle or to grow crops. (Exposure to Agent Orange also caused serious health problems for tens of thousands of Americans and Vietnamese after the war.) Another terrifying aerial weapon used in South Vietnam was napalm, a form of jellied gasoline that exploded with intense heat, incinerating woodlands, hamlets, and fields in seconds. The use of such weapons, along with conventional bombs dropped by B-52s flying high above the battle zone, made South Vietnam the most heavily bombed country in the history of warfare.

The Light at the End of the Tunnel

As the war dragged on, momentum did seem to be with the United States and South Vietnamese in some respects. In South Vietnam's major cities, the U.S. military had imposed a measure of security and control. Out in the countryside, meanwhile, American forces continued to punish the enemy with terrible losses. These losses came from major engagements such as the 1965 battle of Ia Drang as well as from hundreds of smaller firefights in remote jungles and mountainsides. The military strength of the Viet Cong thus became increasingly dependent upon fresh troops provided by North Vietnam.

Yet somehow it did not feel like the United States was winning. American combat deaths climbed steadily, from 147 in 1964, to 1,369 in 1965, to 5,008 in 1966, to 9,377 in 1967. Viet Cong attacks remained common occurrences across the South, and North Vietnam continued to transport troops and ammunition to their Communist colleagues—despite enduring 643,000 tons of bombs between 1965 and 1968 from the Rolling Thunder aerial campaign.

Why Not Peace?

Critics of the Johnson administration often claim that the Vietnam War could have been avoided or shortened if only Johnson and his negotiators would have more aggressively pursued peace talks. In fact, Johnson sought a negotiated settlement to the war in Vietnam throughout his last few years in office. Historian George C. Herring, writing in *America's Longest War,* notes that American officials tallied nearly 2,000 attempts to begin peace talks from 1965 to 1967 alone. Despite all these attempts to fight the war at the negotiating table rather than the battlefield, though, little progress toward peace was made during Johnson's years in the White House. Why?

Some historians assert that although both American and Communist leaders pledged themselves publicly to peace, they refused to offer meaningful compromise. Both sides demanded concessions that the other was not willing to make, and offered concessions that were of little importance to their adversaries. In April 1965, for example, President Johnson offered "unconditional discussions" and massive economic assistance to North Vietnam, yet he also vowed his continued support for a South Vietnam free of Communism. Since a reunified Vietnam under Communist rule was the single greatest goal of the North Vietnamese government in Hanoi, Johnson's offers of economic aid were meaningless. Henry Kissinger, the architect of the peace talks that began in 1968 and eventually ended the war, wrote in *Ending the Vietnam War* that "the North Vietnamese Communists had not spent a lifetime in mortal struggle to end it by sharing power or by de-escalating the guerrilla war, their most effective means of pressure." Failing to find any basis for compromise, both sides continued to try to advance their cause on the field of battle, with huge costs for all involved.

Within the United States, critics of the Johnson administration grew louder and more numerous. They demanded to know how much longer it would take—and how many more lives it would cost—for America to end this war. Some wanted the United States to increase its military commitment in Vietnam and adjust its strategy in order to win the war; others wanted a rapid withdrawal of American forces. Most wanted some reassurance that progress was being made. With that in mind, Johnson called Westmoreland home from Vietnam in 1967 to join other administration officials in a campaign to reassure Americans and their elected representatives that the war was going well. In a series of press conferences, speeches, and televised interviews, Westmoreland defended the American war effort. He told the National Press Club that "We have reached an important point when the end begins to come into view," and then said in a televised news conference that he could see "the light at the end of the tunnel."

What neither Westmoreland nor others in the Johnson administration knew at that time was that North Vietnamese military commander Vo Nguyen Giap was planning a sustained offensive for the early months of 1968. Convinced of the weakness of the South Vietnamese government, Giap felt that a major assault might sway the South Vietnamese people to revolt against Thieu's regime and rise up in support of reunification with the North. As preparations advanced, Giap and his generals decided to launch the assault so that it coincided with the traditional Vietnamese celebration of the lunar new year, known in Vietnam as "Tet."

Chapter Four

TET: THE TURNING POINT

Who won and who lost in the great Tet Offensive against the cities? I'm not sure. The Viet Cong did not win by a knockout, but neither did we. The referees of history may make it a draw.... We have been too often disappointed by the optimism of the American leaders, both in Vietnam and Washington, to have faith any longer in the silver linings they find in the darkest clouds.

—CBS Journalist Walter Cronkite, February 27, 1968

North Vietnam and its Viet Cong allies launched the pivotal Tet Offensive, the most important military action of the entire Vietnam War, on January 31, 1968. This was the traditional starting date for Tet, the beginning of the lunar new year and a major national holiday of the Vietnamese people. In years past, fighting had lessened dramatically or even ceased altogether during this holiday. South Vietnamese President Nguyen Van Thieu thus gave many South Vietnamese (ARVN) troops leave from duty during the holiday so that they could celebrate with their families. But in the early morning hours of January 31, Viet Cong and North Vietnamese (NVA) forces launched a surprise assault on locations all across South Vietnam, including many places that U.S. strategists believed were safe from enemy attack. The invaders struck dozens of provincial capitals, five of South Vietnam's six largest cities, and smaller towns and villages all across the beleaguered country. The major targets of these attacks in most cases were South Vietnamese government installations, military bases, and communications strongholds. The Communists avoided targets with large concentrations of

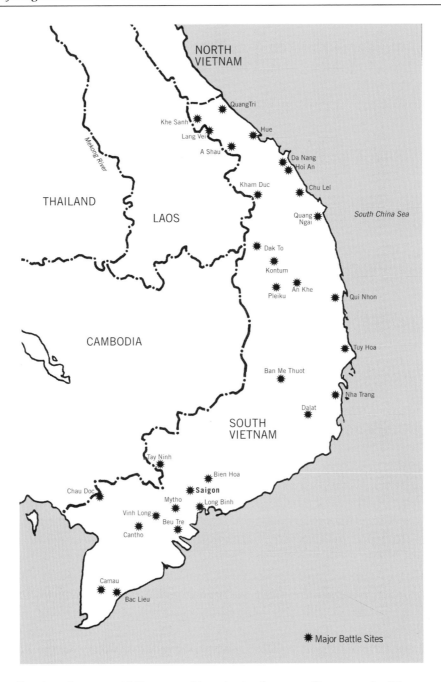

The Tet Offensive of January 1968 targeted hundreds of towns, villages, and military installations across South Vietnam, as well as these major cities and bases.

U.S. forces except in a few select cases where the symbolic importance of the target was irresistible. In Saigon, for example, Viet Cong soldiers used an underground tunnel to seize control of the U.S. Embassy for several hours before being wiped out by American forces.

The Battle for Hue

For the next 25 days, battles small and large raged across the South as stunned American and South Vietnamese forces tried to repulse the invasion. Perhaps the most important and costly battle was fought in the city of Hue, in the northern part of South Vietnam. Hue held symbolic importance for all Vietnamese people. The seat of the ancient imperial government and home to many historic sites of interest, it was also widely regarded as the most beautiful city in all of Vietnam. The Tet Offensive, though, left the once-lovely city in ruins.

Communist forces stormed the city and seized control of much of it on the very first night of Tet. In one of the most atrocious acts of the war, Viet Cong soldiers then rounded up thousands of people believed to have been sympathetic to the South Vietnamese government—including teachers, priests, soldiers, and civil servants—and shot them, clubbed them to death, or buried them alive. It is believed that at least 3,000 people were murdered in this fashion.

On February 12, U.S. forces launched a grim campaign to retake the city. Departing from their usual strategy, Communist fighters did not quickly give ground and retreat into the countryside: in Hue, they stood and fought. As a result, the struggle for control of Hue turned into a vicious nightmare in which seemingly every street became a battle zone. On March 2, American Marines backed by aerial bombing, heavy artillery, and ARVN troops finally drove the Communists out of Hue. But by this time nearly half the city had been destroyed, turning most of the population of the city into homeless refugees. "When the American marines and ARVN forces finally retook the city," wrote Robert D. Schulzinger in *A Time for War,* "they found a moonscape of charred remains of wooden buildings, rotting corpses, and starving abandoned animals."

By February 24 the last of the Communist attacks had been repelled and American and ARVN forces had retaken the territory lost in Tet's opening days. By virtually any military measure, the Viet Cong and NVA forces had been dealt a major military defeat. In all, it has been estimated that between 37,000 and 45,000 Communist soldiers and guerrillas lost their lives in the offensive (out

President Lyndon B. Johnson (at right, with Secretary of State Dean Rusk) was stunned by the scale of the Tet Offensive, which was a public relations nightmare for his administration.

of a total invasion force of 84,000 men). Meanwhile, the United States suffered approximately 1,100 killed and South Vietnam lost another 2,300 soldiers.

The Viet Cong forces that had led the fighting were decimated and ceased to be a major factor in the South for the remainder of the war. In addition, Hanoi's belief that an invasion would spark a popular revolt against South Vietnam's national government failed to materialize. This reality cast doubt on Communist claims that ordinary South Vietnamese supported their cause. Finally, many ARVN units—which had long experienced troubles as an effective fighting force—acquitted themselves well and gained a measure of respect for their fierce defense of their homes and families.

Interpreting Tet

The fact that Tet was a Communist military defeat did not necessarily mean that it was an American and South Vietnamese victory, however.

Though South Vietnam's army had performed better than expected, the government of President Nguyen Van Thieu still enjoyed little public support or respect. In addition, Tet left the government with a huge refugee problem, as upwards of half a million people (some historians place the figure at more than 800,000) uprooted from their homes by the violence sought food and shelter. Most of these desperate people ended up in crowded urban slums or in awful refugee camps.

The United States' reaction to its "victory" was even more complicated. General William Westmoreland, who commanded U.S. forces in South Vietnam, claimed that Tet proved that American forces were clearly superior to the enemy, and that the United States was truly on the path to victory. Westmoreland and other "hawks" in Washington, D.C. wanted to capitalize on Tet and launch new offensive operations that would completely destroy the Viet Cong—and perhaps even force North Vietnam to concede defeat. To this end, Westmoreland requested another 200,000 U.S. troops for deployment in Vietnam.

Political leaders and the American public did not see Tet in the same light. Americans had wanted to believe Westmoreland's claims, made in the fall of 1967, that victory was near at hand, but the surprise Tet attacks told a different story. Television and newspaper coverage of Tet played up the drama and scope of the surprise attack. One newspaper headline proclaimed "WAR HITS SAIGON," and television film crews captured footage of frantic American soldiers defending the embassy in South Vietnam's capital. When news coverage showed the location of Viet Cong attacks on maps of South Vietnam, Americans were alarmed to see that they occurred from one end of the country to another, making it appear that the country had been overrun.

Some coverage of the war was particularly unsettling to the American public. On February 2, NBC aired shocking footage of a South Vietnamese police chief executing an unarmed Viet Cong prisoner in the streets of Saigon. This footage cast America's South Vietnamese allies in a very unfavorable light. Five days later, an American Air Force Major who had helped carry out a devastating attack on a rural village told a newspaper reporter that "it became necessary to destroy the town to save it." To many Americans, this sort of crazy logic seemed symbolic of the U.S. military's whole approach to Vietnam.

As the Tet Offensive went on, major media outlets increasingly questioned American progress in the war. The *Wall Street Journal,* long a supporter of American military intervention in Vietnam, warned in an editorial that

Televised footage of the Tet Offensive, including this execution of a Viet Cong soldier at the hands of South Vietnamese National Police Chief Nguyen Ngoc Loan on the streets of Saigon, shocked and demoralized many members of the American public.

"the American people should be getting ready to accept, if they haven't already, the prospect that the whole Vietnam effort may be doomed." And on February 27, CBS News anchorman Walter Cronkite declared on national television that it seemed "more certain than ever that the bloody experience of Vietnam is to end in a stalemate."

Taking Stock After Tet

Even before Tet, top figures within the Johnson administration had begun to express doubts about the war. Secretary of Defense Robert McNamara, a chief architect of American strategy in Vietnam throughout the mid-1960s, gradually became convinced that the United States could not win in

Vietnam. But even though he privately urged Johnson to change course through much of 1967, when the carnage and violence in Vietnam was spiraling to new heights, he never publicly disclosed his fears or disillusionment. Later, McNamara wrote in his memoir *In Retrospect* that he and his fellow policymakers "acted according to what we thought were the principles and traditions of this nation. We made our decisions in light of those values. Yet we were wrong, terribly wrong."

In early 1968 Johnson replaced McNamara with long-time advisor Clark Clifford, who had once been a big supporter of the war. By the time he took over the helm at the Defense Department, however, he also had come to harbor doubts about U.S. strategy in Vietnam. Clifford promptly pulled together a task force of Pentagon analysts. He told them to examine every part of the existing U.S. strategy and review the overall status of the war in Vietnam. Clifford's task force returned with a grim assessment of the war and a series of recommendations aimed at getting the United States out of Vietnam. These recommendations included a halt to new deployments to Vietnam, an end to the air war, and new efforts to initiate peace talks.

"[We in the Johnson administration] acted according to what we thought were the principles and traditions of this nation," said Secretary of Defense Robert McNamara. "We made our decisions in light of those values. Yet we were wrong, terribly wrong."

This advice was not welcomed by Johnson, who was angry about the Tet Offensive. Part of him wanted to follow the advice of "hawks" and send in more troops. But Johnson came to recognize that neither the Congress nor the American people favored such an approach. This realization was due in no small part to a historic March 1968 meeting that Clifford arranged between Johnson and a group of assembled statesmen and retired military leaders collectively known as the "Wise Men." Over dinner and a long evening of conversation, Johnson was shaken by the sense of futility and defeat that hung over the group. In the ensuing weeks, Johnson reluctantly concluded that withdrawal from Vietnam was the only possible course of action to pursue.

A Stunning Announcement

After the Tet Offensive, the Vietnam War loomed as a huge political problem for Johnson as well. Many Americans still supported the decision to enter Vietnam, but even among supporters, frustration with the war was growing.

During this March 1968 address to the nation, President Johnson announced his intention not to run for re-election.

After all, U.S. casualties were soaring, with no apparent progress toward long-promised victory. In addition, many Americans viewed the antiwar demonstrations taking place on college campuses and in major cities as representative of the larger cultural changes that were shaking American society during the 1960s. These changes—in attitudes toward sex, gender roles, drug use, and acceptance of traditional symbols and institutions of authority—were deeply alarming to many Americans.

Sensing Johnson's political vulnerability, several Democratic candidates lined up to run against their party's sitting president in the upcoming fall 1968 elections. Anti-war candidate Senator Eugene McCarthy performed well in the New Hampshire primary on March 12, and Senator Robert F. Kennedy announced his candidacy shortly thereafter. With polls showing his popularity shrinking and support for his war policies at record lows, Johnson wondered if he could even win the Democratic nomination, let alone the presidency.

On March 31, 1968, Johnson delivered a nationally televised speech to the American people. The contents of that speech reflected not only changing U.S. perceptions of the Vietnam War after Tet, but also his weakened political standing. Johnson told Americans that he intended to dramatically scale back the aerial bombing campaigns against North Vietnam. He also called for a new round of negotiations with the Communists, rejected military requests for additional troops, and assured the American public that the U.S. military would put a new emphasis on training South Vietnam's military so that it could soon take over primary responsibility for the war's prosecution.

Finally, after a dramatic pause, Johnson made an announcement that startled most Americans: "With America's sons in the fields far away, with America's future under challenge right here at home, with our hopes and the world's hopes for peace in the balance every day, I do not believe that I should devote an hour or a day of my time to any personal partisan causes or to any duties other than the awesome duties of this office—the Presidency of your country. Accordingly, I shall not seek, and I will not accept, the nomination of my party for another term as your President." Johnson's shocking decision to forego another campaign for the White House assured that America's future course in Vietnam would be determined by new political leadership.

Chapter Five
"VIETNAMIZATION"

⚜

The U.S. has no choice at the moment but to give Viet-namization a fair try.... A key element in the Vietnamization program may be time. If Richard Nixon, in response to domestic pressure, feels compelled to accelerate U.S. with-drawals, the program could fail. If the pullout is gradual, it might work. "It is a very hopeful idea," said a Pentagon offi-cial of Vietnamization. "It is the only one that will let us get out of there eventually. But please, let's not go too fast."

—*Time,* September 26, 1969

The tenor of the Vietnam War changed dramatically in the spring of 1968. With over half a million soldiers stationed in South Vietnam and billions of dollars of aid flowing into the country, the United States was deeply committed to defending the government of South Vietnam against Communist North Vietnam. Moreover, the Tet Offensive of early 1968 had decimated the Viet Cong guerrilla force that been wreaking havoc in South Vietnam over the past several years. The losses suffered by the Viet Cong left the North Vietnamese Army (NVA) with almost sole responsibility for carrying on the fight against the regime in Saigon and its American allies.

But Tet was widely interpreted as a defeat back in the United States. The offensive revealed that the U.S. government had not been providing an accurate picture of the war in Vietnam, and it convinced many analysts that the war had degenerated into a bloody stalemate. These factors led U.S. President Lyndon Johnson to order a dramatic shift in the course of America's involvement in Vietnam. In March 1968 he announced several measures designed to lure North Vietnam to the negotiating table, including an unconditional halt to U.S. bombing sorties over the North. He also declared that he would not seek reelection in November 1968. These announcements made it clear that the next president of the United States would inherit a war that was far different from the one that had existed only a few short months before.

Johnson's Last Months in the Oval Office

In July 1968 the Pentagon announced that Army General Creighton Abrams would replace General William Westmoreland as commander of U.S. forces in Vietnam. As Westmoreland's deputy, Abrams had spent the previous year building the strength and readiness of South Vietnam's military forces, the Army of the Republic of Vietnam (ARVN). The unexpectedly strong performance of the ARVN during the Tet Offensive thus convinced Johnson and many others that Abrams was an ideal replacement for Westmoreland, who had become enormously controversial in the wake of Tet.

Abrams immediately set about shoring up South Vietnamese positions in urban areas. He also devoted more resources to training South Vietnamese troops to play a larger role in "pacification"—the preservation of peace and security in the many rural villages scattered through the countryside. Abrams also scaled back U.S. combat activity, placing a greater emphasis on small-unit missions at the local level. Abrams' first months in charge were eased by the weakness and disorganization of the Viet Cong in the aftermath of Tet. In fact, American and South Vietnamese forces made genuine progress in expanding the territory under their control by the end of 1968.

Johnson, meanwhile, was disappointed by North Vietnam's response to his peace overtures. Communist Party strategists were smarting from the military defeats of Tet and were in no mood to negotiate from a position of relative weakness. Henry Kissinger, who would later become Secretary of State under President Richard Nixon, wrote in *Ending the Vietnam War* that negotiators in Hanoi "were convinced that the fate of Vietnam would be settled by the balance of forces on the ground." They were thus prepared to wait until they regained the military advantage before moving ahead with peace talks. What's more, Kissinger noted that Johnson's approaching departure from the White House meant that North Vietnam "had no incentive to settle with Johnson, and every temptation to repeat the same test of strength with his successor."

Hamburger Hill

Most North Vietnamese bases were established in remote jungle or mountain areas, and attacks on these positions were extremely dangerous. In the spring of 1969 American units became entangled in a particularly grim assault on one of these positions, along the A Shau Valley near the border with Laos. Over the course of two weeks in May, American troops overcame torrential rains, mountainous terrain, and intense enemy opposition to capture an enemy stronghold. More than one million pounds of bombs were dropped by the U.S. Air Force in support of the assault, including more than 150,000 pounds of napalm. Even so, the base was not captured until U.S. troops cleared the area in vicious close-quarters fighting. By the time the fighting ended, more than 500 North Vietnamese soldiers had been killed, while American casualties numbered more than 470 (56 killed and 420 wounded). The battle was so bloody that surviving U.S. soldiers called the site "Hamburger Hill."

The Battle of Hamburger Hill might have quickly been forgotten. But it became notorious when the exhausted American soldiers who had taken the hill were quickly ordered to abandon the position. The bewildered troops left, and the North Vietnamese returned to the site a few weeks later. When news of these incidents reached American shores, public reaction was swift and angry. Critics demanded to know why the military had spent millions of dollars and fifty-six American lives to capture a position, only to willingly leave the position a few days later. The Battle of Hamburger Hill thus came to be seen by many as a symbol of the futility of American military action in Vietnam.

The Race for the White House

The 1968 presidential campaign was one of the most dramatic presidential contests in U.S. history. On the Democratic side, antiwar candidate Eugene McCarthy's early primary success contributed to Johnson's decision not to run for re-election and reinvigorated the antiwar movement, which staged demonstrations throughout the summer. These events also convinced

Democratic Senator Robert F. Kennedy—the younger brother of President John F. Kennedy, who had been slain by an assassin five years earlier—to enter the race. More moderate than McCarthy but also pledged to ending the war, Kennedy was a formidable candidate. But he was himself assassinated by a gunman on June 6, 1968, mere hours after he learned that he had won the all-important California primary.

Robert Kennedy's death was another shocking blow to the American people, who were also grappling with the assassination of civil rights leader Martin Luther King Jr. in April 1968. Over the next several weeks, Vice President Hubert Humphrey emerged as the candidate to beat for the Democratic nomination. But the candidacy of Humphrey, who was closely linked in the public mind with Johnson and Vietnam, got off to a horrible start.

When the Democratic Party met for its nominating convention in Chicago on August 26, 1968, they were greeted by thousands of antiwar protestors—including a large contingent of bearded, long-haired radical hippies who called themselves "Yippies." Chicago Mayor Richard Daley, a Democrat, ordered a violent crackdown on the demonstrations. Over the next few nights, Chicago police and National Guard troops repeatedly clashed with protestors as TV cameras broadcast the events to the nation. Though Hubert Humphrey eventually received the nomination as expected, the chaotic scene in Chicago enabled opponents to paint his Democratic Party as the party of disorder, anarchy, and violence.

Republican nominee Richard M. Nixon had a far easier time controlling his campaign message. A former vice president under Dwight D. Eisenhower and avowed anti-Communist, Nixon appealed to Americans as the champion of "law and order." This message struck a chord with many Americans who disapproved of the social unrest and turbulence associated with the antiwar movement (some of these same voters also held a negative view of the civil rights movement for the same reason).

Regarding the war in Vietnam, Nixon was a hawk. He believed that America's military might had been foolishly squandered by the Johnson administration, and that more effective use of military power could bring victory. But he did not campaign on this platform because he knew that American voters were sick of continued U.S. involvement in Vietnam. Instead, he told Americans that he had a "secret plan" that would allow him to "end the war and win the peace."

The August 1968 Democratic National Convention in Chicago was tainted by demonstrations within the convention hall and violent clashes between police and demonstrators on the city streets.

In November, voters elected Nixon to the White House in one of the most closely contested elections in U.S. history. Nixon took 43.4 percent of the vote, barely nosing out Humphrey, who earned 42.7 percent of the vote (American Independent Party candidate George Wallace, a former Democratic governor of Alabama who ran for president on a segregationist platform, won a surprising 13.5 percent of the vote).

Nixon's Bid to End the War

When Nixon took the oath of office in January 1969, both he and his lead foreign policy advisor, Secretary of State Henry Kissinger (see Kissinger biography, p. 143), remained convinced that the United States could not allow South Vietnam to fall to Communism. They also believed that admitting military defeat in Vietnam would be a crushing blow to U.S. prestige, American self-confidence, and Nixon's own political fortunes. Yet the Nixon administration also inherited Johnson's promises to reduce American troop levels and negotiate an American withdrawal from Vietnam—promises that reflected the American public's disillusionment with the war.

Despite all these seemingly contradictory goals, Nixon and Kissinger believed that they had a plan that would bring America "peace with honor." The administration's opening move was to extend the hand of peace while simultaneously reminding the Communist regime in North Vietnam of the power of American bombing. Nixon sent a letter to Communist leaders in Hanoi proposing that both the United States and North Vietnam remove their troops from South Vietnam and permit remaining parties within South Vietnam to negotiate a political settlement. Simultaneously, the United States approached the Soviet Union—still North Vietnam's largest source of financial aid and military supplies—with an offer to move forward on U.S.-Soviet arms reduction treaties in return for Soviet pressure on North Vietnam to give ground at the bargaining table.

As in the past, these early diplomatic efforts went nowhere because of North Vietnam's refusal to relinquish conquered territory or recognize the legitimacy of South Vietnam's government. At this point, Nixon and his advisors approved a new wave of bombing against Communist targets in the region. One of North Vietnam's great strategic advantages over the course of the war had been its ability to stage troops in Cambodia, just across the border from South Vietnam and within striking distance of the capitol, Saigon. American and South Vietnamese forces had always stopped their military operations at the Cambodian border, but Nixon waved off this self-imposed restriction. In response to attacks near Saigon, Nixon ordered a sustained bombing campaign against Communist forces within Cambodia starting on March 18, 1969. These aerial operations were accompanied by cross-border raids into Cambodian territory. In addition, Nixon approved a resumption of bombing of power plants, military installations, and other strategically important targets in North Vietnam itself.

Nixon knew that the U.S. Congress and American public would interpret these military actions as a widening of the war. For this reason, Nixon ordered that these new bombing campaigns be kept secret. On May 9, 1969, however, a *New York Times* reporter broke the story. Nixon retaliated by ordering wiretaps on the phones of those suspected of leaking the story. Two years later, after the *Times* revealed another round of secret bombings and then published a series of secret government documents about the Vietnam

War known as the "Pentagon Papers," Nixon ramped up his administration's domestic spying operations against political opponents, "hostile" journalists, and antiwar leaders. (This illegal behavior led to other criminal acts by Nixon and his political allies, including the burglarization of Democratic Party headquarters in 1972. Nixon's efforts to cover up his administration's links to the burglars erupted into the so-called "Watergate scandal." The Watergate affair eventually engulfed Nixon's presidency, and in August 1974 he was forced to resign from office in disgrace.)

The "Nixon Doctrine" and Vietnamization

By the summer of 1969, many Americans were expressing impatience with Nixon's apparent lack of progress in extricating the United States from Vietnam. Congressional pressure to unilaterally begin troop withdrawals from Vietnam was growing, and large antiwar demonstrations continued to flare up around the country. Nixon responded on June 8, 1969, by announcing that he was ordering the withdrawal of 25,000 American combat troops from Vietnam.

The withdrawal, Nixon proclaimed, was part of a new American foreign policy called the "Nixon Doctrine." Under this doctrine, the United States would no longer commit to sending combat troops to support wars against Communism in developing countries, but it would offer economic assistance and military supplies to its allies. In part, this doctrine was intended to encourage the other Cold War powers—the Soviet Union and China—to also lessen their involvement in conflicts beyond their borders. But the doctrine also reflected the sober recognition that even the wealthiest, most powerful nation in the world had become overextended, and that the American public was weary of war.

Nixon also explicitly linked the gradual withdrawal of U.S. troops in Vietnam to a parallel policy called "Vietnamization." Under this plan, the United States intended to gradually hand over more and more responsibility for the war to South Vietnam and its ARVN troops. This policy, crafted by U.S. General Creighton Abrams, had actually begun to take root in 1967 under President Lyndon B. Johnson. By the end of 1969 the Nixon administration was firmly committed to this path of action.

Nixon and Kissinger recognized that North Vietnam was likely to interpret the reduction of U.S. troop strength as a signal that the Americans were

After taking office in January 1969, President Richard M. Nixon (seen here with U.S. troops) promised that his policy of "Vietnamization" would bring "peace with honor."

Nixon's "Madman" Strategy

The Nixon administration's frustration at North Vietnam's refusal to offer meaningful concessions in peace talks eventually led to one of the strangest episodes in the Vietnam War. Desperate to force North Vietnam out of its uncompromising negotiating position, President Nixon told aide Robert Haldeman about his "Madman Theory": "I want the North Vietnamese to believe I've reached the point where I might do *anything* to stop the war. We'll just slip the word to them that, 'for God's sake, you know Nixon is obsessed about Communism. We can't restrain him when he's angry—and he has his hand on the nuclear button'—and Ho Chi Minh himself will be in Paris in two days begging for peace."

In the end, the United States never reached the point of employing nuclear weapons against North Vietnam, and it is unclear if the threat had any impact on the negotiating stance taken by North Vietnamese negotiators in Paris. After the war, though, Nixon insisted that his approval of massive bombing campaigns against the North was a key factor in getting the Communists to sign off on the 1973 Paris Peace Accords.

losing their will to fight. They knew that if they were to keep any advantages at the bargaining table they needed to do something to counteract the impact of troop withdrawals. In late summer 1969 Kissinger formed a study group of high officials to study the issue, telling them: "I can't believe that a fourth-rate power like North Vietnam doesn't have a breaking point." The group sought out what Nixon called a "savage, punishing" blow that would shift the tide of war and convince the Communists to negotiate in good faith.

Changing Responsibilities and Attitudes

The ongoing process of American troop withdrawal and Vietnamization changed the nature of American involvement in Vietnam. Prior to Vietnamization, large American units went out in search of Viet Cong and North Vietnamese Army units to attack; now, much smaller American units provided air and combat support to ARVN troops who shouldered more of the actual responsibilities for fighting.

With each passing year, the number of U.S. military personnel stationed in Vietnam steadily declined. In April 1969 the number of U.S. troops deployed in the war-torn country reached an all-time high of 543,400, but by the end of the year 475,200 Americans remained. This number declined to 334,600 by the end of 1970, 156,800 by the end of 1971, and just 24,200 by the end of 1972.

American combat deaths dropped dramatically as a result of Vietnamization—from 14,589 in 1968, to 9,414 in 1969, 4,221 in 1970, 1,381 in 1971, 300 in 1972, and 237 in 1973. Most soldiers were filled with relief when their tours were over and they could return home. But American morale suffered during this time as well. Many soldiers expressed deep bitterness at the thought that thousands of American troops had sacrificed their lives in the conflict, only to have the United States leave before victory was won.

This anger was further heightened by a lack of respect for the South Vietnamese military and the national government. In the case of the ARVN troops, their performance actually improved somewhat as the war went on, especially during the Tet Offensive. But their early reputation as poorly trained cowards shadowed them throughout the war. Racism also played a role: many American soldiers simply did not trust or respect their Vietnamese counterparts, in part because they looked the same as the feared Viet Cong.

Finally, American soldiers deployed in Vietnam from 1969 onward knew that the larger American strategy was withdrawal, not military victory, and they did not want to lose their lives for such a diminished goal. American soldiers were haunted by the prospect of dying for nothing, and growing numbers of troops refused to go out on patrol, feigned injury and illness, and even murdered or "fragged" American patrol leaders who urged men into combat.

Despite the reductions in force, American soldiers continued to play several important roles in the war effort in South Vietnam. Many American troops, for example, were used in support of "pacification," an ongoing series of programs intended to win support for President Nguyen Van Thieu and his regime within the villages of rural South Vietnam. Many of these programs aimed to provide security, health care, education, and jobs to war-weary South Vietnamese, while others were used to support ongoing combat operations. Other American troops provided training and air support to ARVN forces.

The Invasion of Cambodia

In early 1970 the Nixon administration unexpectedly launched a military operation into neighboring Cambodia using large numbers of American ground troops. This controversial operation, which involved nearly 12,000 U.S. Army troops and 8,000 South Vietnamese soldiers, was meant to destroy Viet Cong sanctuaries and North Vietnamese positions hidden in Cambodia's jungles. But its unintended impact was to arouse the American antiwar movement, which had quieted considerably once Nixon began withdrawing U.S. troops from Vietnam, to never before seen heights of outrage and rebellion.

In the early 1960s, Cambodia had avoided direct entanglement in the Vietnam War by maintaining a policy of neutrality. During the mid-1960s, however, the government of Prince Norodom Sihanouk drifted toward the orbit of Communist China and North Vietnam. During this period, Sihanouk permitted Communist troops to travel through eastern Cambodia along the Ho Chi Minh Trail. But NVA infiltration of Cambodia became so great that the Cambodian government re-established communications with the United States.

In 1969 Nixon approved the covert bombing of Viet Cong camps in Cambodia. This aerial offensive had the unintended impact of driving the Communist insurgents deeper into Cambodia rather than out of the country. In March 1970, Cambodian General Lon Nol overthrew Sihanouk's government when the president traveled to France for medical treatment. Fearful that a North Vietnamese-backed Communist group known as the Khmer Rouge posed a growing threat to his rule, Lon Nol invited American military and economic assistance.

Nixon was so certain of Lon Nol's dependence on the United States that he approved plans for a major assault on Viet Cong and North Vietnamese military camps scattered up and down the Vietnamese border with eastern Cambodia. He thought that a display of America's military power might pay dividends in peace negotiations with North Vietnam, and he also believed that elimination of these enemy sanctuaries would advance the United States' Vietnamization efforts.

During the next several weeks, American and ARVN troops roamed through Cambodia, striking at NVA bases and securing the major port of Sihanoukville, which had been used by the Communists to import war supplies. U.S. and ARVN units forced the Communists out of many of the key

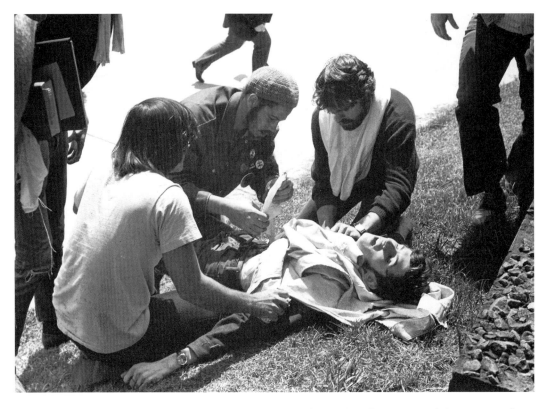

Kent State University students attend to wounded student John Cleary, one of the victims of an infamous May 1970 National Guard attack on unarmed demonstrators on the Kent State campus in Kent, Ohio.

areas they had used to stage attacks within South Vietnam, and they captured large amounts of Communist weapons and ammunition. Administration officials such as Henry Kissinger claimed that the invasion disrupted enemy operations so much that Nixon was able to order the withdrawal of 150,000 American troops. Additionally, the American incursion seemed to lend some additional stability to the government of Lon Nol.

But the 1970 invasion of Cambodia ultimately failed to remove the threat. North Vietnamese units returned to abandoned areas and resumed their activities after the Americans left in early June. More importantly, the U.S. incursion drove many enemy combatants into previously peaceful areas of Cambodia, creating chaotic conditions that helped the Khmer Rouge recruit more angry peasants to its banner (the Khmer Rouge ultimately seized control of the nation in 1975, whereupon they launched a nightmarish five-year reign of terror that claimed an estimated one million Cambodian lives).

On April 30, 1970, Nixon informed the American people that he had sent American troops into Cambodia in order to enhance security in South Vietnam. This revelation triggered a huge uproar in the United States. Many Congressmen complained that they had not been consulted about—nor had they authorized—the use of U.S. forces outside South Vietnam. More dramatically, the invasion of Cambodia sparked protests on college campuses across the United States. On May 4, 1970, Ohio National Guard troops opened fire on protestors at Kent State University, killing four students and wounding nine others. The Kent State killings fueled additional protests across the nation—eventually prompting dozens of universities to shut their doors for the remainder of their spring terms—and through May and June millions of people voiced their anger with the widening of the war in Southeast Asia. Nixon hastily withdrew American ground forces from Cambodia in June. One month later, the U.S. Senate sent a clear signal of displeasure about the invasion when it overturned the Gulf of Tonkin Resolution by a vote of 85 to 10.

Chapter Six

THE FALL OF SAIGON

When Thieu withdrew his troops from Pleiku, we realized suddenly that there was no trap, and there was no plan, and the South was not up to fighting anymore. That is when we decided to chase them as fast as we could.

—North Vietnamese General Tran Cong Man,
Tears Before the Rain

The Cambodian incursion was the last major action engaged in by U.S. combat troops, and it provided ample evidence that the highly trained, technologically advanced United States military was still a fearsome machine. The American objective in Vietnam was never just to win battles or capture territory, however, but to pressure North Vietnam into ending its efforts to unify Vietnam under Communist rule. In this respect, the Cambodian incursion failed because it did not halt North Vietnamese attacks on South Vietnam. One year later, an invasion of Laos, another neighboring country that was used as a supply and infiltration route by the Communists against the South, also failed to achieve desired results.

The invasion of Laos was carried out by South Vietnamese (ARVN) units and involved no U.S. combat troops, though American helicopters and planes provided air support. Ultimately, this offensive proved to be a significant setback for South Vietnam—and for America's efforts to negotiate an end to the war. The ARVN performed poorly in this offensive, retreating with heavy losses. The clash in Laos further reassured North Vietnam that if it waited for the Americans to leave, military victory over South Vietnam was inevitable.

Negotiation and Diplomacy

Peace negotiations between the United States, North Vietnam, and South Vietnam took place against this backdrop of continuous warfare. These talks had begun back in May 1968, when delegations from all three parties commenced official negotiations in Paris, France. From the beginning of these discussions, North Vietnam stuck firm to its negotiating position: the United States must withdraw from Vietnam, and the "illegitimate" South Vietnamese government of President Nguyen Van Thieu must be disbanded and replaced with a coalition government that included the Communist-led National Liberation Front (NLF; later known as the Provisional Revolutionary Government, or PRG). The United States was willing to withdraw troops, but it wanted to be free to continue to offer aid to South Vietnam. Even more importantly, it insisted that Thieu's government remain in place.

These official peace talks were riddled with breakdowns and wasteful arguments over unimportant issues. When it became clear that no meaningful progress was being made, Secretary of State Henry Kissinger initiated secret meetings with North Vietnamese lead negotiator Le Duc Tho in August 1969. Kissinger hoped that if the pressure of official diplomatic negotiations was removed, he and his counterpart might be able to broker a mutually acceptable back-room agreement. By 1971, though, neither set of negotiations had shown any real progress in ending the bloodshed in Vietnam.

On January 25, 1972, President Richard Nixon announced the existence of the secret talks between Kissinger and Le Duc Tho. At the same time, he revealed a softening in the American position. He announced that the United States was willing to withdraw its forces from South Vietnam, but only after "free elections" in which both Thieu and the PRG could participate.

Nixon's announcement was applauded at home, as he had hoped it would be: Nixon was running for reelection in 1972 and he wished to be seen as making progress in ending the war. The announcement was also welcomed by both the Soviet Union and China. Nixon and Kissinger had been working for months to open the door for better relations with these leading Communist powers, and in 1972 this work bore fruit. In February 1972 Nixon made a historic visit to Communist China, the first for an American president. Later that spring, he visited the Soviet Union. In both countries, he and his Communist counterparts spoke about the importance of avoiding direct military clashes. These visits boosted Nixon's popularity during an election year.

America's "Secret War" in Laos

During the 1960s and early 1970s, the Vietnam War spilled over into several neighboring countries including Laos. Like Vietnam, Laos had been a colony of France until the mid-1950s. In 1953 Laos received completed independence, but the nation became gripped by political instability almost immediately. This instability stemmed from a violent struggle for power between two factions: the Royal Lao, which was allied with the United States, and the Pathet Lao, a Communist movement strongly supported by North Vietnam.

By the early 1960s, Laotian efforts to maintain neutrality in the Vietnam War—and the larger Cold War that was being waged at that time—lay in tatters. American analysts were disturbed by growing Soviet and North Vietnamese assistance to the Pathet Lao, and their concerns about events in Laos were further heightened when its forested eastern territory became home to large sections of the Ho Chi Minh Trail. This trail, which was actually a complex network of trails, roads, and waterways, delivered huge numbers of supplies and reinforcements to Communist forces operating in South Vietnam and Cambodia throughout the war.

When the Pathet Lao, backed by Vietnamese Communists, launched new efforts to remove the U.S.-supported government in Laos, American officials approved a "secret war" against Communist elements in the country. From 1962 to 1973, the United States carried out a wide range of secret activities in Laos. These actions included clandestine deliveries of military and economic assistance to the Royal Lao government and relentless aerial bombing of Communist targets throughout the Laotian interior. Communist groups responded with violence of their own, and by the late 1960s many Laotians found that they were living in a vast war zone.

In the early 1970s, both the American public and the U.S. Congress reacted extremely negatively when information about the "secret war" emerged. In 1973 the United States ended almost all of its involvement in Laos. Two years later, Communist forces seized control of the war-battered nation and established the Lao People's Democratic Republic.

Of equal importance, according to Spencer G. Tucker, author of *Vietnam,* they showed that "both Communist powers wanted *détente* and agreement with the West … more than escalation of the war in Vietnam. [North Vietnam] was largely abandoned by its allies."

The Easter Offensive and Linebacker

North Vietnam was unhappy about the emergence of *détente* because it raised the possibility that the great Communist powers, eager to show their new cooperative spirit with the West, might force Hanoi to accept a negotiated settlement in the war before it could achieve its goal of reunification. With this in mind, North Vietnam decided to seek a swift and decisive military blow that would hasten an end to the conflict once and for all.

North Vietnam's Easter Offensive prompted President Nixon to approve "Linebacker," one of the most intense U.S. bombing campaigns of the entire Vietnam War. During this six-month campaign, American pilots dropped huge numbers of bombs on bridges, roads, tunnels, factories, ammunition depots, and military bases all across North Vietnam.

In March 1972 North Vietnam launched the Easter Offensive, a major assault that featured more than 120,000 troops supported by artillery and tanks. North Vietnamese and Viet Cong troops spilled into the South from multiple points along the demilitarized zone, as well as bases in Laos and Cambodia. Their goal was to capture provincial capitals in parts of northern and western South Vietnam, seize the Central Highlands that ran on a north-south line through the interior, and thus divide the nation in two. Communist strategists believed that if these goals were achieved, they might constitute fatal wounds to the government in Saigon.

The North Vietnamese did manage to capture some desired territory in the opening weeks of fighting. But the offensive did not go as expected. It failed to capture any provincial capitals in the South, and it failed to break the Army of South Vietnam. Champions of Vietnamization held this up as proof that South Vietnam could stand on its own. The truth, however, was that most ARVN successes came as a result of punishing American air support and skillful direction from U.S. military advisors like John Paul Vann, who played a pivotal role in keeping the Central Highlands out of Communist hands.

The Easter Offensive also prompted President Nixon to approve "Linebacker," one of the most concentrated and effective American bombing campaigns of the entire Vietnam War. From May 8 to October 23, 1972, Americans dropped huge numbers of bombs on a wide array of targets within North Vietnam: bridges, roads, tunnels, factories, ammunition depots, military barracks, and other targets. The bombing was accompanied by the laying of mines in Haiphong Harbor, North Vietnam's main sea port. Together, the bombing and the mining radically disrupted the flow of war supplies to North Vietnamese Army troops fighting in the South and brought the Easter Offensive to a halt. More importantly, it severely damaged the North Vietnamese capacity to wage war and thus convinced them to resume serious peace negotiations.

The Paris Peace Accords

For all the death and destruction that wracked Vietnam during the spring and summer of 1972, the overall balance of power remained unchanged. North Vietnam's leaders now recognized that they could not achieve a military victory as long as the United States remained willing to use its awesome air power, but American officials were well aware that public impatience with continued U.S. involvement in Vietnam was rising with every week. These pressures brought concessions from both sides during meetings in Paris in October 1972.

At that time, the two sides reached a tentative agreement that permitted North Vietnam to retain territory it had gained within South Vietnam and keep troops there. The agreement also allowed North Vietnam to continue to receive aid from China and the Soviet Union. In return, North Vietnam promised to allow Thieu's government to remain in place. In addition, the terms of the agreement gave the United States its long-sought chance to withdraw its troops from the South. Moreover, it provided for the return of American prisoners of war. Finally, the agreement clearly stated that the United States would return if North Vietnam violated the terms of the accords. Kissinger jubilantly announced on October 26 that "peace was at hand." This proclamation, which occurred just days before the 1972 presidential election in the United States, has been widely credited as a factor in Nixon's landslide victory over Democratic nominee George McGovern.

There was one problem with the October agreement: South Vietnamese President Nguyen Van Thieu would not agree to the terms. Recognizing that neither his government nor his army could survive without American support, Thieu claimed that the agreement would do little more than provide a "decent interval" between the American departure and South Vietnam's demise. The deal collapsed, and when North Vietnam balked at giving more ground at the bargaining table, Nixon ordered another round of intensive bombing.

This bombing campaign, which began on December 18, was known as "Linebacker II." Like the first Linebacker bombardment, this campaign rained down a tremendous number of bombs on North Vietnamese infrastructure, including rail yards, ports, and power plants in Hanoi and Haiphong. Peace activists called it the "Christmas Bombings," and accused Nixon of expanding a war that most Americans opposed. In the end, however, many historians believe that the bombings did help bring the North Vietnamese back to the peace talks.

The final round of talks proceeded quickly. The negotiations included delegates from the United States, North Vietnam, the Thieu government in South Vietnam, and the Provisional Revolutionary Government (PRG). The PRG had been created by North Vietnam in 1969 to be Hanoi's "legal" voice in South Vietnam. Composed of Viet Cong and other insurgent leaders, it directed affairs in Communist-controlled areas of the South. North Vietnam and other socialist countries recognized it from the date of its creation as the truly legitimate government of South Vietnam.

On January 27, 1973, representatives from the four sides signed the Agreement on Ending the War and Restoring Peace in Vietnam, otherwise known as the Paris Accords. The Accords were full of provisions spelling out an end to military hostilities and the process by which peaceful elections would be held within South Vietnam. For example, the agreement created a National Council for Reconciliation that included political representation for the Provisional Revolutionary Government. This Council was given the responsibility to arrange new elections in South Vietnam in which representatives of the PRG could participate.

For the Americans, though, the only one thing that mattered was that their long and costly involvement in Vietnam was over. Nixon addressed the American people, telling them that all American troops would leave the country within 60 days and that "South Vietnam has gained the right to determine its own future. Let us be proud that America did not settle for a peace that betrayed an ally."

Thieu remained deeply unhappy with the accords, though. He had been coerced into signing the agreement only after Nixon granted South Vietnam huge amounts of military equipment, including planes and tanks—and warned him that the United States was prepared to "seek a settlement with the enemy which serves U.S. interests alone."

American officials promised Thieu and his supporters that the United States would not allow his nation to be overrun by the Communists. But the South Vietnamese were not reassured. They knew that public opinion in America would make it virtually impossible for any administration to send U.S. troops back into Vietnam. South Vietnamese politician Nguyen Cao Ky, a high-ranking figure in Thieu's government until 1971, summarized the South Vietnamese reaction when he said: "I could not stomach [the Paris Accords], so nauseating was its hypocrisy and self-delusion.... This is an enormous step toward the total domination of Vietnam and there is no reason why the Communists should stop now.... I give them a couple of years before they invade the South."

North Vietnamese lead negotiator Le Duc Tho and U.S. diplomat Henry Kissinger shake hands after finalizing the 1973 Paris Agreement on Ending the War and Restoring Peace in Vietnam.

America on the Sidelines

One provision of the Paris Accords was strictly honored: American troops quickly withdrew. By March 30, 1973, only 240 American personnel remained in South Vietnam. These troops were assigned primarily to the American embassy in Saigon. In addition, the North Vietnamese turned over hundreds of American prisoners of war (although claims that some U.S. prisoners were kept by the Communists have persisted ever since).

Almost every other provision of the Paris Accords, however, was abandoned or ignored. Efforts to produce a blueprint for national elections quickly

The Paris Peace Accords provided for the release of hundreds of American prisoners of war (POWs). Here, former POW Robert L. Stirm is greeted by his family at Travis Air Force Base in California as he returns home.

bogged down as Communist and non-Communist members became deadlocked over election procedures. Meanwhile, both sides violated the cease-fire agreement. Thieu was particularly aggressive during this time, using military resources left behind by the United States to launch attacks on territory controlled by the PRG. North Vietnam retreated and used the next several months to rebuild and recover from the damage inflicted by the American weaponry. Thieu also imposed a devastating "economic blockade" of rural areas believed to have been infiltrated by Communists. This ruthless and foolish measure sparked malnutrition and outright starvation in many areas of South Vietnam and destroyed the regime's already shaky reputation with the populace.

In the United States, meanwhile, lawmakers signaled that the Vietnamese would be left to settle their differences on their own. Congress slashed funding to South Vietnam from $2 billion in 1973 to $1 billion in 1974, then reduced it to $700 million the year after that. In August of 1973 Congress passed a resolution halting all bombing in Cambodia, and three months later it enacted the War Powers Act to limit the power of a president to wage war. The War Powers Act required the president to notify Congress of any use of military forces within forty-eight hours and to end military action within sixty days unless specifically authorized by Congress to do otherwise. (The War Powers Act remains a source of friction between the executive and legislative branch to this day.)

These new limits on presidential authority reflected not only deep American unhappiness with the whole Vietnam War, but also growing uneasiness with the Nixon administration itself. In 1973 the Nixon White House became mired in the Watergate affair. This scandal eventually revealed that Nixon had covered up his knowledge of burglaries and other illegal activities carried out by political allies. Watergate mesmerized the American public and pushed events in Vietnam off the front page, especially after the United States completed its military withdrawal from that war-torn nation in mid-1973. Nixon ultimately resigned the presidency on August 9, 1974, rather than face certain impeachment and removal from office. He was replaced by Vice President Gerald Ford.

The Reunification of Vietnam

By late 1974 North Vietnamese leaders were convinced that the Americans would not return. They also recognized that the Thieu regime had virtually no popular support left. With these factors in mind, the Communists began making plans to conquer South Vietnam once and for all. North Vietnamese Army troops were sent flowing south along the Ho Chi Minh Trial to build up strength along the perimeter of the Southern defenses. North Vietnam also replenished its army with new recruits and the latest Soviet weaponry.

In December 1974 the NVA stormed the provincial capital of Phuoc Long in the Central Highlands, easily defeating ARVN forces and taking the city. North Vietnamese leaders then waited to see what the American reaction would be. Thieu pleaded with the United States to help turn back the invasion, but to no avail. President Ford called on Congress to come to the aid of the ARVN, but lawmakers had no appetite for further involvement in Viet-

As the Communist offensive moved into the outskirts of Saigon, thousands of South Vietnamese refugees crowded onto boats to seek safety on U.S. war ships patrolling the coastal waters of the South China Sea.

nam. On March 10, 1975, it flatly denied an aid package to the beleaguered South Vietnamese. The vote was the clearest sign yet that the government of South Vietnam was now on its own.

From there the end came quickly. On March 10 North Vietnam pressed a massive offensive, called the Ho Chi Minh Campaign, deeper into South Vietnam's Central Highlands. Hoping to preserve territory for his government, Thieu ordered his troops to abandon the central highlands and consolidate their forces around the major cities. But these instructions triggered chaos throughout the northern provinces. Entire divisions of ARVN troops disintegrated in panic and fled southward. They were joined by terrified civilians who fled toward Saigon and the southern coast by the tens of thousands. Thousands of Vietnamese died from shelling or starvation in this awful exodus, which came to be known as the "Convoy of Tears."

Within a matter of days, major cities such as Danang and Hue had fallen to the wave of Communist troops sent from the North. Stunned by the lack of resistance to their offensive, North Vietnamese generals adjusted their goals and decided to conquer the entire country in one final push. By the end of March, the NVA controlled the northern half of the country, leaving the Thieu regime to defend the area around the capital city of Saigon.

Attacking from the north and the west, the North Vietnamese brought the full force of its military to bear on the remaining ARVN forces surrounding Saigon in April 1975. Those ARVN forces still willing to fight took a pounding, losing thousands of men as their circle of control constricted around Saigon. On April 21 President Thieu gave a tearful resignation speech in which he condemned America for its "irresponsible" treachery; Vice President Tran Van Huong took his place (he was in turn replaced a few days later by General Duong Van Minh, the man who officially surrendered to North Vietnam).

Saigon's last days as the capital of South Vietnam were nightmarish. A frantic airlift delivered the last few thousand U.S. citizens, as well as U.S. Ambassador Graham Martin and other embassy personnel, to the safety of American naval ships lying offshore. Many Vietnamese officials and assistances were also whisked to safety with their families. But hundreds of thousands of desperately frightened Vietnamese people were left behind in the now lawless streets of Saigon to face the approaching Communist tanks.

On April 30, 1975—one day after the last American helicopter disappeared over the horizon—jubilant North Vietnamese troops marched into the presidential palace in the center of Saigon. By nightfall the flag of Communist North Vietnam flew over the city, which the conquerors renamed Ho Chi Minh City. Finally, after eight decades of French colonialism and two decades of civil war, Vietnam had been reunified as a single independent country under Communist rule. One year later, the entire country was renamed as the Socialist Republic of Vietnam.

Chapter Seven

PATIENCE OVER POWER IN VIETNAM

⬤

Again and again, the Saigon regime ... came to the end of its natural life.... But again and again the United States hoisted the cadaver to its feet and tried to breathe artificial life into it. Like a ghost that is denied a grave to rest in, this regime stalked the earth posthumously.

—Jonathan Schell, *The Real War*

When American military forces entered Vietnam, they were known to be the best-equipped, best-trained, and most formidable fighting machine in the world. Yet they were ultimately unable to achieve a decisive victory against the Communist armies of North Vietnam and the Viet Cong, armies variously described as rag-tag, motley, and—in the words of one American secretary of state—"fourth-rate." A multitude of factors kept the Americans and their South Vietnamese allies from taking advantage of their military superiority to win the war. Political pressures, flawed military strategies, declining troop morale and performance, and the inadequacies of South Vietnam's government and army have all been blamed for the outcome in Vietnam. Conversely, the Communist North Vietnamese and their allies in the South, the Viet Cong, enjoyed a number of advantages that compensated for their disadvantages in wealth and firepower. Their methodical approach, their intense commitment to their cause, and the battlefield strategies they employed all contributed to their eventual victory.

A Limited War with a Limited Ally

From the first commitment of American military personnel under President Dwight D. Eisenhower in 1954, U.S. policy in Vietnam was to limit its involvement in the country to the minimum necessary to achieve its goal: the preservation of South Vietnam as an anti-Communist ally in the region. Under President John F. Kennedy, America tried to keep South Vietnam from succumbing to the rising Communist threat by incrementally increasing its military and financial assistance to Saigon. By 1965, however, American analysts decided that it was necessary to take stronger measures to counter the growing Communist military menace. That year, President Lyndon Johnson ordered the first American combat troops into Vietnam. Johnson's goal was to utilize the smallest number of American soldiers needed to preserve South Vietnam's independence. The United States did not enter Vietnam to claim new territory. Rather, it wanted to convince the Communists that 1) the United States was serious about preserving the existing government of South Vietnam, and 2) the Communists would suffer enormously if they chose to continue their insurgency.

The American desire to wage a limited war in Vietnam was the product of a variety of domestic and international political considerations. When Johnson took office in late 1963, his fondest wish was to address civil rights, poverty, housing, and other pressing social justice issues in America. He knew that the situation in Vietnam required attention, but he was determined that it not derail his goal of building a "Great Society." Therefore, Johnson did not make a strong and early public case for going to war in Vietnam, and his administration took limited actions that it hoped would persuade the North Vietnamese and Viet Cong to back off.

International pressures also inclined Johnson to pursue a limited war. Though the United States wanted to stop the spread of Communism, it did not want a direct conflict with either of the Communist giants, the Soviet Union or China. Concerned that overly aggressive military action—such as direct bombing of Hanoi, North Vietnam's capital—might draw one of these Communist giants into the war, Johnson placed strict limits on American military options in Vietnam. Some analysts and historians have asserted that Johnson's decision to forego a major early offensive against North Vietnam gave the enemy confidence that it could continue the war without fear of truly damaging reprisals from the United States.

Perhaps the greatest factor hindering the American war effort in Vietnam was its ally: South Vietnam. Politically, the United States felt that it had little choice but to support South Vietnam, but the country's political and military problems were numerous. The political leadership in South Vietnam from 1954 to 1975 was ineffective at best and thoroughly corrupt at worst. In the

U.S. President Lyndon B. Johnson (right) confers with South Vietnamese President Nguyen Van Thieu at a 1968 conference in Hawaii. Thieu has been widely criticized for his leadership of South Vietnam during the war.

latter years of the war, for example, the government was led by Nguyen Van Theiu and Nguyen Cao Ky, two generals who American assistant secretary of state William Bundy characterized as "the bottom of the barrel, absolutely the bottom of the barrel." Each of these wartime leaders focused on securing the allegiance of the South Vietnamese military and preserving power, often by ruthless means that turned the Vietnamese population against them. The American forces that backed these corrupt leaders were thus widely distrusted by the people of South Vietnam.

The armed forces of South Vietnam suffered greatly from the corruption and instability that afflicted the national government. When American engagement in Vietnam began, the U.S. emphasis was on training and equip-

Atrocities on Both Sides

Even under the best of conditions, war is brutal, horrid, and inhumane. It is, by definition, organized killing. Over the years, armies have developed "rules of war" to try to shield non-combatants from the viciousness of war. But in all wars there are incidents when the rules of war are ignored or trampled and civilians pay the price. These incidents are called atrocities, and the Vietnam War saw more than its fair share. "Whether committed in the name of principles or out of vengeance, atrocities were as common to the Vietnamese battlefields as shell craters and barbed wire," wrote Vietnam veteran Philip Caputo in *A Rumor of War.*

By far the most notable American atrocity of the war was the My Lai massacre, which took place in South Vietnam's Quang Ngai province. On March 16, 1968, an American unit was sent out on a search-and-destroy mission in an area suspected of harboring Viet Cong. Once they entered "My Lai 4" (one of several hamlets that made up Song My village), a platoon led by Lieutenant William Calley launched a systematic slaughter of unarmed women, children, and the elderly. Old people were bayoneted in the backs while they prayed; dozens of people were herded into a ditch and machine-gunned; and several women were raped and then murdered. By the time American helicopter pilots spotted the ongoing massacre and intervened, hundreds of people had been killed (estimates vary from as low as 128 to as high as 504). For over a year the military covered up the incident, but eventually the massacre came to light. An investiga-

ping the armed forces of South Vietnam to carry out the war against North Vietnam and the Viet Cong themselves. Yet from the early 1960s on, it was apparent that the South Vietnamese military was incapable of winning its own war. The ARVN grew in size over the course of the war, reaching nearly one million soldiers by 1975. But few soldiers felt any real loyalty to the government, and desertion rates were very high throughout the war. In addition, corruption was rampant in the army, and many of its top ranking officers had achieved their positions from political connections rather than merit. As the war ground on, the ARVN's inconsistent performance aroused the distrust

tion led to the court martial and murder conviction of Calley, but 24 other officers and enlisted men charged in the case never received prison sentences; they were either acquitted or had charges dropped on technicalities. Calley, meanwhile, was originally sentenced to life in prison. But his case became so heavily tangled in national politics that he gained his release from prison in late 1975.

The most heavily publicized atrocities committed by the Communists occurred in the city of Hue during the Tet Offensive of 1968. For years, Communists had used murder and kidnapping to terrorize those who lent their support to the South Vietnamese regime or to the Americans. In the days after they captured the city of Hue in early February, Viet Cong and NVA soldiers reportedly butchered thousands of civilians suspected of having cooperated with the South Vietnamese regime. The extent of the slaughter in Hue has since been a subject of considerable debate, but scholars agree that civilian executions were undoubtedly an element of the early 1968 Communist occupation of that city.

Some scholars have asserted that the officially sanctioned quality of the executions committed by Communist forces in Hue and other places make those incidents even more despicable. "It is important to note that for American forces [atrocities] were aberrations in direct violation of U.S. military law," wrote Colonel Harry G. Summers in *Vietnam War Almanac*. "For the Viet Cong and the North Vietnamese Army, however, atrocities were a deliberate, sanctioned tactic."

and anger of American generals and soldiers—and convinced the United States that it would have to shoulder most of the military burden if it hoped to claim victory. (By contrast, American troops recognized the tenacity and skill of the enemy Viet Cong and North Vietnamese Army-NVA troops.)

American War Strategies

By 1965 it had become clear that the ARVN alone could not defeat the Communists and that the mere threat of American force would not be sufficient. American combat troops subsequently were placed in Vietnam, and their numbers grew dramatically over the next several years. During that period of deepening involvement, U.S. General William Westmoreland, consulting closely with high-ranking civilians in the Johnson administration (especially Secretary of Defense Robert McNamara), devised a strategy known as attrition, which was intended to punish North Vietnam into submission. Some of that punishment was delivered through aerial bombing campaigns, but U.S. strategists also relied on ground campaigns designed to kill so many Viet Cong and NVA soldiers that the enemy would lose its will to fight.

The strategies devised to fight in Vietnam reflected the unique conditions of that conflict. Early in the war, the Communists tried concentrated, conventional attacks on South Vietnamese positions, only to be soundly beaten by superior American firepower. The Communists adapted quickly, however. They rolled out a new strategy of guerilla warfare, dispersing their forces across the Vietnamese countryside in smaller groups. These units focused on taking one village at a time through a combination of intimidation, violence, and propaganda. Faced with this new strategy, the United States turned to search-and-destroy missions.

In a typical search-and-destroy mission, a small unit of soldiers (usually between 40 and 80 men) would venture beyond an established U.S. position to seek out and eliminate Viet Cong camps or mobile units. Often, U.S. units were airlifted into targeted areas by helicopter, but most of these missions placed a heavy emphasis on overland foot travel. Soldiers called these multi-day expeditions "humpin' the boonies" or simply "humpin' it."

The tension of a search-and-destroy mission could be excruciating. Walking through a steaming jungle or hip deep in a rice paddy, soldiers listened and watched intently for any sign of enemy action. At any moment a unit might stumble across an enemy camp or a Viet Cong ambush and a quiet afternoon would ignite into an intense "firefight" or gun battle. Other times a unit might go for days without encountering an enemy, yet still lose men to hidden booby traps, land mines, or poisonous snakes or scorpions. Veterans of these search-and-destroy missions (or, as the U.S. military preferred to call them, "search and clear missions" or "pre-emptive operations") grew increasingly hardened to the danger, but also to the act of killing. "I know my happiest moment in Vietnam was when I was hit, because I 'knew' I was homeward bound," recalled Vietnam veteran John J. Fitzgerald, co-author of *The Vietnam War: A History in Documents*. "I have never wanted to be out of a place

A U.S. soldier throws a rice basket into the flames of a burning house during a "search and destroy" mission in October 1967.

more than Vietnam. The place filled me with dread and I have never known the kind of fear I felt there any place else."

Determining the effectiveness of search-and-destroy missions was a difficult process. Over time, though, the U.S. military tried to quantify the success of its attrition strategy by relying on "body counts." A body count was a simple count of the number of enemy killed and wounded in battle. Measured against the number of American or ARVN soldiers lost, the body count produced a "kill ratio." U.S. commanders rated the success of a mission by this kill ratio; a ratio of 10:1 was considered average, while a ratio of 50:1 was rated excellent. For much of the war, these casualty figures were regularly released to the U.S. news media and public to show them how the war was progressing.

"Body count" statistics gave the surface impression that American troops were faring well: they were killing Communists at a far greater rate than they were being killed. But this statistical measurement was useless as a tool for measuring North Vietnamese and Viet Cong dedication to their cause. Nor could it measure the rural population's growing anger and despair over the ways in which the attrition strategy employed by U.S. and ARVN troops disrupted, endangered, and claimed the lives of friends and family members.

The logging of body counts was detrimental to the American cause in other ways as well. It rewarded officers and units for producing "body count" numbers which could not be verified, thus encouraging U.S. troops to fabricate or elevate counts. When it was revealed that these statistics could not be trusted, the American public (and news media) became even more suspicious of optimistic official reports on the war. In addition, it has been widely claimed that the reliance on body counts as a statistical indicator of the war's progress encouraged American soldiers to take lives unnecessarily. According to this charge, U.S. troops patrolling the dangerous South Vietnamese countryside became more likely to fire on rural Vietnamese civilians on mere suspicion that they were Viet Cong (VC) or VC sympathizers because the soldiers understood that their superiors held the view that "If it's dead, it's VC."

Declining Morale

When the Vietnam War began and American troops first entered the country, they did so with confidence and pride. Polls, interviews, news stories, and letters all showed that most soldiers, as well as the American public, believed that U.S. troops were fighting in Vietnam for a valiant cause: to prevent Communist forces from overthrowing a legitimate democracy. American soldiers thus entered Vietnam with the same can-do spirit that had accompanied U.S. actions in World War II. Yet over the course of the war this confidence leached away, undermining the troops' morale and fighting efficiency.

One of the most frequently cited factors that negatively influenced morale and performance in American combat units was U.S. policy regarding tours of duty. Instead of being stationed in Vietnam permanently—which might have allowed soldiers to better understand local conditions, become accustomed to the nature of warfare in Vietnam, and improve unit cohesion—most U.S. soldiers were placed in Vietnam for a thirteen-month tour of duty. This created a situation in which soldiers were constantly being rotated in and out of units. This lack of continuity sapped the effectiveness of entire units. Indeed, veteran GIs dreaded the arrival of new soldiers, who were often the first to get killed or to give away the unit's location to the Viet Cong.

Meanwhile, "short-timers"—soldiers reaching the end of their tours—counted the days until their assignment ended and they could return home to America. Many of these soldiers naturally became more reluctant to place themselves in danger when they knew that they would be delivered from the war zone in a matter of days or weeks.

Adding to the problems created by troop rotation were tensions created by the draft and by racial divisions among the troops. Throughout the Vietnam era, all American boys who reached age 18 were required to register with the Selective Service to make themselves eligible for required military service. But while there were no exceptions regarding registration, draft-age men could avoid induction into the armed services if they met certain criteria. Young men attending college, raising families, or pursuing certain professional occupations, for example, could all secure deferments.

"I know my happiest moment in Vietnam was when I was hit, because I 'knew' I was homeward bound," recalled one American war veteran. *"I have never wanted to be out of a place more than Vietnam."*

These policies—especially the college deferment—enabled many young men from middle- and upper-class economic backgrounds to avoid serving during the war. By contrast, young men who were poor, less educated, or black were much more likely to be drafted to fight in Vietnam. As a result, U.S. casualties during the war were disproportionately from these demographic groups. African Americans, for example, accounted for 31 percent of total U.S. combat troops in Vietnam and approximately one quarter of combat deaths before 1970—even though they made up only 11 percent of the U.S. male draft-age population.

The clear social inequities of the draft did not escape the notice of antiwar and civil rights protestors in the United States. The antiwar movement portrayed this state of affairs as another example of the moral failure of U.S. leadership. Protestors encouraged young men to resist the draft, and many of these draft resistors fled to Canada to avoid going to war. Back in Vietnam, meanwhile, the antiwar movement in the United States caused considerable pain and anger among many U.S. troops.

Ultimately, all of these factors contributed to the steady decline in the morale of American soldiers. In 1971, *New York Times* reporter B. Drummond Ayers Jr. wrote: "The bitter Vietnam experience has left the United States Army

"Fragging" in Vietnam

One of the most troubling indicators of the decline in American military order and morale during the Vietnam War was the increased incidence of "fragging," a term used for an attack on one's own commanding officer. These incidents got their name from the fact that some murder attempts took the form of tossing a fragmentation grenade into a tent or latrine. They most often occurred when gung-ho officers gave orders that put men in potential danger. Some American combat units even put cash bounties on the heads of their officers. For the American military, fragging represented the ultimate breakdown in order and discipline.

During the height of U.S. involvement in Vietnam, hundreds of fragging incidents were being documented each year. The years 1970-1971 were especially bad. Even though U.S. troops were being brought home by that time, those left behind in the jungles of Vietnam felt abandoned. Determined not to lose their lives in the last months of a war that America clearly wanted out of, some soldiers came to see assassination of inexperienced, incompetent, or overzealous superior officers as a legitimate act of self-preservation.

with a crisis in morale and discipline as serious as any its oldest and toughest soldiers can remember…. The men themselves are fed up with the war and the draft, questioning orders, deserting, subverting, smoking marijuana, shooting heroin, stealing from their buddies, hurling racial epithets and rocks at their brothers." Certainly not all American soldiers serving in Vietnam behaved in this fashion; many carried out their duties professionally, despite the frightening and chaotic environment that surrounded them. But there is a general consensus that breakdowns in military discipline and performance in the armed forces became much more common in the final years of U.S. involvement in Vietnam.

Race Relations in Vietnam

In many cases, morale problems and the vicious nature of the war in Vietnam further inflamed the racial bias that some American troops carried against

South Vietnamese civilian survivors of a clash between Viet Cong and government forces huddle together in shock.

the Vietnamese. The differences in language, culture, and physical appearance between Vietnamese and Americans were significant and difficult to bridge, especially in an environment where it was often impossible for U.S. soldiers to tell if a Vietnamese was a "friendly" or a Viet Cong agent. The Vietnamese people, meanwhile, came to see American forces as a single great juggernaut that was rolling over their country, leaving ruined forests, fields, and villages in its wake.

Importantly, many Vietnamese also saw the Americans as agents of destruction in the realm of Vietnamese culture and tradition. These changes were most obvious in Saigon and other major population centers that were completely transformed by the arrival of the Americans. "The rapid process of modernization and the impact of the American presence had unsettled traditional Vietnamese social relationships and standards of behavior," explained Edward Doyle and Stephen Weiss in *A Collision of Cultures*. "In a society of limited resources and communal arrangements, a new materialism had emerged, an unfettered pursuit of wealth and luxury that strained families, fostered crime, and … accentuated the contrast between the cities and the rural areas" of Vietnam. Or, as U.S. Senator J. William Fulbright charged in 1967, "Saigon has become an American brothel."

But the American military's incursion into Vietnam also brought U.S. troops into contact with rural Vietnamese. These encounters rarely ended positively for the Vietnamese. At worst, peasants saw their homes and crops destroyed by American units, and even if their possessions were left intact, they were often subjected to humiliating treatment. "The war had already been lost by the time I got there in the spring of 1967," claimed soldier-turned-author Tobias Wolff in *Time*. "The suspicion that this was so came upon me not as a thought but as a deepening unease at the way we treated the Vietnamese and the way they treated one another…. Everywhere I went I saw Americans raining contempt on Vietnamese, handling them roughly, speaking to them like badly behaved children, or dogs. In time I learned to do it myself. Fear was our teacher; it taught us some bad lessons, and taught them well."

The physical damage done to Vietnam by American military actions also darkened Vietnamese attitudes toward the United States and the government it supported in Saigon. "By the end of the war there were an estimated 21 million bomb craters in South Vietnam," asserted James William Gibson in *The Perfect War*. "Air force planes sprayed 18 million gallons of herbicide containing dioxins on some six million acres—around one-seventh of South Vietnam's total land area…. An additional 1,200 square miles of territory were bulldozed flat, stripped of all life." An untold number of Vietnamese villages—the traditional cornerstone of Vietnamese culture—were destroyed as a result of these actions. But as Jonathan Schell noted in *The Real War*, "victories … won at the expense of pulverizing the country physically … provid[ed] a poor foundation for the creation of the strong, independent regime in the South that American policy required. The moral absurdity of 'destroying' the society we were trying to 'save' was often pointed out; the strategic absurdity of the same policy was less often noted."

A People's War: The Communist War Effort

Looking back on the Vietnam War, Americans have sometimes marveled that their rich and powerful nation was unable to defeat an enemy that, by comparison, was as poorly equipped and poorly funded as Communist North Vietnam and the Viet Cong. But the Communists actually enjoyed significant political, social, and tactical advantages. These advantages were further strengthened by a shared sense of purpose that nurtured the Communists even during the darkest days of the war.

To U.S. policymakers, North Vietnam was a symbol of the Soviet and Chinese effort to spread Communism throughout the world. But to many Vietnamese the existence of North Vietnam was an inspiration, one that stood in contrast to the "puppet" governments of South Vietnam. For all its shortcomings, Communist North Vietnam was free and independent from foreign rule. This simple fact gave it legitimacy and respect among Vietnamese who looked back on the nation's colonial past with anger and resentment.

North Vietnamese military commander Vo Nguyen Giap, who oversaw the ultimately successful Communist strategy of guerrilla warfare.

Ho Chi Minh, military commander Vo Nguyen Giap, and the Communist leaders who followed in their path adeptly managed the contrasting appeals of nationalism and Communism to mobilize their followers for war. Within North Vietnam, the Communist Party eliminated political rivals and insisted upon complete obedience to the government. There were no antiwar marches in Hanoi. Within South Vietnam, however, the Communist-backed National Liberation Front (popularly known as the Viet Cong) downplayed Communism in favor of nationalism. Rather than calling for a Communist revolution in South Vietnam, it called for free and fair multi-party elections (which it was confident of winning). This political strategy muted resistance to Communism in the South and helped win over politically undecided peasants who made up the majority of the Vietnamese population.

Giap parlayed this political advantage into a simple but brutally effective war strategy. Ever since he had helped found the Viet Minh nationalist group in the 1940s, Giap had worked to find ways for a poor but committed people to defeat a rich and heavily armed foe. He put his studies to the test in the Viet Minh's long and ultimately successful contest against the French. Giap published some of his insights into this war in *People's War: People's Army* (1961). "Our strategy was ... to wage a long-lasting battle," he wrote. "Only a long-term war could enable us to utilize to the maximum our political trump cards, to overcome our material handicap and to transform our weakness into strength.... From the military point of view, *the Vietnamese people's war of liberation proved that an insufficiently equipped people's army, but an army fighting for a just cause, can, with appropriate strategy and tactics, combine the conditions needed to conquer a modern army of aggressive imperialism.*"

Throughout the Vietnam War, both North Vietnam and the Viet Cong used the various elements of Giap's war strategy to advance their cause. For example, they successfully enlisted the citizenry in their struggle—sometimes through violence and intimidation. Villagers provided food and shelter for troops, acted as sentries and observers of enemy activity, transported supplies, and assisted the insurgents in a host of other ways. This development was daunting to American forces, for it was impossible for them to tell friend from foe among the South Vietnamese population. Americans naturally became suspicious that every Vietnamese person they met might be Viet Cong or a Viet Cong sympathizer.

The nature of service in the Communist armies was also quite unlike that in the U.S. ranks. At the peak of war, 40 percent of North Vietnamese between the ages of eighteen and thirty-four were in the North Vietnamese army. North Vietnamese society thus became suffused with the feeling that an entire generation was joined in a common cause.

In addition, North Vietnamese troops knew that they would remain with the military until they were wounded, killed, or the war was won. Unlike their American counterparts, their personal involvement in the war had no "end date." As a result of this level of commitment, soldiers became very skilled at their tasks. Communist soldiers also worked hard. When they were not actively engaged with the enemy, they were digging tunnels, ferrying military equipment to distant locations, training new recruits, or placing booby traps near American bases. This dedication to the cause clearly contributed to the Communists' eventual triumph.

Chapter Eight

THE AMERICAN ANTIWAR MOVEMENT

⊸⪽⫯⪾⊷

I have worked too long and hard now against segregated public accommodations to end up segregating my moral concern. Justice is indivisible.... Now it should be incandescently clear that no one who has any concern for the integrity and life of America today can ignore the present war.

—Martin Luther King Jr., 1967

Thumbing through the pages of American history books, one can find wildly different interpretations of the character, morality, and influence of the antiwar movement that roiled American society and politics during the years of the Vietnam War. According to some historians—and many participants—the antiwar protests that rocked U.S. campuses, the halls of government, and American living rooms were patriotic, politically influential, and founded on the highest moral convictions. This antiwar movement pulled together the efforts of millions of Americans, from college students to business people. Proponents say that antiwar outrage was a key factor in bringing down the presidency of Lyndon B. Johnson in 1968 and forcing Johnson's successor, Richard M. Nixon, to withdraw American combat forces beginning in 1969. According to some participants and observers, the American antiwar movement also was pivotal in weaning American society from decades of stifling conformity and blind faith in governmental institutions.

But other analysts, joined by millions of Americans who lived through the turbulent years of the 1960s and 1970s, continue to describe the antiwar movement as destructive, incoherent, shockingly self-absorbed, and fundamentally anti-American. According to these voices, the antiwar movement had "more clowns than heroes, more ignominy than virtue," wrote Gerard J. DeGroot in *A Noble Cause? America and the Vietnam War*. People holding this view insist that America's understandable concern about the Vietnam War was hijacked by a radical minority who made villains of American soldiers serving their country, aided the enemy, and did lasting damage to trust and civility in American politics and society.

There was, of course, just one antiwar movement, and while its essential qualities remain in dispute, observers of all ideological stripes are in basic agreement about its arc of growth and influence. Taking its inspiration from other influential social movements of the era, the antiwar movement emerged as a significant force in 1965 as a scattered series of teach-ins and events on college campuses. It became much larger and more diverse, however, as the American war effort expanded. The movement achieved its greatest impact from 1967 through 1970, when massive protests were held in Washington, D.C. and other major American cities, as well as on hundreds of university campuses. After 1970 the movement became less visible and influential, its main message somewhat negated by Nixon's withdrawal of combat troops from Vietnam. But even after the antiwar movement ceased to exist, its cultural impact remains a source of great debate among historians—and ordinary Americans—to this day.

Roots of Youth Protest

Prior to 1964, when President Johnson persuaded Congress to pass the Gulf of Tonkin Resolution granting him authority to wage war in Vietnam, few Americans knew or cared about the distant Southeast Asian nation of Vietnam. Nor was Vietnam a subject of conversation among the record number of students who were pouring into American colleges and universities at that time. Within the general American population, only a tiny number of pacifist and socialist groups, such as the War Resisters League, the Fellowship of Reconciliation, and the American Friends Service Committee, were registering concerns about the growing presence and influence of American military advisors in Vietnam during the late 1950s and early 1960s.

Yet American ignorance about Vietnam was not due to any apathy toward current events or foreign policy among the general populace. In fact, the early 1960s had already proven to be a time of momentous political and social activism driven by high ideals. Starting in the American South, the civil rights movement had energized African Americans (and their many white allies) to protest against the racial injustice and entrenched discrimination that characterized so many American political and social institutions.

During the early 1960s, meanwhile, President John F. Kennedy had also appealed to American idealism. He urged ordinary people to take an active role in improving American institutions and exporting the best parts of American life to nations abroad through such groups as the Peace Corps. When Lyndon B. Johnson took over the presidency after John F. Kennedy's tragic assassination in November 1963, he similarly encouraged Americans to commit themselves to creating a better world. The centerpiece of Johnson's whole domestic agenda, in fact, was the creation of what he called a "Great Society," one that would eradicate poverty and other social problems that had long bedeviled the United States.

These and other reforms took place against the backdrop of the Cold War, a tense political, military, and economic rivalry between democratic nations, led by the United States, and Communist nations, especially the Soviet Union. Their self-proclaimed status as the world's leading promoter of freedom, democracy, and individualism caused many Americans to think deeply about these values—and to ask whether they were really living up to them.

American youths entering college in the late 1950s and into the 1960s were filled with the reforming energies of the era and generally embraced an idealistic vision of American values at home and abroad. In some of the most prestigious American universities, groups of students founded organizations that challenged limits on student freedom and probed into the nature of authority in American institutions in general. In 1959 students at the University of Michigan in Ann Arbor formed the Students for a Democratic Society (SDS); three years later they issued their famous political manifesto, "The Port Huron Statement," which called for fundamental reforms of American government and educational institutions, among other objectives.

At the University of California, Berkeley, meanwhile, students led by Mario Savio formed a group called the Free Speech Movement and made national headlines protesting limits on student political organizing and academic freedom. Hundreds of students were arrested before the university changed its regulations. On these campuses and many others which looked to Ann Arbor and Berkeley as examples, students exhibited an increased willingness to use political organization and protest to challenge perceived shortcomings in American society.

An antiwar "sit-in" at the University of Michigan in Ann Arbor, where some of the earliest organized antiwar demonstrations took place.

Early Antiwar Demonstrations

The first significant national demonstrations against American military involvement in Vietnam took place within months of the Gulf of Tonkin Resolution, which gave Johnson wide latitude to expand U.S. military operations in Southeast Asia. In December 1964 the War Resisters League organized an early demonstration. Four months later, on March 24, 1965, organizers unveiled the first major expression of the antiwar movement in direct response to the arrival of the first American ground troops (3,000 Marines) in South Vietnam. This "teach-in" at the University of Michigan featured politically active professors, peace activists, and organizers who led classes and all-night discussions about the nature of the emerging American war effort in Vietnam.

Word of the teach-ins spread, and soon they were happening on college campuses across the country. Because there was no centralized organization behind the antiwar efforts, the messages at the teach-ins differed from campus to campus. Yet they contained a common thread: antiwar activists argued that the South Vietnamese government that was being supported by U.S. dollars was corrupt, brutal, militaristic, and anti-democratic. These demonstrators asserted that supporting such a regime was a betrayal of the very values Americans prized at home.

From the seeds of these teach-ins came the first organized antiwar protest to garner truly national attention. The March on Washington to End the War in Vietnam took place on April 17, 1965. The leaders of the Students for a Democratic Society (SDS), which organized the demonstration, only expected a few thousand participants. But instead, between 15,000 and 25,000 protestors spent the day marching and listening to speeches against the war. Paul Potter, then president of the SDS, asked the crowd: "What kind of system is it that justifies … seizing the destinies of the Vietnamese people and using them callously for its own purposes? What kind of system is it that disenfranchises people in the South, leaves millions upon millions of people throughout the country impoverished ... that consistently puts material values before humane values—and still persists in calling itself free and still persists in finding itself fit to police the world?" It was this kind of message that motivated protestors throughout the years-long antiwar effort that followed.

As Troop Strength Escalates, So Do Demonstrations

From 1965 through 1968, the American presence in South Vietnam expanded dramatically and so too did antiwar demonstrations. A variety of groups joined in the antiwar cause, representing a broad range of interests. In addition to student groups, religious and pacifist groups such as Clergy and Laity Concerned About Vietnam (CALCAV), the National Emergency Committee of Clergy Concerned About Vietnam, and the Catholic Peace Fellowship emerged as vocal critics of the war. CALCAV, in particular, was a formidable group, because as the war dragged on it expanded beyond its liberal Protestant roots to gather a number of conservative religious leaders to its banner. At around the same time, civil rights leaders like Martin Luther King, Jr., explicitly linked the Vietnam War, which was being fought disproportionately by lower-class African Americans, with the larger civil rights struggle still being waged in America.

These leaders and organizations pointedly questioned why the United States was willing to lend its support to military governments in South Vietnam that had no popular support. And as the number of American and Vietnamese dead and wounded in the conflict continued to escalate, they asked a simple question: Was "saving" South Vietnam worth the cost paid in human lives?

By 1967, the numbers of people motivated to participate in antiwar protests—often called peace protests—were truly impressive. On April 15, 1967, 125,000 people showed up for a protest in New York City staged by an antiwar coalition collectively known as the Spring Mobilization Committee to End the War in Vietnam; on that same day, 70,000 gathered in San Francisco,

"What kind of system is it that disenfranchises people in the South, leaves millions upon millions of people throughout the country impoverished ... that consistently puts material values before humane values—and still persists in calling itself free and still persists in finding itself fit to police the world?"
— SDS Leader
Paul Potter

Demonstrations of support for the Johnson Administration, such as this 1966 rally in Indianapolis, Indiana, were dwarfed by antiwar protests across the country.

California. These huge and generally peaceful protests were widely publicized across America by the news media, and they were undoubtedly a factor in convincing growing numbers of liberal Congressmen and other political figures to declare their opposition to the war. In May 1966, for example, former Marine Corps general David Shoup, who had commanded the entire U.S. Marine Corps during the Kennedy administration, publicly asserted that "I don't think the whole of Southeast Asia, as related to the present and future safety and freedom of this country, is worth the life or limb of a single American."

Buoyed by the surging momentum of the antiwar movement, a group calling itself the National Mobilization Committee to End the War (or MOBE for short) pulled together the most dramatic protest yet. In late October 1967, some 100,000-250,000 people traveled to Washington, D.C. Unlike many past demonstrations, this protest event featured large numbers of businessmen, housewives, and blue-collar workers alongside the long-haired hippies and casually dressed college students that had long been the movement's foundation. At the height of the protest, some 50,000 people formed a human ring around the Pentagon, the headquarters of the U.S. military. Television cameras captured the dramatic scenes as college students placed flowers inside the raised gun barrels of the military police guarding the building; all the while folksingers sang protest songs and activists lectured on the evils of war. The surreal, carnival-like images from this event remain some of the most compelling of the entire Vietnam era.

Johnson's Last Months

President Johnson was cut deeply by the outraged rhetoric of the antiwar movement. After all, these young, socially conscious Americans were the very

One of the most notable antiwar demonstrations of the Vietnam era took place in October 1967, when thousands of protestors marched on the Pentagon.

ones that he counted on for support of his Great Society programs. In late 1967, Johnson called General William Westmoreland, the head of military operations in Vietnam, back to the United States to assure the American public that "the end was coming into sight." Johnson bolstered these claims, proclaiming that when it came to the war, he could see the "light at the end of the tunnel." In January 1968, though, the North Vietnamese and Viet Cong armies launched the Tet Offensive deep into South Vietnam. The size and scope of this assault stunned both South Vietnam and the United States. It also sparked a chorus of new accusations that the Johnson administration was cynically misleading the American people about the war's progress.

Though American and South Vietnamese troops turned back the Tet Offensive and actually made gains on the field of battle, Tet proved to be a fatal wound for the Johnson presidency. Many Americans felt that Johnson had lied to them, and that the war was doomed to churn on for years to come. This

During the late 1960s, burning draft cards became a popular means of expressing defiance and anger over U.S. policies in Vietnam.

prospect incited the antiwar movement to even greater action. In the wake of Tet, demonstrations flared up on campuses across the nation. Most dramatically, in April and May some 1,000 students took over five buildings on the campus of Columbia University in New York City. They held the buildings for ransom, demanding an end to the war for their return. Eventually police stormed the facilities with clubs flying, arresting nearly 700 students.

It was not just committed antiwar students who turned against the war following the Tet Offensive. As the campaign season for the 1968 presidential elections kicked off, Democratic Senator Eugene McCarthy's condemnations of the "hollow claims" of the Johnson administration made him an early front-runner for his party's nomination. Meanwhile, mainstream American newspapers and television commentators spoke more critically about the war. The *Wall Street Journal,* one of the more conservative American newspapers, suggested that the American war effort "may be doomed." America's most trusted television anchorman, Walter Cronkite, announced on his CBS nightly news program that it is "more certain than ever that the bloody experience of Vietnam is to end in a stalemate." Reeling at the combined impact of the antiwar movement, the loss of mainstream support, and the continued difficulty of waging war, Johnson announced on March 31, 1968, that he would not seek reelection to the presidency. The antiwar movement, crowed supporters, had toppled a president.

The Chicago Convention

Johnson's withdrawal from the presidential race gave new momentum to supporters of an American withdrawal from the Vietnam War. Many activists looked to the upcoming Democratic National Convention in Chicago as their chance to secure the nomination of a candidate pledged to end the war. Yet the events of 1968 conspired against any great political victory. In the months before the convention, two of America's most prominent political figures were assassinated. On April 4, 1968, civil rights leader Martin Luther King Jr. was shot in Memphis, Tennessee. Two months later, on June 5, 1968, Democratic presidential hopeful Robert "Bobby" Kennedy was gunned down in Los Angeles (he died the next day).

The year 1968 also was marked by growing fissures within the antiwar movement itself. In the first few years of the antiwar movement, philosophical differences between mainstream opponents of the war and radical organizations had been suppressed. But as the war ground on, the violent and sometimes anarchic messages of radical antiwar figures increasingly alienated pacifists, mainstream liberals, and other Americans who had grown disillusioned with the war.

This splintering within the antiwar movement intensified after the August 1968 Democratic National Convention. The protest activities surrounding the convention hall were dominated by the more radical and disorderly groups in the wider American reform movement, including the Black Panthers, a militant black separatist group, and a new group calling itself the Yippies, led by Jerry Rubin and Abbie Hoffman. The Yippies called for open drug use in the streets and nominated a pig for president. Sensing the potential for anarchy, Chicago Mayor Richard Daley announced in the weeks before the convention that his hard-nosed police force would crack down hard on civil disorder. The stage was set for an epic confrontation.

Inside the convention center, Democratic party officials battled over their platform on the Vietnam War. After a tough fight they nominated Vice President Hubert Humphrey and pledged their support to continue Johnson's war policies. Outside the convention center, protestors defied police orders to stay off the streets. The city's Grant Park became the epicenter of the protests, and clashes between protestors and law enforcement flared up throughout the first days of the convention. Order finally broke down on the final day of the convention as heavily armed police charged into throngs of protestors. "[Police] used clubs, fists, blackjacks, and brass knuckles," wrote Richard L. Wormser in *Three Faces of Vietnam*. "They swept through gatherings of people chanting, 'kill! kill! kill!', clubbing demonstrators, bystanders, and journalists." Protestors scrambled to get away, running wildly through the streets. And television cameras captured it all. In the final analysis, it was hard to say whose reputation was injured most by the events in Chicago: the antiwar movement, which seemed to have been hijacked by violent revolutionaries; Daly's Chicago police, who came off as jackbooted thugs; or the Democratic Party, which found itself portrayed in many quarters as symbolic of a divided and chaotic America.

The violence that swirled around the Democratic Convention confirmed the beliefs of many Americans that the antiwar protestors had gone too far. The emerging Republican presidential frontrunner, Richard M. Nixon, spoke to their fears about social disorder when he promised that as president he would bring a return to "law and order." Regarding Vietnam, Nixon agreed with President Johnson that it was time to seek negotiations to end the war in Vietnam and bring American soldiers home, but he pledged to Americans that he would not accept an American defeat. His stated campaign goal was to bring "peace with honor." In one of the closest elections up to that point in American history, Richard Nixon won the November presidential election with 43.4 percent of the popular vote. Humphrey won 42.7 percent, and third-party candidate George Wallace claimed most of the remaining votes.

Last Act of the Antiwar Movement

Nixon's pledges to end the war and bring American troops home brought an immediate decrease in antiwar protests in the United States—but the quiet did not last for long. When Nixon accelerated the bombing of North Vietnam in mid-1969, protests erupted anew as critics charged that the president was actually expanding the war. On October 15, 1969, a "Moratorium Day" organized by two antiwar organizations—the New Mobilization Committee to End the War and the Vietnam Moratorium Committee—who were dissatisfied with the pace of U.S. withdrawal was honored by millions of Americans across the country. The largest Moratorium Day demonstrations were held in Boston and New York City, but smaller gatherings were reported from coast to coast. One month later, another Moratorium Day attracted even bigger crowds.

Nixon responded to these protests on November 3, 1969, with his famous "Silent Majority" speech, in which he attempted to tie American patriotism to support for his strategy of "Vietnamization." Nixon's assurances of eventual American withdrawal, combined with a relatively quiet couple of months in Vietnam and infighting among antiwar groups, led some to wonder whether the energy and influence of the antiwar movement was ebbing. In April 1970, though, Nixon suddenly announced that he had ordered American troops to attack Communist forces in the neutral nation of Cambodia, bordering South Vietnam.

Opponents of the war all across the United States decried this further expansion of the war. The most explosive reaction to the Cambodian incursion took place on college campuses. Protests erupted at colleges and universities across the country, including Kent State University in Ohio. At Kent State, protesting students set fire to a building used by the Reserve Officers' Training Corps (ROTC), and Ohio Governor James Rhodes called out the National Guard to restore order. Two days later, on May 4, students rallied against the war in the center of campus. When the National Guard was ordered to break up the protest, the clash spiraled out of control, culminating with the deaths of four unarmed students from Guard gunfire. Less than two weeks later, violent protests broke out on the campus of Jackson State University in Mississippi, and police there killed two protestors and injured twelve. In the weeks that followed, as many as four million students across the United States participated in protests at 1,300 universities. More than 530 campuses were closed temporarily, and 51 of them closed for the rest of the academic term.

As it turned out, these proved to be the last major antiwar demonstrations in the United States. There were more protests, right up until the removal of the last American troops in 1973, but there were no more great demonstrations, no marches numbering in the tens of thousands. In June 1970 Nixon announced the first of the massive troop withdrawals that he had promised. By the end of that year, 140,000 American troops had been recalled

Vietnam Veterans Against the War

The movement against the Vietnam War has often been criticized for its treatment of American soldiers. Some opponents of the war condemned all U.S. soldiers for their involvement in the conflict, even though many conducted themselves honorably in Vietnam. Reports of harassment of returning soldiers at the hands of protestors proliferated during and after the war, and many veterans experienced hostility from neighbors, coworkers, fellow students, and professors when they tried to resume their lives back in America.

In the final years of American involvement in Vietnam, however, opponents of the war willingly made room in their cause for U.S. soldiers who themselves had turned against the war. Beginning in 1967, a small number of American veterans formed an antiwar group of their own. After forming a connection at a protest march in New York, the group came to realize that many of their fellow soldiers, active and inactive, also opposed the war. Over the next several years, hundreds of Vietnam veterans joined the group that came to be known as the Vietnam Veterans Against the War (VVAW). In 1971, after Americans had become alarmed at

from Vietnam. The following year, U.S. troop deployments in Vietnam fell by another 180,000. Intense aerial bombing of Communist targets continued during this time, but the troop withdrawals assured most Americans that the nation's unhappy involvement in Vietnam was finally drawing to a close. By mid-1973, when the United States completed its military withdrawal from Vietnam, media coverage of events in Southeast Asia had fallen dramatically, and the antiwar movement was no more.

Nixon, however, was by no means solely responsible for the dissolution of the antiwar movement. Most of the groups that had staged protests over the years were campus-based, and when students graduated and moved on, many of the organizations simply fell apart. Leaders of many groups embroiled themselves in bitter infighting, arguing over tactics and whether one protest method or another was sufficiently "radical"; other leaders found themselves in prison or simply burned out on constant conflict. Finally, many

growing reports of American soldiers committing atrocities in Vietnam, the VVAW held a series of hearings in Detroit. During this event, called the Winter Soldier Investigations, many veterans publicly confessed to witnessing or participating in terrible acts that violated their conscience.

The group's most public demonstration was called Operation Dewey Canyon III. Several hundred VVAW members and supporters set up a camp in Washington, D.C., in April 1971 and spent several days giving talks, holding memorial services, and providing testimony at Congressional hearings. The most heavily publicized testimony came from VVAW spokesman John Kerry, who later became a Senator from Massachusetts and won the Democratic presidential nomination in 2004. Kerry presented a long list of arguments against the U.S. war, charging that the war was being prosecuted so that "President Nixon won't be, and these are his words, 'the first President to lose a war.'" He then asked the assembled Congressmen, "how do you ask a man to be the last man to die in Vietnam? How do you ask a man to be the last man to die for a mistake?" The VVAW demonstration was capped in highly symbolic fashion when Kerry and hundreds of other veterans threw medals that they had earned in combat in Vietnam onto the steps of the Capitol.

of those who had joined the movement in the heyday of its idealism in the mid-1960s had simply become exhausted by the early 1970s, or were just ready to move on to another stage in their lives. One way or another, the antiwar movement died a quiet death just as its ultimate goal—the U.S. withdrawal from Vietnam—was being realized in 1973.

The Legacy of the Antiwar Movement

To this day, historians and ordinary Americans alike argue over the impact and legacy of the antiwar movement, both in terms of its immediate impact on the Vietnam War and its long-term influence on American politics and society. Those arguing for the movement's influence suggest that both Johnson and Nixon limited their military actions for fear that overly aggressive actions would spark greater protest; that antiwar protests helped make resisting the draft a legitimate option; and that the growing antiwar protests were a major factor in Johnson's decision not to run for reelection in 1968. Those who argue against the movement's influence discount most of these assertions. They contend that the biggest factor limiting American military action was the desire to keep China and the Soviet Union out of the war, and that it was only the lack of military success that made the antiwar movement seem like a real participant in policy-making. Further, they contend that the media overplayed the importance of the protests, and that both Johnson and Nixon knew that the vast majority of Americans never participated in protests or supported the agenda of the antiwar movement.

In the longer term, however, it is harder to discount the influence of the antiwar movement. Along with the civil rights movement and the women's liberation movement, the antiwar movement demonstrated that Americans working together to advocate for an issue that concerned them could have a significant impact on the political process. Further, it contributed to growing American skepticism about the authority and integrity of bedrock American institutions and political leaders. Even if the movement only involved a minority of Americans, and even if the greatest claims for its impact are open to argument, there is no doubt that the antiwar movement contributed substantially—for better or worse—to the decline of trust in government and authority in general that took place during the 1960s and 1970s.

Chapter Nine

LEGACY OF THE VIETNAM WAR

───⸱⸱⸱───

When you defeat someone on the battlefield or they defeat you, and later you help the other person up, at that time the war is truly over.

—Vietnam veteran Fred Downs, 2001

For both the United States and Vietnam, the post-war era was turbulent and unsettling. But the character of this turbulence was quite different within the two nations. In Vietnam, the primary struggle was to emerge from the rubble and devastation of the war and create a viable state. In America, the only physical scars left from the war were the ones that veterans carried on their bodies. But the Vietnam War also wreaked profound damage on American confidence and self-image, and it sparked significant and enduring changes in how the United States conducted its foreign policy and maintained its military.

Vietnam and American Foreign Policy

Today, most Americans recognize that when it comes to global politics, we live in a world of great complexity. We accept that any decision made by American strategists about the application of military force must involve careful analysis of a stunning variety of political, economic, cultural, and military factors. In the years leading up to the American involvement in Vietnam, however, the world did not appear quite so complex. Presidents Truman, Eisenhower, Kennedy, Johnson, and Nixon all subscribed to the idea that the primary geopolitical role of the United States was to contain the spread of

113

U.S. President Ronald Reagan, shown here at a press conference, embraced a foreign policy that placed great emphasis on "saving" Latin America from Communism.

Communism. This belief made it both a moral and strategic obligation for the United States to intervene militarily when small nations were in danger of "falling" to Communism. Such intervention was dictated by widespread belief in the so-called "domino theory," which held that if one nation became Communist, neighboring countries would be at greater risk of suffering the same fate.

Over the course of fighting the war in Vietnam, however, it became readily apparent that defending South Vietnam from Communism was a formidable and complex task. The succession of South Vietnamese regimes that the United States worked to defend during the Vietnam War were unpopular with their citizens, and they engaged in corrupt and brutal practices that were directly counter to stated American principles of governance. Moreover, an apparent majority of South Vietnamese wanted reunification with North Vietnam and the end to foreign intervention in their country, even if it meant accepting Communist rule. This underestimation of the nationalist character of the conflict in Vietnam would haunt the United States throughout the war years. Meanwhile, America's role in driving the conflict's deepening spiral of violence and destruction triggered widespread disillusionment among U.S. citizens who had once seen intervention in Vietnam as compatible with traditional American ideals and values.

In the years following the Vietnam War, the United States, the Soviet Union, and China tried to avoid letting smaller nations become Cold War battlegrounds. But although deploying actual U.S. troops in political "trouble spots" was seen as political suicide, some American policymakers remained determined to confront Communism whenever it was perceived to threaten U.S. security. In the 1980s, for example, the administration of President Ronald Reagan became alarmed at political developments in several Latin American states. Reagan publicly assured Americans that he would not lead them into "another Vietnam." Rather than openly committing American troops, though, Reagan ordered the Central Intelligence Agency and other covert operations groups to support pro-American governments and political groups in those nations. These operations in El Salvador, Nicaragua, and Honduras were highly controversial, and in some cases clearly in violation of American law. The most glaring example of this was the Iran-Contra affair, in which several Reagan administration officials secretly armed Nicaraguan "freedom fighters" seeking to topple the nation's socialist government.

By 1991 the Soviet Union had ceased to exist, Communist governments had collapsed throughout eastern Europe, and Communism was no longer considered a major threat to the United States. One year earlier, however, Iraqi dictator Saddam Hussein had ordered his army to invade neighboring Kuwait. President George H.W. Bush responded by helping to organize a broad coalition of countries to defeat Iraq. Moreover, Bush and his military strategists defined a limited but clear objective and applied overwhelming military force to reaching that objective. When the U.S.-led coalition chased Iraq out of Kuwait in the 1991 Persian Gulf War, Bush happily proclaimed, "By God, we've kicked the Vietnam Syndrome once and for all." Policymakers embraced the idea that the United States had finally put the unpleasant memories of Vietnam behind it.

But Vietnam continued to cast a long shadow over American foreign policy, as President Bill Clinton found out several times during his presidency (1993-2001). During his years in the White House, ethnic and tribal violence in the collapsing former Communist state of Yugoslavia and in the African nations of Rwanda and Somalia seemed to call out for foreign intervention. The world looked to the United States, the lone remaining superpower, for guidance and intervention. But American reluctance to commit its mighty military machine to any conflict that had any potential for turning into a "quagmire" remained strong. In these cases, the fear of "another Vietnam" clearly lingered in the minds of policymakers and ordinary Americans alike (in the case of Yugoslavia, Clinton eventually helped convince the North Atlantic Treaty Organization-NATO to carry out massive air strikes against Serbian forces that had refused to participate in peace talks; these U.S.-led air strikes were widely credited with convincing Serb leaders to accept a negotiated end to the conflict).

In March 2003 the United States embarked on its largest extended military operation on foreign soil since the Vietnam War. American forces entered Iraq and overthrew the government of dictator Saddam Hussein (a small number of troops from several other nations, most notably Great Britain, also participated). President George W. Bush and officials in his administration stated that removing Hussein was necessary because he possessed weapons of mass destruction. The Bush White House and its supporters also implied a linkage between Hussein and the Al Qaeda terrorist network that was responsible for the devastating attacks of September 11, 2001, in New York City and Washington, D.C.

Since that time, American troops have remained in Iraq for the stated purpose of helping the Iraqi people establish a democratic government there. But the claims used to justify the invasion of Iraq have been mostly discredited, and the U.S. occupation has been a troubled one. Sectarian warfare between ethnic groups within Iraq has soared, as has terrorist activity by Al Qaeda and other groups. As of mid-2006, more than 2,500 American troops have lost their lives in Iraq, and the Iraqi civilians claimed by the violence number in the tens of thousands. The guerrilla nature of the violence that is wracking Iraq, combined with the uncertainty about how much longer American troops will remain in the region, has led some analysts to conclude that the Iraq War is becoming what policymakers dread most: "another Vietnam." Defenders of U.S. policy in Iraq, however, firmly reject such claims. They claim that the occupation, although difficult and challenging, is giving Iraqis the time they need to establish a stable, democratic government.

The American Military After Vietnam

Few segments of American culture were more devastated by the experience of the Vietnam War than the American military. Prior to the war, the military had been the pride of the nation, a strong and efficient fighting force that had helped America win World War II and save the world from the forces of fascism. Yet over the course of the Vietnam War, civilian perceptions of the military declined dramatically, as did morale within the different branches of the armed services. Protestors condemned the military for adopting fighting strategies that led to "body counts," heavy use of Agent Orange and napalm, and atrocities such as the My Lai massacre. Within the military, soldiers grew to distrust both their civilian and military leadership. And the knowledge that American forces withdrew from Vietnam without victory was tremendously upsetting to soldiers, U.S. veterans of earlier wars, and members of the American public alike. By the end of the war the armed services faced real crises in their ranks.

After the war, the American military spent a lot of time and effort trying to determine exactly where its efforts in Vietnam had gone wrong. The explanations that emerged did much to shape the military in the coming years. A favored explanation within the military was the idea that U.S. forces had fought the war "with one hand tied behind their back." According to this thesis, civilian politicians had placed limits on the military that kept it from doing its job; soldiers pointed to presidential interference in choosing bombing targets so as not to provoke the Chinese, President Johnson's decision not to call up additional reserve troops, longstanding limitations on attacking Viet Cong positions within Cambodia and Laos, and a general civilian hesitation to allow the military to press forward to victory. The more introspective generals acknowledged that they bore some of the blame for these decisions because they had told civilian leadership what they wanted to hear, rather than giving them their full military assessment of the situation. The lesson learned, according to supporters of this analysis, was that the military had to reassert its authority over battlefield decisions. No longer would political considerations drive planning on the field of battle; no longer would military leaders tell politicians only what they wanted to hear.

These conclusions led the U.S. military to adopt a number of significant changes from top to bottom. At the top, the Goldwater-Nichols Defense Reorganization Act of 1986 greatly enhanced cooperation between the separate branches of the military and made the Chairman of the Joint Chiefs of Staff (a general who represented the combined wisdom of the heads of the Army, Navy, Air Force, and Marines) the primary military advisor to the president. General Creighton Abrams, who led the Army from 1972 to 1974, changed the structure of his branch of the service. For example, he made the reserves responsible for most support actions, thus ensuring that the reserves would be utilized more extensively as a resource in future conflicts.

Another major reform was the 1973 elimination of the draft and the creation of all-volunteer armed forces. Not only did this reform eliminate protests against forced military service, but it created a military filled with soldiers who wanted to be there. Advocates of this change stated that the all-volunteer armed forces have been more receptive to demands of military professionalism. Finally, military training, both in the service academies and in boot camp, changed to reflect the way that wars were being fought. Soldiers received more extensive training in dealing with insurgencies and guerilla warfare, as well as in the high-tech weapon systems being developed by the United States.

One of the most difficult and pervasive problems facing the military after Vietnam was the diminished morale of soldiers and the decreased respect Americans gave to military personnel. Late in the war, order and respect for superior officers had declined dramatically among soldiers serving in Vietnam. A big push in the immediate aftermath of the war was the restoration of discipline and order. Each of the services cracked down on misbehavior and insubordination, while simultaneously pushing efforts to reclaim the discipline and pride that had once characterized the military. Under President Reagan, publicity campaigns depicting the various armed forces as skilled, professional fighting squads—the "Be All You Can Be" campaign for example—helped lift the public image of soldiers. The Persian Gulf War of 1991 was also a huge boost to the reputation of the armed forces. American troops performed admirably in that successful military operation, and they returned home to the heroes' acclaim that was so notably absent during Vietnam.

Despite all the progress made by the military, however, the prosecution of the Iraq War (2003-) has reawakened memories of Vietnam for some observers. U.S. troops have struggled to deal with insurgent warfare, in part because it is often impossible to tell friend from foe in the occupied nation. In addition, the mistreatment of Iraqi detainees by American soldiers at the Abu Ghraib prison and the charges made by a number of retired generals and other critics that civilian Secretary of Defense Donald Rumsfeld has exerted too much influence over military strategy all echo perceived problems in Vietnam. Meanwhile, media coverage of the Iraq War has been criticized by some proponents of the U.S. invasion of Iraq as excessively gloomy—a charge that was also frequently leveled at American news organizations during the Vietnam era. Journalists and other defenders of the coverage, however, insist that they are objectively reporting events both in Iraq and the United States, where public opinion had shifted firmly against the war as of mid-2006.

Vietnam and the American Psyche

In addition to the known costs of the Vietnam War—the terrible loss of life, the economic damage to all sides, the political tumult—many argue that the biggest price paid by the United States was a jarring loss of confidence. Over the course of the war, Americans came to understand that presidents and lawmakers were willing to manipulate the truth to advance their agendas. They learned that their vaunted military was, for a multitude of reasons, incapable of defeating an enemy with far less conventional firepower. They saw the antiwar movement become mired in bitter infighting. And they witnessed the heavy toll that deep differences over the war took on countless American families and communities. For many historians, wrote Brian Balogh in *After Vietnam: Legacies of a Lost War,* "Vietnam has come to represent the decline of authority, a new level of social and political conflict, and the fragmentation of national identity" in America.

The Vietnam War also continues to cast a long shadow over American politics, more than three decades after the fall of Saigon. Political candidates for state and national office from both parties have been ruthlessly examined and criticized for their actions during the Vietnam years. Both Democratic President Bill Clinton and Republican President George W. Bush avoided military service in Vietnam during the war. While both survived politically, they both have been condemned by political opponents for their actions during that war. Senator John Kerry, who ran for president in 2004, compiled an impressive war service record in Vietnam, but his candidacy was bitterly opposed by some veterans who never forgave him for his leadership position in the antiwar group Vietnam Veterans Against the War. Of all the Vietnam-era politicians, war hero Senator John McCain, who was tortured during several years of imprisonment in a North Vietnamese prison camp, has perhaps fared best in the public eye.

Of course, it also should be noted that the Vietnam War was not the only force responsible for the wrenching changes in American society that took place in the 1960s and 1970s. Changing demographics, the various other social movements of the 1960s (including the youth movement, the women's movement, the civil rights movement, and the environmental movement), the Cold War, and the increase in wealth and consumerism all have been cited as major factors in the decline of civility and consensus in American political life.

Consolidating Communist Power: Vietnam and Its Neighbors

Nowhere has the legacy of the Vietnam War been felt more deeply than in the nation in which it was fought. Over the course of the war, some two million Vietnamese (from both the North and South) were killed, and millions more were wounded or forced from their homes and into refugee camps. There were huge economic costs as well. More than a decade of intense American bombing and spraying of defoliants like Agent Orange destroyed countless Vietnamese villages, roads, shops, and factories and left prime agri-

---

Refighting the War: Vietnam on Film

From the time the United States entered the Vietnam War in 1964, television cameras and newspaper and magazine photographers followed soldiers into their camps and into battle. These journalists returned with searing firsthand images from the war. After the war's end, filmmakers used similarly searing imagery to offer their own interpretations of the legacy of Vietnam.

Some of the first movies about the war explored the psychological impact of the conflict on returning soldiers. *The Deer Hunter* (1978), directed by Michael Cimino and starring Robert De Niro, John Savage, and Christopher Walken, explores the dreadful Vietnam experiences of three hunting buddies from a small town in Pennsylvania. The film won several Academy Awards, including Best Picture. Another major Vietnam film from 1978 was *Coming Home,* starring Jon Voight as a handicapped Vietnam veteran and Jane Fonda as his girlfriend. *Coming Home* picked up the Academy Awards for Best Actor and Best Actress (the latter award was extremely controversial because of Fonda's well-publicized antiwar activities during the war).

Another film that delved deeply into the psychological impact of the Vietnam experience was *Apocalypse Now* (1979). The film's director, Francis Ford Coppola, patterned his dark vision of the war after Joseph Conrad's classic novella *The Heart of Darkness.* Now considered one of the classic war movies, *Apocalypse Now* leads the viewer gradually into a jungle world of drugs, violence, and madness. Another version of the "psychological damage" school of Vietnam War films was *First Blood* (1982). This film starred Sylvester Stallone as a Vietnam vet named John Rambo who unleashes his war-honed fighting skills on an unfriendly civilian world. Its popularity spawned a series of increasingly outlandish "Rambo" movies during the 1980s.

cultural land barren and ruined. By 1975 Vietnam had become a unified, independent nation for the first time since the mid-1800s, when France brought all of Southeast Asia under its control … but at what price?

There have been dozens of other Vietnam movies released over the years as well. Some explored the prisoner-of-war issue, suggesting that American soldiers remained within Vietnam. These films ranged from the serious (1983's *Uncommon Valor*), to the absurdly sensational, such as the *Missing in Action* Chuck Norris action films. Other films have explored the nature of combat in Vietnam. Some of the best from this genre are director Stanley Kubrick's *Full Metal Jacket* (1987), Oliver Stone's *Platoon* (1986), John Irvin's *Hamburger Hill* (1987), and Randall Wallace's *We Were Soldiers* (2002).

Actors Martin Sheen and Laurence Fishburne (background) in a scene from Francis Ford Coppola's controversial Vietnam film *Apocalypse Now*.

The immediate goal of the victorious Communists was the consolidation of power. Within a short time of the fall of South Vietnam in 1975, the two Vietnams were reunited under the banner of the Socialist Republic of Vietnam.

Vietnam after reunification under Communist rule in 1975.

Thousands of people who had previously displayed loyalty to the South Vietnamese government were rounded up and killed in the wake of the war's end; several hundred thousand other Vietnamese were "re-educated" to follow Communist doctrine and toil for the new single-party regime. Many of the best and the brightest from South Vietnam fled the country to evade this crackdown. The largest number of these refugees made their way to France and the United States, where they established thriving immigrant communities.

The neighboring countries of Laos and Cambodia were also deeply scarred by the Communist victory in Vietnam. North Vietnam backed the bloodthirsty Pathet Lao party, which took control of Laos in November 1975 and killed hundreds of thousands of ethnic Hmong people. This party remained loyal to its Vietnamese allies for years afterward. In Cambodia, the Communist-backed Khmer Rouge, led by the dictator Pol Pot, seized power in 1975 and purged the country of anyone associated with the previous regime or with ties to the capitalist West. The Khmer Rouge renamed the country Democratic Kampuchea and declared that it was now "Year Zero" in the country. During the next three years of Pol Pot's rule, as many as two million Cambodians lost their lives to systematic executions, crushing workloads at labor camps, starvation, and disease. Educated people, including doctors, engineers, teachers, military officers, and government officials, were special targets for torture and murder.

But relations between the bloodthirsty Khmer Rouge and the Socialist Republic of Vietnam quickly soured. Border skirmishes, combined with

Collected skulls of Cambodian victims of the Khmer Rouge's brutal reign of terror in Cambodia during the late 1970s.

growing Vietnamese anger over Pol Pot's resistance to its dictates, prompted Vietnam to invade Cambodia in 1979. Though Vietnam was in turn attacked by China, which supported the Khmer Rouge, it succeeded in placing a pro-Vietnamese government in Cambodia. In 1993 elections sponsored by the United Nations created a coalition government—which did not include representatives of the Khmer Rouge—to rule over the devastated country.

The Fall and Rise of the Vietnamese Economy

Following the war, the dedicated Communists who had long labored to reunify their country set about placing it under a pure form of socialist organization. All land, property, and businesses were placed under state control and the Communist Party orchestrated all economic activity through a series of "Five Year Plans." Villagers were told which crops to grow and which manufactured goods to produce.

123

As in so many socialist nations, the Vietnamese economy quickly fell apart. As agricultural productivity declined, the nation experienced widespread hunger and poverty and became one of the poorest nations in the world. The grim situation was made worse by the government's insistence on maintaining a huge standing army, the fourth largest in the world. This military investment left the nation with little money to address poverty, malnutrition, and other social problems. In 1981 Pham Van Dong, who served as premier of North Vietnam from 1955 to 1975 and premier of the Socialist Republic of Vietnam from 1975 to 1987, grudgingly acknowledged the nation's economic woes: "Yes, we defeated the United States. But now we are plagued by problems. We do not have enough to eat. We are a poor, underdeveloped nation. Waging war is simple, but running a country is very difficult."

> *"Yes, we defeated the United States," said Vietnamese Premier Pham Van Dong. "But now we are plagued by problems. We do not have enough to eat. We are a poor, underdeveloped nation. Waging war is simple, but running a country is very difficult."*

Vietnam's only saving grace through the late 1970s and 1980s was the patronage of the Soviet Union. Over this period the Soviet Union provided nearly $2 billion a year in aid, keeping the country afloat. By the mid-1980s, however, even the Soviets were acknowledging that market-style reforms were needed if socialist nations were to survive. The Vietnamese Communist Party responded with experiments in small-scale capitalist enterprise and private ownership of farmland. It was during this time that a generational change took place in the nation's leadership. Many of the older Communist leaders who had led the country during the war years died or retired, and they were replaced by a new generation of administrators and officials—including some with South Vietnamese backgrounds. Still, membership in the Communist Party was mandatory for any Vietnamese with political aspirations.

The collapse of the Soviet Union in 1991 finally ushered in large-scale changes within Vietnam. Deprived of their longtime source of economic support, Vietnam was forced into broader economic engagement with the rest of the world. With an impoverished work force willing to work for very low wages, and an agricultural sector that had recovered from the war to become a leading rice producer, Vietnam began to attract greater levels of foreign investment from Japan and other nations. Economic growth rates grew from the 1-2 percent averages of the 1980s into the realm of 5 to 7 percent a year. According to Patrick J. Hearden, author of *The Tragedy of Vietnam,* "Vietnamese leaders still claimed to be socialists, but they talked and acted more like capitalists."

Reconciliation with the United States

By the early 1990s, the only thing that kept Vietnam from full participation in the world community was its continued estrangement from the United States. Ever since the war, relations between the two countries had been strained. Vietnam demanded that the United States pay war reparations, while the United States insisted that Vietnam account for all American soldiers missing in action during the war. Even these strains had become muted with time, however, and in 1991 the Vietnamese government began to pass along additional information about missing American soldiers in hopes that the Unites States would relax an economic embargo that had long hobbled the Vietnamese economy.

In 1991 Vietnam offered assistance in determining the fate of 2,265 missing American soldiers. One year later, U.S. President George H.W. Bush allowed the sale of some goods to Vietnam for humanitarian purposes. In October 1992 Vietnam offered additional information on thousands of missing American soldiers, and in return the United States allowed American corporations to open offices in Vietnam. After several more exchanges of information, U.S. President Bill Clinton offered full diplomatic recognition of Vietnam in July 1995. This opened the door for the country to engage in a range of activities with the United States and other nations.

Though socialist economic planning has been largely abandoned in Vietnam, single party Communist Party rule remains the norm. Yet even this is showing signs of change. By the late 1990s, half of the nation's population had been born after the war. This younger generation was not as motivated by the language of independence and revolution that had inspired their elders, and they increasingly pressed the government to open up the political process to allow more participation by people, especially at the local level. Buddhists began to re-emerge as a political force during this period as well. The Buddhists are untainted by any association with the former South Vietnamese regimes, they can claim to be long-time supporters of Vietnamese nationalism, and they have widespread support among the nation's youth. Though the Communist Party has cracked down on Buddhist political leaders, some observers believe that Buddhists will be a significant factor in the future of Vietnamese politics.

Western tourists, including one sporting a Vietnamese flag t-shirt, walk along a busy commercial street in Ho Chi Minh City, formerly known as Saigon.

Today, peace exists between the two nations that fought such a long and bitter war between 1964 and 1975. Americans can find "Made in Vietnam" labels on food products, items of clothing, and other manufactured goods they purchase in U.S. stores, and American tourists are warmly welcomed in Vietnam. Like Japan and Germany, who were enemies of America in earlier wars, Vietnam has now become an important trading partner for U.S. business interests.

BIOGRAPHIES

George Ball (1909-1994)
U.S. Undersecretary of State, 1961-1966

George Wildman Ball was born on December 21, 1909, in a small town outside Des Moines, Iowa. His parents—Amos Ball, Jr., an oil company executive, and Edna Wildman Ball, a teacher—later moved the family to the upscale Chicago suburb of Evanston, Illinois. Ball attended Northwestern University, where he received a bachelor's degree in 1930 and a law degree in 1933. While at Northwestern, Ball studied under Bernard DeVoto, who encouraged his students to range far and wide in their intellectual interests, and to use their critical intelligence to scrutinize the decisions of their fellow man. Ball used these skills again and again during his subsequent career of public service. But they came to naught in the mid-1960s, when he waged an unsuccessful campaign to keep the United States from escalating its involvement in the Vietnam War.

Between Law and Politics

Though he had never before even visited a farm, Ball began his political career in 1933 with the Farm Credit Administration, one of the many programs established by Democratic President Franklin D. Roosevelt to help Americans cope with the Great Depression. By 1934 he had moved to the Treasury Department, where he got his first taste of policymaking in the nation's capital.

Though he impressed many colleagues with his rational approach to difficult issues, Ball did not necessarily want a career in politics, so he returned to Chicago to practice law from 1935 to 1942. In 1942, though, Ball was called back to Washington, D.C., first with the Lend-Lease Administration and then with the U.S. Strategic Bombing Survey. During the latter research program, Army officials urged Survey members toward one conclusion: that the Allied bombing of Germany had broken the will of the German people to wage war. Ball's interviews with German officials, however, convinced him that the bombing had not been a conclusive factor in ending the war. Ball's quiet insistence on considering all the evidence won him the respect of many in Washington, and indicated his willingness to take a position that ran counter to majority opinion.

In the years after World War II, Ball balanced his time between law and politics. He helped found a legal firm, Cleary, Gottlieb, Steen and Ball, that emerged as a force in American law. He also worked closely with international agencies involved in the economic reconstruction of European countries devastated by World War II. In addition, he helped craft the Trade Expansion Act of 1962, which was designed to ease trade barriers between the United States and its major trading partners in Europe. Finally, Ball worked on the presidential campaigns of Democratic candidate Adlai Stevenson in 1952 and 1956.

In 1961 Ball joined the administration of incoming Democratic president John F. Kennedy as undersecretary of economic affairs. Within the year he was reappointed as undersecretary of state. Shortly after taking the reins of his new job, Ball joined Secretary of State Dean Rusk, Secretary of Defense Robert S. McNamara, and several other high-ranking officials in "ExCom," a group that advised Kennedy during the October 1962 Cuban Missile Crisis. Some in the administration urged Kennedy to launch direct attacks against Cuban and Soviet sites during the crisis, which erupted after Soviet missiles were discovered in Cuba. But Ball was among those who advised the more cautious, diplomatic course chosen by Kennedy. The president's strategy ultimately led to the peaceful resolution of one of the most dangerous standoffs in America's long Cold War with the Soviet Union.

Weighing Events in Vietnam

One of the pressing issues facing diplomats in the Kennedy administration in the early 1960s was the question of U.S. support for the endangered government in South Vietnam. The French had withdrawn from Vietnam in 1954 after years of colonial rule. They left behind a divided nation: a Communist North Vietnam and a non-Communist South Vietnam. South Vietnam's government was both weak and corrupt, and in the late 1950s and early 1960s it was buffeted by attempts from insurgents within the South (known as Viet Cong) to unite the country under Communist rule.

This development deeply alarmed the American foreign policy establishment, which believed that if one small state in Southeast Asia fell to Communism, others would swiftly follow. Accepting this so-called "domino theory," the majority of presidential advisors urged strong American support for the South Vietnamese government. This support first took the form of economic aid and military advisors. In 1964, though, President Lyndon B. Johnson approved aerial bombing campaigns and massive U.S. troop deployments in Vietnam. For the next several years after that, American military involvement in the Vietnam conflict steadily deepened.

George Ball strongly disagreed with this strategy from the outset. From the moment that the first American military units were stationed in Vietnam in 1961, Ball advised against American escalation. He argued that Vietnam was not essential to American interests and that further actions there would strain U.S. military and economic resources. After 1964, when American involvement in Vietnam intensified, his opposition to U.S. military and political policies in the region became even more pointed.

Between 1964 and 1966, Ball wrote twenty strongly worded position papers outlining his arguments for halting U.S. escalation and hastening American withdrawal. In October 1964, Ball warned that U.S. ground troops operating in Vietnam would "bog down in the jungles and rice paddies—while we slowly blow the country to pieces." After ground troops were stationed in Vietnam in 1965, he accurately predicted that America was at grave risk of "bogging down an indeterminate number of American troops in a protracted and bloody conflict of uncertain outcome." Ball also urged the Johnson administration to reassess the political stakes involved. "The world knows that the government in Saigon [South Vietnam] is a joke," Ball declared, "and if our withdrawal resulted from an effort to face this problem squarely, friendly nations would not interpret it as a U.S. failure to keep its commitments."

Ball's advice, given over and over during the course of two years of escalation, was that the United States should withdraw from South Vietnam, which he described as "a lost cause." But his arguments were consistently ignored. In fact, he was often criticized by those within the government who advocated increases in U.S. troop deployments, new bombing campaigns, and other military actions. McNamara considered his advice "out of line," and presidential advisor McGeorge Bundy suggested that Ball's arguments were never very persuasive.

Despite his increasing irrelevance within the Johnson administration, Ball remained loyal to the president and did not make public his criticisms of

131

U.S. policy. "I figured that I could do better remaining on the inside," he later commented. By 1966, however, Ball became convinced that Johnson had become trapped in a strategy of continuing escalation. He resigned and returned to the private sector. He continued to offer informal advice to policymakers, however, and his counsel may have contributed to the decision of Johnson and his successor, Richard Nixon, to begin withdrawing U.S. ground troops from Vietnam in 1968.

Ball left public life and became an investment banker with Lehman Brothers in New York City until his retirement in 1982. He remained an informal advisor to several presidents, most notably in 1978 when he urged President Jimmy Carter to modify U.S. policy toward Iran. Ball recognized that if the U.S.-backed Shah of Iran was toppled, an Islamic fundamentalist regime would likely follow (one year later, Ball's forecast came true). Ball also wrote several books about American foreign policy, including *The Discipline of Power: Essentials of a Modern World Structure* (1968) and a volume of memoirs, *The Past Has Another Pattern* (1982). He struggled financially toward the end of his life, and died of abdominal cancer on May 26, 1994, in New York.

Sources

Ball, George. "Cutting Our Losses in South Viet-Nam (1965)." *Foreign Relations of the United States, 1964-1968. Vol 3*. Washington, DC: Department of State.

Bill, James A. *George Ball: Behind the Scenes in U.S. Foreign Policy*. New Haven, CT: Yale University Press, 1997.

DiLeo, David L. *George Ball, Vietnam, and the Rethinking of Containment*. Chapel Hill: University of North Carolina Press, 1991.

Macarthur, John R. "The Columns of Liberty." *Harper's Magazine Online*. Available online at www.harpers.org/TheColumnsOfLiberty.html.

Ho Chi Minh (1890-1969)
Communist Revolutionary and President of North Vietnam, 1945-1969

The man who would become Ho Chi Minh was born Nguyen Sinh Cung on May 19, 1890, in the central Vietnamese village of Kim Lien. Cung was raised in a family with deep respect for education. His father, Nguyen Sinh Sac, was a local teacher who continued to pursue his studies during Ho's youth; his mother, Hoang Thi Loan, was the daughter of a respected local schoolmaster. When he was eleven, Cung was given an adult name, Nguyen Tat Thanh, meaning "he who will succeed." During these years, his father instilled in him a strong sense of patriotism toward his country—and an equally strong dislike for French colonial rule over Vietnam.

For a time, Ho followed in the professional footsteps of his father. After graduating in 1909 from Quoc Hoc, a French-run national academy in the regional capital of Hue, he taught in village schools. During this time, his resentment of French colonial rule over Vietnam increased. Frenchmen in Vietnam held all the important jobs and kept most of the nation's wealth, while Vietnamese peasants worked long hours in the rice fields for little gain. This state of affairs led Ho to engage in a variety of anti-French political activities. Within a matter of months, he became concerned that he might be targeted for arrest by French authorities. In 1911, Ho began a long and remarkable journey for a poor Vietnamese teacher. He signed on as a crew member on a French ocean liner and left his home. He did not return to Vietnam again until thirty years had passed.

Embraces Communism

Ho lived in England and France during the tumultuous years of World War I. Two events related to that war influenced his later politics. One was the Versailles Peace Conference of 1919, during which American President Woodrow Wilson spoke persuasively about the right of nations to pursue democracy and self-determination. These were the things Ho wanted for his country, but when he attempted to present a proposal for Vietnamese freedom from French colonial rule to Wilson, he was turned away. The other influential event that shaped Ho's world view was the 1917 Communist Revolution in Russia. In this momentous event in world history, landless peasants violently removed the Russian aristocracy that had long ruled the country and set about creating a "worker's paradise" based on the ideas of Karl Marx and Vladimir Lenin. Ho became a student of Communist ideas, and in 1920 he even helped to found the French Communist Party.

Through the early 1920s, Ho advanced his knowledge and training in Communist ideology. He wrote a series of pamphlets and articles protesting French rule of his homeland, and several of these writings were smuggled into Vietnam. He also spent time in the Russian capital of Moscow, studying at the University of Oriental Workers, and in Canton, China, where he trained in revolutionary tactics with other young Vietnamese dissidents. While in China, Ho organized the first Vietnamese group dedicated to Marxist revolution: the Revolutionary Youth League of Vietnam, or Thanh Nien. Five years later, in 1930, he led a group that created the Indochinese Communist Party. This organization was dedicated to bringing independence and Communist rule to all of Indochina, the cluster of nations located in the southeast peninsula of Asia.

These were tumultuous years for Ho. His writings and political activities had made him an underground hero in Vietnam. But he found himself in hostile territory during much of his travels. Only in Russia and its satellite states was Communism an accepted political view. In other nations where he spent time—China, Hong Kong, Malaya, Singapore, the Dutch East Indies—Ho's movements were continually monitored by authorities, and he was actually arrested several times for his political activities. In June 1931, for example, Ho was arrested in Hong Kong by British colonial police and spent the next two years in prison. Upon gaining his release on a technicality, Ho promptly fled to Moscow. But Soviet leader Joseph Stalin distrusted Ho both for his intelligence and his independent streak, so the Vietnamese Communist leader was forced to curtail his activities for most of the rest of the decade.

Leads Viet Minh against French

In 1941 Ho—who had finally embraced the name Ho Chi Minh, meaning "He Who Enlightens"—and the Indochinese Communist Party created

134

the League for the Independence of Vietnam, better known as the Viet Minh. The Viet Minh brought together a range of smaller nationalist groups who had been seeking Vietnamese independence. It bound them together under strict Communist organizing principles, and united a wide range of seasoned Vietnamese Communist figures, such as Vo Nguyen Giap. It was during this period that Ho finally ended his three decades of exile and returned to Vietnam.

The Viet Minh hoped to use the chaos of World War II, during which Japan had supplanted France as the colonial administrator in Vietnam, to seize control of their homeland once and for all from foreign occupiers. Eager to court U.S. support for their cause, the Viet Minh downplayed their Communist roots and aided U.S. military forces against Japan. In August of 1945 the United States dropped atomic bombs on the Japanese cities of Hiroshima and Nagasaki. As Japan reeled from these attacks, Viet Minh forces seized control of many of Vietnam's major cities. On August 14 Japan surrendered to the Allied forces, and on September 2, 1945, the Viet Minh declared the independence of the Democratic Republic of Vietnam. Their new president, Ho Chi Minh, read a declaration of independence that was based on the United States' own beloved Declaration of Independence.

The victories of 1945 seemed to signal the realization of Ho's lifelong dream of Vietnamese independence, but France quickly announced that it was not ready to relinquish control of its long-time colony. The United States then decided that it would not support Vietnam's campaign for independence against French wishes. In 1946 France began a military campaign to regain control of Vietnam. The fledgling Vietnamese Army, known as the People's Army of Vietnam (PAVN), wilted in the face of French firepower and quickly lost control of Vietnam's major cities. But rather than give up, the Viet Minh turned to guerrilla warfare, locking the French into a bloody war for control of Vietnam.

Though the Viet Minh seemed outmatched against the French, Giap trained the growing Viet Minh army in guerilla tactics that frustrated the French military. Meanwhile, Ho rallied Vietnamese across the country to the Viet Minh cause, emphasizing the nationalistic aspects of the struggle.

Ho also negotiated with other Communist nations for support. He received the active backing of the Soviet Union, and after the Communists seized power in China in 1949, he also won the support of Chinese leader

Mao Zedong. Ho skillfully used the Communist giants' distrust for one another to maximum advantage, winning crucial military, economic, and tactical support along the way. By allying the Viet Minh independence movement so closely with these Communist nations, however, Ho alienated the United States, which had become determined to stop the spread of Communism around the world.

By 1954 the Viet Minh had fought France to a standstill and forced it to the negotiating table. But they were not strong enough to negotiate for a fully independent Vietnam. Instead, the Geneva Accords of 1954 called for the "temporary" creation of two Vietnams: the Democratic Republic of Vietnam, or North Vietnam, which was headed by Ho Chi Minh and his Communist allies; and the Republic of Vietnam, or South Vietnam, which was supported by the United States. Had elections been held to unify the country in 1956, as the Geneva Accords stipulated, Ho Chi Minh and the Communists would likely have won because of their leading role in ending French colonial rule. But the United States intervened. South Vietnamese President Ngo Dinh Diem and his American allies flatly refused to hold the promised elections.

War with the United States

In the years immediately following the war with France, Ho and his advisers focused on building the economy and solidifying their rule in North Vietnam. By 1959, however, they were strong enough to begin infiltrating South Vietnam with both soldiers and guerillas who preached the glories of Communist revolution. Through the early 1960s, North Vietnam encouraged revolution and resistance to the U.S.-supported Diem regime throughout South Vietnam. It did so partly through its National Liberation Front (NLF), a political organization that stressed national independence and democratic reforms to rural South Vietnamese (while hiding its links to Communist North Vietnam). Another weapon used by Ho's government to destabilize Diem's government was the Viet Cong, a guerrilla organization that essentially served as the military arm of the NLF.

By 1964 it was estimated that nearly half of South Vietnam was under Communist control. Late that year, President Lyndon B. Johnson approved a massive escalation of U.S. military involvement in Vietnam. American bombing campaigns against North Vietnam (such as Operation Rolling Thunder) were initiated early the following year, and U.S. troop deployments steadily rose, reaching more than 500,000 troops by 1968.

Ho's strategy from the beginning was to exhaust the United States into giving up the war. "You can kill ten of our men for every one we kill of yours. But even at those odds, you will lose and we will win," he famously predicted. Ho's confidence was so great that he rebuffed any attempt to negotiate peace that did not give Vietnam complete independence.

During the mid-1960s, however, Ho's health declined significantly. Out of necessity, key decisionmaking responsibilities fell to other North Vietnamese leaders. By the late 1960s his role in the North Vietnamese government was, according to some reports, largely ceremonial. Ho died on September 3, 1969, well before the 1973 withdrawal of U.S. troops from Vietnam and the final Communist victory over South Vietnam in 1975. One of the first acts of unification undertaken by the Communist conquerors was to rename the South Vietnamese capital city of Saigon as Ho Chi Minh City in honor of the legendary revolutionary figure.

Today, Ho Chi Minh remains one of the most controversial figures in recent world history. To many Vietnamese people, he was a humble but determined revolutionary who bravely promoted Vietnamese freedom from foreign domination. For many who revere him, Ho is primarily a nationalist who used Communism as the best tool to bring about independence for his country. Some historians share this basic view of him as well. Others characterize him as a ruthless opportunist who used nationalism as a wedge to advance his Marxist beliefs and increase his personal power, even if it brought death to millions of his countrymen. Finally, some scholars contend that this undeniably gifted leader was *both* a devoted patriot and a calculating Communist ideologue; according to these historians, Ho Chi Minh's foremost motivations will always remain somewhat of a mystery.

Sources

Duiker, William J. *Ho Chi Minh*. New York: Hyperion, 2000.

Ho Chi Minh. *On Revolution: Selected Writings, 1920-1966*. Edited by Bernard Fall. New York: Praeger, 1967.

Quinn-Judge, Sophie. *Ho Chi Minh: The Missing Years, 1919-1941*. Berkeley: University of California Press, 2002.

Lyndon B. Johnson (1908-1973)
President of the United States, 1963-1968

Lyndon Baines Johnson was born on August 27, 1908, in Stonewall, Texas. His parents worked hard to provide for their family of five children, but the family lacked electricity, running water, or a flush toilet for the first years of Johnson's childhood. What the family lacked in wealth they made up for in charm and intelligence: Johnson's father, Sam Ealy Johnson Jr., was a talkative and well-liked farmer and state politician known for protecting the interests of the poor, and his mother, Rebekah Baines Johnson, was a college graduate who taught her children to love art and literature.

From the time he was a boy, friends and neighbors speculated that Johnson was destined to become a politician. He loved talking politics with the local men, and he spent hours wandering the chambers and hallways of the Texas state house where his father worked, soaking in the sights and sounds of the legislature at work. As early as the ninth grade he boasted to friends that he would be president one day. But Johnson's path to politics was not without difficulty: he graduated from Johnson City High School in 1924 at the age of fifteen, but it took two years of working at dead-end jobs to convince him to go to college. He earned a teaching degree at nearby Southwest Texas State Teachers College. While earning his degree he taught at an impoverished school near the Mexican border, and after graduating in 1930 he taught at a large Houston high school. But it was politics that truly fired his blood.

Became Master Politician

Johnson's first meaningful involvement in politics came as a campaign manager for Texas state Senate candidate Welly Hopkins. Johnson's skill at giving speeches, organizing campaign events, and convincing voters to turn out for his candidate helped lift Hopkins to victory. It also convinced state Congressman Richard Kleberg to hire Johnson for his 1931 campaign for a seat in the U.S. House of Representatives. When Kleberg won, he took John-son to Washington, D.C., with him. In 1934, Johnson married Claudia Alta "Lady Bird" Taylor, who remained one of his closest advisors throughout his life; the couple later had two daughters, Lynda Bird and Lucy Baines.

Johnson arrived in Washington, D.C., at the height of the Great Depres-sion. He soon became directly involved in federal efforts to alleviate the poverty that was wracking the nation. In 1935 he was appointed to head the Texas office of the National Youth Administration (NYA), a youth education and vocational training program that was part of President Franklin D. Roo-sevelt's New Deal. Under Johnson's direction, the Texas branch of the NYA became one of the most successful in the nation.

Johnson then decided to seek office on his own. In 1937, at the age of twenty-eight, Johnson ran for a seat in the U.S. Congress as a representative of Texas's Tenth District. His opponents charged that he was too young, but Johnson outworked them, speaking at every town in his district, and won the race. As a Congressman, Johnson allied himself closely with Roosevelt and his New Deal policies, and proved himself a loyal supporter of the Democrat-ic Party. Johnson served in the House for twelve years until 1948, when he mounted a successful campaign for a seat in the U.S. Senate. Although he won the Democratic primary by a mere 87 votes—earning him the sarcastic nickname "Landslide Lyndon"—the victory launched one of the most illustri-ous Senate careers in American history.

Johnson easily won the general election (Texas was a strongly Democrat-ic state at this time) and returned to Washington, D.C., where he immediately made his presence felt. Energetic and smart, he became known as one of the Senate's most effective young legislators. In 1951 his Democratic colleagues elected him "party whip," an important leadership position within the party. At the start of his second term in 1955, he was elected majority leader, the most powerful position in the Senate.

Johnson used his power to pursue his political ideals. Though he was from the South, Johnson did not support the Jim Crow laws that segregated black and white Americans. Though other Southern leaders fought laws to overturn segregation, Johnson supported them, and he convinced others to do the same. He was also an early supporter of space exploration, and used his power in the Senate to help create the National Aeronautics and Space Administration (NASA). Throughout his tenure as leader of the Senate, he

proved himself to be a skilled back-room bargainer with a knack for shep-
herding legislative bills into law.

Reaches the Presidency

In 1960 Johnson believed the time was right to run for the presidency,
but fellow Democrats did not agree. Political analysts believe that Johnson's
thick Texas accent and raw political style hampered his failed bid for his
party's presidential nomination. Yet these were the very attributes that made
him appealing as a vice presidential running mate for Democratic nominee
John F. Kennedy of Massachusetts. In the general election of 1960, Johnson's
Southern connections helped Kennedy take several key Southern states to
claim a narrow victory over Republican nominee Richard M. Nixon.

Johnson did not relish the role of vice president; he later claimed that he
"detested every minute of it." But he made the best of the office, traveling frequently to meet foreign leaders and loyally carrying out Kennedy's political
wishes. Then, on November 22, 1963, a lone gunman assassinated Kennedy
in Dallas. Under these tragic circumstances, Johnson was thrust into the presidency.

In a speech to the American people shortly after being sworn into office,
Johnson said: "All I have I would have given gladly not to be standing here
today." But he also pledged that he would do his best to carry out Kennedy's
policy goals and build on the fallen leader's legacy. Ever the skillful politician,
Johnson used his powers of persuasion and the outpouring of emotional support from the American public to push through many of Kennedy's legislative
priorities. The most notable of these was the Civil Rights Act of 1964, the single most important piece of civil rights legislation in American history.

Following his reelection in the fall of 1964, Johnson extended the reach of
his domestic programs even further. He declared a "War on Poverty" and
launched an ambitious program of reforms aimed to create what he termed a
"Great Society" of social justice and economic prosperity for all. To this end,
Johnson helped create Medicare, a federal health insurance program for dis-
abled and senior citizens, and Medicaid, a health insurance program for poor
Americans. He also approved extended social security benefits, a boost in the
minimum wage, new measures to better ensure fair housing practices, and legislation to better protect the environment. These programs were the realization
of Johnson's fondest hopes as a politician, and if Johnson were judged on these

domestic accomplishments alone, he might be considered one of the greatest presidents in American history. But the Vietnam War destroyed his presidency.

Johnson and Vietnam

When Johnson took office in 1963, American involvement in the Vietnam War was limited. The United States provided economic aid and military advisors to a South Vietnamese regime that was trying to fight off Communist insurgents who wanted to unite South Vietnam with its communist neighbor, North Vietnam. Johnson was one of many Americans who believed that the United States should combat the spread of Communism, but he was reluctant to send American fighting troops to such a distant and little-known land.

All that changed in the summer of 1964. Steady North Vietnamese and Viet Cong pressure on the South Vietnamese regime was taking its toll, and a significant percentage of the South Vietnamese countryside had fallen under Communist control, at least after nightfall. Johnson wanted to avoid getting too involved, but after a mysterious August 1964 clash between U.S. Navy and North Vietnamese forces in Vietnam's Tonkin Gulf, he asked for and received broad Congressional authorization to take greater military action in Vietnam. Johnson vowed to keep Communism at bay in South Vietnam, but he also assured reporters that "we are not going to send American boys nine or ten thousand miles away to do what Asian boys ought to be doing for themselves."

At first, American involvement in Vietnam was limited to aerial bombings of strategic targets in North Vietnam. When this failed to stop the Communist incursions, Johnson approved the deployment of American troops to Southeast Asia. Over the course of 1965, the number of American troops in Vietnam rose from 23,000 to 184,000. Johnson and his strategists believed that each additional infusion of troops would stop the Communist advance, but the war continued without either side gaining a decisive advantage. Over the course of the next three years, from 1965 to 1968, the number of American soldiers fighting in Vietnam rose to 536,000. Americans deaths increased proportionally, rising from 147 in 1964, to 5,008 in 1966, to 14,589 in 1968.

The war in Vietnam was a disaster for Johnson's presidency. As American casualties mounted, a powerful and increasingly well-organized antiwar movement emerged. Across American campuses and cities, protestors chanted slogans like "Hey, hey, LBJ, how many kids did you kill today?" Military spending to support the war effort increased dramatically, forcing Johnson to accept cuts to some of his beloved domestic programs. Mainstream support for the president dropped precipitously, from 66 percent in early 1966 to just 26 percent by March 1968.

On March 31, 1968, following a winter of heavy fighting in Vietnam that culminated with the Tet Offensive, Johnson announced in a speech to the nation that "I shall not seek, and I will not accept, the nomination of my party for another term as your President." Johnson's vice-president, Hubert Humphrey, secured the Democratic Party's nomination, but he lost the presidential election to Republican candidate Richard Nixon (who also struggled with the Vietnam War for much of his presidency).

Just sixty years old, Johnson retired to his ranch in Texas. He spent his remaining years running a hog farm, playing with his grandchildren, and building a successful presidential library. He died of a heart attack on January 22, 1973. Johnson's legacy is still hotly debated. Supporters claim that he did more for African Americans than any president since Abraham Lincoln, and that he created important "safety nets" for poor and working Americans; detractors charge him with needlessly inflating the size of the federal government and with incompetent and indecisive leadership in the Vietnam War.

Sources

Dallek, Robert. *Lone Star Rising: Lyndon Johnson and His Times, 1908-1960.* New York: Oxford University Press, 1991.

Dallek, Robert. *Flawed Giant: Lyndon Johnson and His Times, 1961-1973.* New York: Oxford University Press, 1998.

Gardner, Lloyd C. *Pay Any Price: Lyndon Johnson and the Wars for Vietnam.* Chicago: Ivan R. Dee, 1995.

Goodwin, Doris Kearns. *Lyndon Johnson and the American Dream.* New York: St. Martins, 1991.

Lyndon Baines Johnson Library and Museum. http://www.lbjlib.utexas.edu.

Vandiver, Frank E. *Shadows of Vietnam: Lyndon Johnson's Wars.* College Station: Texas A&M University Press, 1997.

Henry Kissinger (1923-)
American National Security Advisor (1969-1975) and Secretary of State (1973-1977)

Heinz Alfred Kissinger was born on May 27, 1923, in Furth, Germany. His parents, Louis and Paula, were members of the Jewish lower middle class; his father was a teacher and his mother a homemaker. Over the course of Kissinger's childhood, Jews came to face increasing discrimination in Germany due to the rise of Adolf Hitler's Nazi Party. Kissinger was forbidden from attending public school as a teen because of his religion, and anti-Semitic policies instituted by the Nazis forced his father out of his job as well. The family fled the country in 1938, just before the onset of World War II and the Holocaust. They settled in New York City, in the Manhattan neighborhood of Washington Heights.

Kissinger, who changed his name to Henry upon immigrating to America, held a variety of part-time jobs to pay for his education at the City College of New York. Drafted into the Army in 1943 (the same year he became an American citizen), his knowledge of European politics and proficiency in the German language made him a valuable asset to the American military throughout World War II. He taught German to American officers, served as an interpreter for a general, and helped American officials eliminate the remnants of the Nazi Party from the German government after the war was over. In 1947 Kissinger continued his studies at Harvard University, earning a bachelor's degree in 1950, a master's degree in 1952, and his doctorate in 1954.

A New Voice in American Foreign Policy

Over the course of the next fifteen years, Kissinger established himself as a professor, author, analyst, and advisor. His base was Harvard University, where he began as an instructor in 1954 before rising through the ranks to become a lecturer (1957-1959), associate professor (1959-1962), and professor of government (1962-1971). Kissinger also served as a member of the faculty of Harvard's Center for International Affairs and the director of the university's Defense Studies Program.

In the meantime, Kissinger became a noted analyst and commentator on American foreign policy. He was an unofficial advisor to Presidents Eisenhower, Kennedy, and Johnson, as well as several foreign policy officials within their respective administrations. He also helped shape public opinion through a series of books, several of which became best-sellers despite their complex subject matter. Kissinger's 1957 work *Nuclear Weapons and Foreign Policy*, for example, won several awards as the year's best work in international relations.

Kissinger, though, did not receive an invitation into the inner circles of American government as an official advisor, diplomat, or cabinet member. He remained something of an outsider because his interpretation of American diplomacy—especially as it related to the United States' Cold War struggles with the Soviet Union, China, and other Communist nations—differed from the prevailing view of that era. During the 1950s and into the mid-1960s, most American politicians, Democrat and Republican alike, agreed that America's international role was to promote the idealistic goals of freedom and democracy, and to halt the spread of Communism. In order to meet these goals, the United States had developed a massive arsenal of nuclear weapons capable of obliterating any aggressive enemy.

Kissinger viewed America's role in the Cold War differently. He believed that the United States should take careful and pragmatic consideration of all the political and economic costs and benefits before engaging in armed conflict. He believed that some situations warranted American involvement. But he also believed that the United States needed to take a more realistic approach to the struggle against Communism. With this in mind, he emphasized stability in international relations and policies that were first and foremost concerned with protecting American interests.

Architect of a Changed Foreign Policy

In his unofficial advisory role, Kissinger counseled President Lyndon B. Johnson during the military buildup that he carried out in Vietnam from 1964 through 1968. He was initially supportive of Johnson's policies, but eventually became alarmed about the direction of the war. Kissinger visited Vietnam on several occasions in the mid-1960s, and these trips helped convince him that even the deployment of hundreds of thousands of American troops would not save South Vietnam from its Viet Cong and North Vietnamese enemies. Nor did he believe that nuclear weapons should be considered as an option against the Communists. Kissinger instead advocated a negotiated peace with North Vietnam, and he actually began exploring options for peace talks under Johnson in 1967. But it was not until the following year that a leading American politician gave Kissinger's proposal his full attention. In Richard Nixon's presidential election campaign of 1968, he repeatedly assured voters that he had a "secret plan" to win the Vietnam War. Most historians now recognize that Henry Kissinger was a big part of that secret plan.

After his election, Nixon named Kissinger the head of his National Security Council (NSC). In an unprecedented move, Nixon also ordered all federal agencies to coordinate their foreign policy decisions through Kissinger and the NSC. Kissinger spent much of the next several years traveling around the world as America's leading diplomatic representative. As he carried out this so-called "shuttle diplomacy" from capital to capital, he transformed and reoriented American foreign policy. He oversaw important nuclear arms control negotiations with the Soviet Union, including the momentous 1972 Strategic Arms Limitations Treaty (SALT). Kissinger also masterminded the opening of diplomatic relations with Communist China, a triumph that culminated with Nixon's historic visit to that country in 1972. Kissinger also played an important role in Middle East politics. In 1973, for example, he helped broker a cease fire in the Arab-Israeli War (also known as the Yom Kipper War), which pitted Israel against the Palestinians and surrounding Arab states.

Nixon named Kissinger as Secretary of State in 1973, and he remained in that role under President Gerald Ford until 1977. Kissinger became an unlikely celebrity during these years. He was known for courting the press, and for keeping company with a procession of young starlets (he divorced his first wife, Ann Fleischer, in 1964). With his dour face, heavy build, and thick accent, he was not a conventionally attractive man. But as he once told a reporter, "power is the ultimate aphrodisiac," and by this time Kissinger certainly ranked as one of the most powerful figures in American politics.

Orchestrates Nixon's War

Of all the challenges facing Kissinger in the Nixon and Ford White Houses, the war in Vietnam was undoubtedly the most controversial and explosive. He knew that the United States could not just suddenly withdraw from Vietnam, because that would deprive Nixon of the "peace with honor" he had promised the American people. Instead, Kissinger promoted "Vietnamization" of the war, a plan whereby the American military would gradually hand over primary responsibility for fighting the Communists to South Vietnamese forces. In the meantime, Kissinger pursued diplomatic options for ending the war. These efforts encouraged some Americans to think that U.S. involvement in the bloody war might finally be drawing to a close.

Yet Kissinger and other administration officials believed that these efforts alone would not convince the North Vietnamese—who continued to insist on a unified Vietnam under Communist rule—to sign a peace treaty. The Nixon administration thus carried out a series of military actions designed to remind North Vietnamese negotiators about the costs of continuing the war. Kissinger was directly involved in decisions to approve the secret bombing of Cambodia in 1969 and the invasion of that country in 1971, the South Vietnamese invasion of Laos, and the massive bombing campaigns of North Vietnam in 1972, known as Linebacker I and II. These actions against Communist forces also led to the deaths of thousands of civilians in Cambodia, Laos, and North Vietnam, and have led some critics to label Kissinger a war criminal (Kissinger's political tactics and maneuvers in the early 1970s toward Latin America have also triggered condemnation from human rights activists and other critics).

In October 1972 Kissinger and North Vietnamese lead negotiator Le Duc Tho reached a preliminary peace agreement after more than two years of secret talks. Kissinger's subsequent announcement that "peace is at hand" has been cited by historians as a factor in Nixon's easy re-election one month later. But the deal fell apart when South Vietnamese President Nguyen Van Thieu refused to agree to it.

Determined to bring North Vietnam back to the bargaining table, Nixon ordered—with Kissinger's encouragement—a massive "Christmas bombing" of cities all across North Vietnam. At the same time, the Nixon administration put enormous political pressure on Thieu to accept the terms of the treaty. One month later, on January 27, 1973, U.S., North Vietnamese, and South Vietnamese officials signed the Paris Peace Accords. This treaty to end U.S. involvement in the Vietnam War was identical in many respects to the one that had been hammered out the previous October. Under the terms of the agreement, the United States agreed to withdraw its forces in exchange for

North Vietnamese guarantees that it would stop trying to overthrow South Vietnam's government.

Kissinger and his North Vietnamese counterpart, Le Duc Tho, were awarded the Nobel Peace Prize as a result of their efforts. Scarcely two years later, though, North Vietnamese troops and Viet Cong fighters launched a major offensive against South Vietnam. Kissinger implored Congress and President Ford to provide U.S. support for its ally, but Ford—and America— had had enough of the war in Vietnam. The United States remained on the sidelines as North Vietnam captured the South Vietnamese capital of Saigon and unified the battered country under a Communist government.

When Jimmy Carter came into office following the 1976 presidential elections, Kissinger left government and began a long and lucrative career in the private sector. He founded a consulting firm, Kissinger Associates, that offers services to both businesses and governments, and became a professor of diplomacy at Georgetown University in Washington, D.C. Kissinger has remained a behind-the-scenes advisor on American foreign policy, and he was especially influential during the administration of Ronald Reagan. He has continued to write extensively, and his memoirs and commentaries on international politics have drawn considerable attention.

Kissinger still has many critics, and their calls of "profiteer" and "war criminal" echo outside the halls where he is paid handsomely to speak. But even though his career in international politics was marked by enormous controversy, historians generally agree that Kissinger ranks as one of the most important and influential diplomats of the twentieth century.

Sources

Hanhimaki, Jussi M. *The Flawed Architect: Henry Kissinger and American Foreign Policy.* Oxford and New York: Oxford University Press, 2004.

Isaacson, Walter. *Kissinger: A Biography.* New York: Simon & Schuster, 1992.

Kissinger, Henry. *Ending the Vietnam War: A Personal History of America's Involvement In and Extrication from the Vietnam War.* New York: Simon & Schuster, 2003.

Kissinger, Henry. *Years of Renewal.* New York: Simon & Schuster, 1999.

Schulzinger, Robert D. *Henry Kissinger: Doctor of Diplomacy.* New York: Columbia University Press, 1989.

Robert McNamara (1916-)
American Secretary of Defense, 1961-67

Robert Strange McNamara was born on June 9, 1916, in San Francisco, California. His father, Robert James McNamara, managed the sales department at a wholesale shoe company and his mother, Clara Nell Strange McNamara, was a homemaker. McNamara later said that the pressure he felt from his parents to succeed was "unbelievable," but he seemed up to the task throughout his youth. He graduated at the top of his high school class, attained the rank of Eagle Scout, and graduated with honors from the University of California, Berkeley, in 1933.

McNamara continued his education at the prestigious Harvard Business School in Cambridge, Massachusetts, where he developed an intense interest in using the tools of logic and statistical analysis to solve the problems that faced mankind. In 1939 McNamara graduated from Harvard Business School with a master's degree. He then became the youngest assistant professor ever hired by the school. In 1940 McNamara married Mary Craig, with whom he eventually had three children.

World War II Vet and "Whiz Kid"

When the United States entered World War II late in 1941, the government turned to Harvard and other leading academic institutions for assistance in managing the complex logistical challenges of fighting a war halfway around the world. McNamara became part of a team of Harvard academics who worked with the War Department to implement statistical analysis as a key tool in managing all areas of the war effort, including arms production, supplying troops, and increasing the effectiveness of aerial bombing campaigns.

McNamara taught Army officers during the first years of the war, then entered the Army as a captain in 1943. He worked closely with General Curtis LeMay to plan American bombing campaigns against Japan, especially the 1945 bombing raids against Tokyo. Thanks to their efforts, American forces were able to increase the number of missions they flew, yet simultaneously reduce the number of pilots lost. One key to the strategy employed by LeMay and McNamara involved bombing from higher altitudes. But this change also made bombing runs less accurate, and this in turn triggered a dramatic surge in Japanese civilian deaths and destruction of non-military targets from U.S. bombing campaigns. Later in his life, McNamara commented that had America lost World War II, he and LeMay could have been charged with war crimes for the bombing of Tokyo. McNamara was released from active military service in April 1946, with the rank of lieutenant colonel.

McNamara's World War II experiences convinced him even more of the potential benefits of statistically based management principles. When he returned to the United States, he established a business consulting company with several other management experts. Within a matter of months, the Ford Motor Company hired McNamara and his colleagues to work under the leadership of Charles "Tex" Thornton. These "Whiz Kids," as the team became known in the press, used their mastery of statistics and management principles to rescue the struggling automaker. Many of the Whiz Kids distinguished themselves during these years, but McNamara's performance was particularly noteworthy. He became known as a brilliant, driven, and supremely self-confident business executive. In 1957 he was made a company vice president and a member of its board of directors. Three years later McNamara became the first person outside the Ford family to hold the role of company president. But he spent just five weeks in the job.

Becomes Secretary of Defense

Upon his election to the presidency in 1960, John F. Kennedy declared his intention to bring the "best and the brightest" into government. This vow led him to ask McNamara to join his cabinet as secretary of defense. McNamara accepted and moved into the Pentagon in early 1961, taking a huge cut in pay in exchange for the challenge of bringing systematic reform to the world's largest bureaucracy.

McNamara immediately launched a comprehensive review of the nation's military resources and strategies. After examining the results, he began making significant changes to the U.S. military machine. For example, he introduced the idea of "mutual assured destruction"—building the United States nuclear arsenal up to the point that America could guarantee the destruction of any enemy that launched an attack. But McNamara also recognized that most conflicts would never involve nuclear weapons. He thus encouraged the development of efficient, limited "strike forces" among the three major branches of the military. McNamara felt that the armed forces existed to provide the president with a variety of options, and he wanted the military to be flexible enough to allow presidents to choose the most efficient application of power for any given conflict.

McNamara also reorganized the budgets and management practices of the U.S. military. He cancelled contracts for weapons systems that he viewed as impractical or unnecessary, shut down military bases, and increased investments in antiballistic missile systems. It became clear that under McNamara, Americans could at least be sure that major military expenditures had been subjected to careful financial analysis.

Over the next five years, McNamara played a key role in shaping the foreign policies of two American presidents. McNamara's first test came in 1961, when he advised President Kennedy to proceed with the Bay of Pigs invasion, a disastrous attempt to oust Communist revolutionary and Cuban President Fidel Castro. Scarcely a year later, McNamara sat at President Kennedy's side during the Cuban Missile Crisis, one of the tensest standoffs in the Cold War between the United States and the Soviet Union. In the immediate aftermath of the crisis, McNamara was credited with helping Kennedy shape the firm but moderate negotiating stance that defused the crisis without violence. Years later, however, recordings of cabinet meetings during the crisis revealed that McNamara was one of several advisors who encouraged Kennedy to stand up to "Soviet aggression" with a full attack on Cuba. Many historians believe today that such a response might well have triggered nuclear war between the two superpowers.

Vietnam: "We were wrong, terribly wrong"

Under Kennedy and later under President Lyndon B. Johnson, McNamara was one of the key architects of American involvement in Vietnam. McNamara believed—as did most American strategists—in the domino theory. According to this theory, if one small nation fell to Communism, others would soon follow, like a line of dominoes. McNamara was thus a strong backer of the government of South Vietnam in the early 1960s, a period when it was struggling against Communist insurgents. He strongly supported U.S.

decisions to send financial aid and military advisors to the South Vietnam regime during these years.

American involvement in Vietnam increased dramatically in late 1964, after North Vietnamese forces allegedly attacked a U.S. Navy vessel in the Gulf of Tonkin off the coast of North Vietnam. After President Johnson received Congressional approval to ratchet up U.S. military efforts in the region, McNamara and his aides devised a strategy for increased military involvement in Vietnam. The plan for American engagement called for the deliberate and measured application of steadily larger measures of U.S. military force. This blueprint for war included sustained aerial bombing campaigns against enemy targets, followed by a gradual escalation of American troops in Vietnam. In McNamara's view, this gradual increase in American pressure against the enemy would inevitably bring about a decisive military victory over the Communist forces seeking to overthrow the South Vietnamese government.

This methodical strategy was based on the idea that the Communists were attempting to overthrow a legitimate South Vietnamese government. It hinged on the assumption that America could win by making the costs of waging that war—in dollars and lives—so high for the Communists that they would relent. But McNamara gradually came to understand that many of the people within South Vietnam were opposed to their own government, and that nationalism—the desire for independence from foreign influence or rule—was a key factor in the war. As the war progressed, it also became clear that Viet Cong and North Vietnamese forces were willing to accept horrible levels of casualties in pursuit of their goals. Years later, McNamara wrote in his memoir *In Retrospect* that "we of the Kennedy and Johnson administrations who participated in the decisions on Vietnam acted according to what we thought were the principles and traditions of this nation. We made our decisions in light of those values. Yet we were wrong, terribly wrong."

It took McNamara many years to come to this conclusion, however. Throughout 1965 and 1966, he called for steady increases in the number of U.S. soldiers sent to fight in Vietnam. He justified these increases with "body count" statistics—arguments that the Communists were suffering far greater casualties than American forces. But as the war dragged on without any conclusive turn in America's favor, McNamara's encounters with the media became increasingly combative. He felt that press coverage of the war was becoming excessively negative and pessimistic. Some journalists, meanwhile, believed that the chief architect of "McNamara's War," as some called it, was refusing to face the fact that the war was not going well.

By 1966 McNamara began to harbor secret doubts about his own policies. Superior firepower was not bringing the enemy to its knees, and years of hard work had failed to transform the South Vietnamese military into an effective fighting force. Publicly, McNamara continued to support the Johnson administration's war policies; privately, he implored Johnson to stop bombing and withdraw U.S. troops. It was advice that Johnson was not yet ready to heed.

By late 1967 McNamara had lost faith in the viability of American policy in Vietnam. He resigned his post in February 1968; to this day it remains unclear whether he resigned voluntarily or was fired. He took a job as president of the World Bank, an international agency interested in reducing world poverty and increasing economic productivity in Third World nations. McNamara served in this role until his retirement in 1981.

Looking Back

After leaving the World Bank, McNamara began to analyze American foreign policy, both past and present. In the 1980s he wrote critically about President Reagan's heavy military investments and praised Soviet Premier Mikhail Gorbachev's efforts to promote peace with the United States. For many years, however, he refused to answer questions about his role in Vietnam.

McNamara finally ended his silence on the war in 1995 with his book *In Retrospect: The Tragedy and Lessons of Vietnam,* a searching examination of American policies in Vietnam and the role he played in making and carrying out those policies. McNamara's book caused a major uproar when it was released, in large part because it seemed to open old wounds in American society about the war. Some Americans praised him for his expressions of regret about the war. But others condemned him for offering apologies three decades late. "It would have been better to go out silently if you could not find the courage to speak when it would have done your country any good," declared *Atlantic Monthly* editor James Fallows.

In 2003 McNamara participated in the making of the film *The Fog of War,* by director Errol Morris. During the course of the documentary, McNamara harshly criticized American policy makers—himself included—for unquestioning acceptance of the domino theory as fact, and for their strategic decisionmaking throughout the war. He also asserted that if the United States had better understood the nationalistic foundations of the conflict, the entire Vietnam War might have been averted.

Sources

Hendrickson, Paul. *The Living and the Dead: Robert McNamara and Five Lives of a Lost War.* New York: Knopf, 1996.

McNamara, Robert, with Brian Van de Mark. *In Retrospect: The Tragedy and Lessons of Vietnam.* New York: Times Books, 1995.

McNamara, Robert, with James G. Blight and Robert K. Brigham. *Argument without End: In Search of Answers to the Vietnam Tragedy.* New York: Public Affairs, 1999.

Morris, Errol. *The Fog of War: Eleven Lessons from the Life of Robert McNamara* (DVD). Sony, 2003.

Richie, Jason. *Secretaries of War, Navy, and Defense: Ensuring National Security.* Minneapolis, MN: The Oliver Press, 2002.

"Robert S. McNamara." *Secretaries of Defense.* http://www.defenselink.mil/specials/secdef_histories/bios/mcnamara.htm (March 29, 2006).

Shapley, Deborah. *Promise and Power: The Life and Times of Robert McNamara.* Boston: Little, Brown, 1993.

Ngo Dinh Diem (1901-1963)
South Vietnamese president and prime minister, 1954-1963

Ngo Dinh Diem was born on January 3, 1901, on his family's estate outside the central Vietnamese city of Hue. He was born at a time when Vietnam was under the colonial rule of France. Diem's father, Ngo Dinh Kha, was part of a class of wealthy landowners known as mandarins, who served as the local representatives of the French bureaucracy. Like their French rulers, the Ngo family were Catholic and had been since the seventeenth century. Their religious faith gave them a significant socioeconomic advantage over the majority of Vietnamese, who were followers of Buddhism. Nonetheless, Diem grew up in a family environment that regarded the idea of a future independent Vietnam as a desirable goal.

Diem's father had been a high-ranking local politician, and Diem soon followed in his footsteps. He graduated from the prestigious secondary school Quoc Hoc (National Academy) in Hue, then attended the French-run School for Law and Administration in Hanoi, graduating at the top of his class in 1921. Bright, dedicated, and intensely hard-working, Diem soon distinguished himself as an able administrator. By the time he was in his mid-20s he had joined the ranks of the mandarins and been given supervisory responsibility for a region around Hue that included some 300 villages. In 1929 he was appointed governor of Phan-Thiet province. His first major task was to put a stop to a revolutionary movement with clear Communist underpinnings that was gaining popularity among Vietnamese villagers.

Seeks Path Between Communism and Colonialism

Like most Catholics in Vietnam, Diem thought that the Communist program of revolution threatened the natural social order, which included a hierarchy stretching from the emperor down through the mandarinate to the peasant class. As governor, he was effective at rooting out Communists, even in the home region of Ho Chi Minh, the man who would later lead the Communist movement in Vietnam. But Diem did not truly want French rule, either. When the French colonial governors appointed him to a new post as the Interior Minister and Secretariat of the Commission on Reforms in 1933, he proposed a series of steps that would reduce French authority and usher in greater Vietnamese independence. But when these proposed reforms were ignored, he resigned, telling the French-backed emperor, Bao Dai, that staying in office would be a "deplorable comedy."

Diem's resignation "established an enduring reputation [among many Vietnamese] for stubborn integrity and uncompromising nationalism," wrote historian Philip Catton in *Diem's Final Failure: Prelude to America's War in Vietnam*. Over the next several years, Diem studied, read, and corresponded with others who sought independence from French rule. For much of World War II, he was regarded as a leader among the growing nationalist movement in Vietnam. His anti-Communist political beliefs, however, put him at odds with Ho Chi Minh and other Communist revolutionaries.

In 1945 Communist forces killed Diem's revered older brother, Ngo Dinh Khoi, governor of Quang Ngai province. After the Communist-led Viet Minh ousted the Japanese government later that year, Ho Chi Minh offered Diem a position within the government he was trying to form to rule over postwar Vietnam. Diem refused the offer, and he spent the next five years mostly on the sidelines as Communist and nationalist forces wrestled with French troops seeking to re-establish French control over the nation.

In 1950 Diem went into self-imposed exile. He spent the next four years in Europe and the United States. During this time, he found highly-placed friends who sympathized with his goal of keeping Vietnam from becoming Communist. In the United States especially, Diem spoke of a "third way" between French colonialism and Soviet- or Chinese-backed Communism. This vision was warmly received in Washington, D.C., where most legislators and policy experts were deeply concerned about the possibility of a Communist-ruled Vietnam.

Diem Assumes Power

By 1954 the Viet Minh had fought France to a standstill and forced it to the negotiating table. The Geneva Accords of 1954 called for the temporary creation of two Vietnams: the Democratic Republic of Vietnam, or North Vietnam, which was headed by Ho Chi Minh and his Communist allies; and the Republic of Vietnam, or South Vietnam, which was supported by the United States.

The United States pressured emperor Bao Dai to appoint Diem as prime minister in June 1954, and one month later Diem returned to his homeland to take the reins of a nation divided by years of war, threatened by Communist insurgents, and riddled with factions vying for power in the vacuum created by the French departure. Diem's consolidation of power was swift and sure. First, he used the country's small army to defeat the armed factions who challenged his rule, defeating the Hoa Hao (a Buddhist movement), the Cao Dai (a popular religious sect), and the forces of General Binh Xuyen. In October of 1955 he staged a referendum that deposed Bao Dai as emperor and declared him president of the newly created Republic of Vietnam (RVN). Diem was finally alone in command.

Had elections been held to unify the country in 1956, as the Geneva Accords stipulated, Ho Chi Minh and the Communists would likely have won because of their leading role in ending French colonial rule. But the United States intervened. South Vietnamese President Ngo Dinh Diem and his American allies flatly refused to hold the promised elections.

Nepotism and Repression

Under Diem, governmental power and control were very closely guarded. He insisted on making most decisions himself, but he deliberated very carefully, so decisions were slow in coming. Rather than creating a system of bureaucrats who could institute policy, Diem limited power to a small number of people, mostly family members. The second most-powerful person in the country was his ruthless brother, Ngo Dinh Nhu, who ran the country's secret police. Another prominent member of Diem's inner circle was Nhu's wife, known as Madame Nhu (maiden name Tran Le Xuan). Her influence, combined with Diem's unmarried status, led Vietnamese and Americans alike to view her as the regime's unofficial "first lady." In addition, Diem filled virtually all of his government's key administrative positions with fellow Catholics, leaving Vietnamese of other faiths—about 90 percent of the total population—without any meaningful representation in Saigon.

Diem and his ruling clique found that force was the most efficient way of achieving their goals. Diem cracked down very sharply on dissent within his country, imprisoning and killing thousands, both Communist and non-Communist. U.S. ambassadors and diplomats frequently implored Diem to introduce American-style political and economic reforms, but Diem brushed aside most of these proposals. He argued that the Americans did not know Vietnam like he did, and that the best path for Vietnam was the slow introduction of democracy, carried out at the hands of a ruling elite. It was a plan Diem called "Personalism," a middle way between American individualism and Communism. But this strategy ultimately proved to be a disastrous failure.

Diem's popularity further plummeted in the early 1960s, when his regime launched a new campaign to end Communist influence within South Vietnam. Communist opposition within South Vietnam was organized by the National Liberation Front (NLF) or Viet Cong, which sought its support from poor villagers scattered throughout the country. Diem's pacification plan called for the removal of peasants from scattered villages and their consolidation in heavily fortified "strategic hamlets." Saigon hoped that this program would prevent the Viet Cong from infiltrating rural villages, and by the end of 1962 South Vietnamese officials were touting the campaign as a success. Their claims, coupled with a deep desire to build stability in the national government, convinced the United States to continue economic and military aid packages to Diem, even as it expressed anxiety about Diem's repressive tactics and failures to broaden his support beyond his Catholic base.

The Fall of Diem

In 1963, however, a series of events convinced the United States that Diem's regime could not be salvaged. First, the Viet Cong registered significant military gains in the countryside, and security in urban areas deteriorated as well. Another major factor was the Buddhist Crisis of 1963. Buddhist protests against governmental repression flared across the country, and on May 8, 1963, South Vietnamese troops killed nine unarmed Buddhist marchers in Hue. One month later, on June 11, 1963, a Buddhist monk named Thich Quang Duc burned himself to death in the streets of Saigon to protest Diem's policies. Other fiery suicides followed, creating a public relations disaster for the regime. The government's reputation absorbed another blow when Madame Nhu proclaimed that "I would clap hands at seeing another monk barbecue show."

U.S. attitudes toward Diem changed dramatically in the aftermath of the Buddhist crisis. The new U.S. ambassador, Henry Cabot Lodge, later commented that the "United States can get along with corrupt dictators who manage to stay out of the newspapers. But an inefficient Hitlerism, the leaders of which make fantastic statements to the press, is the hardest thing on earth for the U.S. government to support." In the days and weeks that followed, the United States signaled its intentions to remain on the sidelines as several generals within the South Vietnamese army plotted to remove Diem from power. On November 2, 1963, the coup plotters kidnapped and executed Diem and his brother, Nhu, and replaced them with a military leadership headed by Duong Van Minh. Madame Nhu, who was out of the country at the time of the coup, angrily declared that "whoever has the Americans as allies does not need enemies."

Historians have not been kind to Diem. Most American scholars have criticized him for his failure to build an effective South Vietnamese government that could win popular support. They also charge that his repressive government drove many South Vietnamese into the hands of the Communists. Today, Diem remains a notorious symbol of America's failed efforts to establish a viable non-Communist government in South Vietnam.

Sources

Bouscaren, Anthony Trawick. *The Last of the Mandarins: Diem of Vietnam.* Pittsburgh: Duquesne University Press, 1965.

Catton, Philip E. *Diem's Final Failure: Prelude to America's War in Vietnam.* Lawrence: University Press of Kansas, 2002.

Prados, John. "JFK and the Diem Coup." National Security Archive. http://www.gwu.edu/~nsarchiv/NSAEBB/NSAEBB101/index.htm (April 4, 2006).

Richard M. Nixon (1913-1994)
President of the United States, 1969-1974

Richard Milhous Nixon was born January 9, 1913, in the southern California town of Yorba Linda. Nixon's parents, Frank and Hannah Nixon, had moved to California from the Midwest, drawn by economic opportunity and by the Quaker religious community that flourished near the town of Whittier. They had five boys, all named after past kings of England; Richard was the second. The entire Nixon family worked hard, first on a lemon farm and later at a gas station and grocery store near Whittier, but they struggled to stay out of poverty.

Richard Nixon was known as a hard worker and a star student, if not a social success. Most of all, Nixon was determined—to get into an elite Eastern college, to enter politics, perhaps one day to be president. This drive to succeed was an important asset, for he wrestled with adversity and disappointment throughout young adulthood. The Great Depression of the 1930s squashed his first dream, for Nixon could not afford to enroll at Harvard or Yale. Instead he attended Whittier College, the local Quaker school, where he graduated second in his class. Nixon attended law school at Duke University in North Carolina, and he finished third in his class in 1937. Unable to land a position at an elite Eastern law firm, he returned to practice law in Whittier. On June 21, 1940, he married Thelma "Pat" Ryan, a local teacher, with whom he eventually had two daughters, Patricia and Julie. In 1942 Nixon enlisted in the U.S. Navy. The highlights of his wartime service in the South Pacific came not on the battlefield but at the poker table, where he reportedly won large sums of money on a regular basis.

Ferocious Political Fighter

Upon returning home from the war in 1945, Nixon was recruited by local Republicans to run for a U.S. House of Representatives seat. Backed with thousands of dollars in wartime poker winnings and fueled by his ambition, Nixon conducted a fierce campaign, painting his incumbent opponent, Jerry Voorhis, as out-of-touch, too liberal, and soft on Communism. Nixon won an easy victory and was seated in 1947. Assigned to the House Un-American Activities Committee (HUAC), Nixon soon built a national reputation as a staunch anti-Communist. This reputation was shaped in large part by his dogged pursuit of Alger Hiss, a prominent State Department official who was accused of being a Communist agent (Hiss denied the charges, but he was eventually convicted of perjury).

Nixon turned his growing national profile to good use in 1950, when he ran for an open Senate seat against liberal challenger Helen Gahagan Douglas. Nixon played to his strengths, repeatedly branding his challenger as "soft on communism." These bruising campaign tactics led Douglas to label her opponent "Tricky Dick," but they also lifted him to victory.

Nixon had barely begun his senate career when he was tapped by Republican Party candidate Dwight D. "Ike" Eisenhower to be his running mate in the 1952 presidential election. Nixon played his role well in the election, helping the ticket win votes in California, attacking Democratic opponents with zeal, and offering the genial Eisenhower his complete loyalty. Nixon also effectively fended off charges of corruption within his campaign finance office in a nationally televised speech. This "Checkers" speech, so named for its reference to his family's pet dog, revealed Nixon to be a skilled orator.

The Eisenhower-Nixon ticket won the election, and for the next eight years Nixon faithfully carried out his vice presidential duties. At several points during this time, Eisenhower's age and his frequent health crises forced Nixon to play a larger role than many previous vice presidents. Many historians give him favorable marks for his performance during these periods.

Nixon earned the Republican presidential nomination in 1960, pitting him against John F. Kennedy, the young, charismatic Democratic senator from Massachusetts. The ensuing presidential campaign was bitterly contested, with neither candidate able to gain a decisive edge. The election may have been ultimately decided by a famous series of television debates. Though radio listeners thought Nixon won the first debate, Nixon appeared pale and anxious on television compared to the tanned, steady Kennedy. In one of the closest elections in American history—and one tainted by possible voter fraud in Illinois and Texas—Kennedy edged out Nixon for the presidency. Many Republicans urged Nixon to challenge the election results, but he decided that "I could not subject the country" to the bitter controversy of a recount. Nixon suffered another bitter defeat two years later, when he ran for governor of California. He was not so gracious after this disappointment. Informing reporters that "you won't have Nixon to kick around anymore," he announced his withdrawal from public life.

Nixon's War

Nixon did not stay away for long, however. He maintained a behind-the-scenes presence in national politics throughout the mid-1960s, supporting Republican candidates and preparing for another presidential run. By 1968 Democratic President Lyndon B. Johnson had become increasingly unpopular because of his policies in the Vietnam War and domestic unrest at home. That year Nixon mounted another bid for the presidency. Nixon hated the anti-Vietnam War protests and marches, and he promised to bring "law and order" back to the United States. He also told voters that he had a secret plan to win the Vietnam War. Running on this platform, Nixon narrowly defeated Democratic nominee Hubert H. Humphrey (Johnson's vice president) to become the thirty-seventh president of the United States.

Upon his election, Nixon told American citizens that "the greatest honor history can bestow is the title of peacemaker," and he quickly set out to earn that title by turning his attention to the Vietnam War. Determined to get U.S. forces out of Vietnam without losing the war, he pursued a policy called "Vietnamization" in which American forces would gradually turn responsibility for the prosecution of the war over to the South Vietnamese military. Nixon brought U.S. troops home by the thousands, eventually reducing the number of combat personnel in Vietnam from 543,000 just after he took office to just 47,000 by mid-1972. However, the United States continued to supply South Vietnam with massive amounts of military arms and other supplies.

Simultaneously, Nixon instructed Secretary of State Henry Kissinger to open secret peace talks with North Vietnam. But the North Vietnamese adopted a tough negotiating stance, in large measure because they had become convinced that they could outlast the Americans and ultimately prevail. After one year, the negotiations had made virtually no progress.

Increasingly frustrated at his inability to fulfill his campaign promise of "peace with honor" in Vietnam, Nixon used America's military might in a variety of ways to pressure North Vietnam. In early 1970, for example, he ordered the bombing and invasion of Cambodia, a nation that North Vietnamese forces used as a base for attacks on neighboring South Vietnam. College campuses erupted in protest against the sudden escalation of the war, and on May 4, 1970, National Guard troops fired on demonstrators at Kent State University in Ohio, killing four. In 1971 Nixon was further embarrassed by the release of the "Pentagon Papers," a set of secret documents that revealed that multiple administrations had misled the American public about various aspects of the war in Vietnam.

In other foreign policy areas, meanwhile, Nixon enjoyed greater success. Recognizing that there could be no victors in a war between the United States and the Soviet Union, Nixon encouraged a period of relaxed relations and direct talks known as *détente*. This policy led to important missile treaties, including the Strategic Arms Limitation Talks (SALT I), signed at a Moscow summit in the summer of 1972. In February of the same year, Nixon became the first American president to visit Communist China, leading to the normalization of relations with that country. These efforts to diffuse Cold War tensions are widely regarded as the high points of Nixon's presidency, and they helped Nixon win handily over Democratic nominee George McGovern in his reelection bid in 1972.

After his reelection, Nixon pressed again for an end to American involvement in the Vietnam War. When a tentative peace treaty announced in October 1972 fell apart, he ordered the massive Christmas bombing of Hanoi, the capital of North Vietnam, to convince North Vietnam to return to the bargaining table. Finally, on January 27, 1973, the United States, North Vietnam, and South Vietnam signed the Paris Peace Accords. This agreement enabled Nixon to bring home the remaining U.S. troops in Vietnam and proclaim that he had secured the long-promised "peace with honor" for America. But after U.S. troops returned home, hostilities quickly resumed between South Vietnam and North Vietnam.

Watergate and Beyond

Nixon's presidency ended in August 1974 under a cloud of scandal. His spectacular fall from grace can be traced back to June 17, 1972, when representatives from the Committee to Re-Elect the President (CREEP) were caught breaking into Democratic National Committee headquarters at the Watergate office complex in Washington, D.C. Nixon denied any connection with the break-in and won reelection later that year, but *Washington Post* reporters Bob Woodward and Carl Bernstein launched an investigation into the burglary that uncovered a pattern of deception, bribery, and corruption within Nixon's reelection committee and in the White House itself.

The Watergate affair, as it came to be known, soon dominated the news and the attention of the president, who had approved a massive cover-up of the links between the burglars and his administration. The U.S. Justice Department ordered a special prosecutor, Archibald Cox, to investigate presidential wrongdoing, and Cox and his staff soon uncovered secret audiotapes that provided critical evidence of presidential wrongdoing. Nixon went on national television and appealed to the American people, telling them "I am not a crook." But his attempts to suppress the tapes ultimately failed, and when their contents became public, his presidency was doomed. On July 27, 1974, Congress began proceedings to impeach the president. Rather than drag the country through a protracted impeachment trial that he was likely to lose, Richard Nixon resigned the presidency on August 9, 1974—the first president in American history to do so.

Nixon's successor, Vice President Gerald R. Ford, focused on restoring public trust in the U.S. government and its institutions. Eager to put the pain and disillusionment of Watergate in the past, he made the controversial decision to pardon Nixon. Ford also expressed great reluctance to re-enter the war in Vietnam, even though Communist forces were making steady gains by the end of 1974. In April 1975 North Vietnam forcefully reunified the country under Communist rule as America remained on the sidelines.

In the first few years after Nixon's resignation, he stayed out of the public eye. In 1977, however, the disgraced ex-president agreed to a series of televised interviews with David Frost, and the following year he published *RN: The Memoirs of Richard Nixon*. During the 1980s Nixon consciously tried to cast himself as an elder statesman of American politics. He wrote a series of books on international politics and occasionally offered his perspective on major American political events and issues. Nixon's efforts to rehabilitate his image were aided by Republican President Ronald Reagan, who consulted with Nixon about several foreign policy issues during his two terms in office.

In 1990 the Nixon Presidential Library and Birthplace opened its doors in Nixon's hometown of Yorba Linda. Nixon died on April 19, 1994.

Sources

Ambrose, Stephen. *Nixon.*3 vols. New York: Simon & Schuster, 1987, 1989, 1991.

Lee, J. Edward. *Nixon, Ford, and the Abandonment of South Vietnam.* Jefferson, NC: McFarland & Co., 2002.

Nixon, Richard M. *RN: The Memoirs of Richard Nixon.* New York: Grosset and Dunlap, 1978.

Nixon, Richard M. *No More Vietnams.* New York: Arbor House, 1985.

Reeves, Richard. *President Nixon: Alone in the White House.* New York: Simon & Schuster, 2001.

Wills, Gary. *Nixon Agonistes: The Crisis of the Self-Made Man.* New York: New American Library, 1971.

Vo Nguyen Giap (1911-)
North Vietnamese senior general (1946-1972)
and minister of national defense (1946-1982)

Vo Nguyen Giap was born on August 25, 1911, in An Xa, a village in the central region of Vietnam. He was one of eight children born to Vo Quang Nghiem, a respected teacher, and Nguyen Thi Kien. Like so many villages in Vietnam, life in An Xa revolved around the rice harvests, and Giap grew up helping with the harvest, tending his family's water buffalo, and attending school. Unlike most other Vietnamese youth, though, Giap received a quality education. He learned to read and write both Vietnamese and French, and at the age of fourteen he enrolled at a French-run school in Hue, the regional capital.

Exposed to Revolutionary Views

During his years in Hue, Giap read classic texts by Communist thinkers Karl Marx and Vladimir Lenin, as well as underground newspapers that spoke out against French colonial rule in Vietnam. In 1926 he read a small book by Ho Chi Minh called *Colonialism on Trial* that inspired him to join the growing nationalist movement to overthrow French rule. Giap protested mistreatment of Vietnamese students by French teachers, and in 1927 he helped organize a student strike that spread to other schools. Giap was expelled for his political activities, but he found a new home in a group called Tan Viet, short for Tan Viet Cach Menh Dang (Revolutionary Party for a Great Viet Nam). Using assumed names, Giap wrote articles criticizing French colonialism and promoting Vietnamese independence. These writings burnished his reputation among Vietnamese nationalists, but deeply alarmed French officials. In 1930 he was arrested and sentenced to two years in jail for his anti-government activities (though he served only thirteen months). During his time in prison he met his future wife, Quang Thai, and cemented his ties with other leaders in the Vietnamese independence movement.

Through the 1930s, Giap worked as a teacher and journalist. He also attended the University of Hanoi, in the north of Vietnam. Though Giap was by this time a committed Communist, his writings and teachings were focused primarily on Vietnamese nationalism. In 1937 Giap joined the Indochinese Communist Party, a group backed by the Soviet Union that promoted Communist-led independence for Vietnam, Cambodia, and Laos. In northern Vietnam especially, Giap and his fellow nationalists enlisted a growing number of followers. In 1939, however, French efforts to crack down on Communists forced Giap to leave the country—and his new wife, who died shortly thereafter in a French prison.

At War with the French

After fleeing Vietnam, Giap worked alongside Ho Chi Minh and Pham Van Dong in southern China to form a new group called the Viet Minh (Vietnam Independence League). During World War II, Japan seized control of Vietnam and imposed its own brand of colonial rule. Giap returned home and worked with other nationalist leaders to develop the Viet Minh into a legitimate revolutionary force.

Giap masterminded a recruiting strategy that emphasized the grassroots development of support for the Viet Minh cause. Person by person, village by village, the Viet Minh built their strength in the north of Vietnam. When World War II ended, the Ho Chi Minh and the Viet Minh made an unsuccessful effort to claim independence. But when the French reasserted control, the Viet Minh did not stop fighting. In 1946 Giap formed a guerrilla fighting force that came to be known as the People's Army of Vietnam (PAVN) or Viet Minh. For the next thirty years, Giap—who had never received any formal military training—directed this army's operations.

Giap's Viet Minh became one of the most effective fighting forces in history. The Viet Minh were outnumbered and poorly armed, but Giap introduced a political indoctrination and education program that turned Viet Minh troops into highly motivated and self-sacrificing soldiers. Giap also made effective use of the guerrillas' strategic advantages. Avoiding direct confrontation, the Viet Minh harassed French forces with quick strikes, often under cover of darkness. They also cultivated support from ordinary villagers throughout the war zone, enabling them to develop a civilian surveillance network capable of tracking French troop movements. Giap later said that he "appreciated the fact that [his enemies] had sophisticated weapon systems but I must say that it was the people who made the difference, not the weapons." Giap made some mistakes, as in 1951 when he ordered a direct attack on French forces and lost some 22,000 men. But he learned from these errors and his army grew ever stronger.

By the early 1950s the Viet Minh had gained control of large parts of northern Vietnam, and France had grown weary of the protracted war. A military action orchestrated by Giap then struck a decisive blow that permanently ended French dreams of re-establishing colonial rule. In the spring of 1954 he trapped 15,000 French and allied troops (including Vietnamese, North African, and Foreign Legion soldiers) in an outpost in northwestern Vietnam called Dien Bien Phu. The remote location of the garrison had convinced French commanders that the position was a safe one. But Giap and the PAVN surrounded the outpost and rained artillery fire down on the French. The artillery had come from China, and had been carried piece-by-piece through the surrounding jungles by well-organized and determined Viet Minh troops. The artillery barrage quickly destroyed the local airstrip, which the garrison depended on for supplies, and for the next fifty-five days the Viet Minh laid siege to the surrounded garrison. On May 7, 1954, Giap's troops took control of Dien Bien Phu. An estimated 2,200 French and allied soldiers died during the siege, and another 6,500 were captured (the Viet Minh suffered an estimated 30,000 casualties, including 8,000 killed).

The disaster at Dien Bien Phu was a fatal blow to the French government that had been in place back in Paris. A new government was installed, and it agreed to negotiate a withdrawal not only from Vietnam, but from all of Indochina. An international conference was held in Geneva, Switzerland, and in July 1954 Vietnam was divided in two at the 17th parallel. Viet Minh forces now ruled over the northern half, the Democratic Republic of Vietnam, or North Vietnam. For Giap and Ho Chi Minh, the job was half done. What remained was to unify the rest of the country under Communist rule.

Waging War Against the Americans

When South Vietnam's President Ngo Dinh Diem refused to hold 1956 elections meant to unify the two Vietnams under a single government, Ho Chi Minh and other North Vietnamese leaders launched a campaign to gain control of South Vietnam by force. They first sought to build centers of support in isolated villages, and then spread that support outward. This development greatly alarmed the United States, which did not want to see South Vietnam fall to Communism. It stepped in with economic and military aid to support the anti-Communist government of South Vietnam.

By 1960 revolutionaries within South Vietnam had formed the National Liberation Front (NLF) to oppose the South Vietnamese government. The NLF called itself a nationalist group and did not trumpet its Communist orientation. But the Americans and the South Vietnamese soon called the NLF and its soldiers Viet Cong, or Vietnamese Communists. Through the early 1960s, the Viet Cong became South Vietnam's biggest problem. Receiving much of their arms and other support from North Vietnam, the Viet Cong made steady gains throughout the South Vietnamese countryside. In 1964 the United States became more directly involved in the growing civil war, committing troops to fight alongside the South Vietnamese military.

Giap had long resisted bringing the North Vietnamese Army (NVA) into direct warfare against the United States and South Vietnam, for he recognized the superiority of American firepower. When political pressures forced him to engage the enemy directly in 1965 and 1966, the NVA usually lost badly. But Giap then returned to the genius of his earlier strategy, conducting a guerilla war against the enemy.

The war took yet another pivotal turn in the opening months of 1968, when the Viet Cong, backed by the NVA, launched the Tet Offensive. Simultaneous attacks were launched throughout South Vietnam, including the capital of Saigon and other major cities such as Hue. This offensive failed to spark a general revolt of the South Vietnamese population against its government, as North Vietnamese leaders had hoped. In fact, American and South Vietnamese forces eventually recaptured most of the territory lost in the opening days of Tet. But Tet showed U.S. strategists—and the American public—that the war was far from over. This realization further eroded support for the war back in the United States.

Final Years of the War

From 1968 to 1972, Giap continued sponsoring guerilla warfare actions within South Vietnam. Though countless North Vietnamese soldiers lost their lives, the army showed a remarkable will to continue fighting. Giap later commented that the Americans "knew little about Vietnam and her people. They didn't understand our will to maintain independence and equality."

Giap's career at the head of the North Vietnamese Army was finally done in by internal politics within the Politburo, the ruling body of the North Vietnamese Communist party. Following the Easter Offensive of 1972—a conventional military attack against South Vietnamese forces within South Vietnam that ended in stalemate—Giap was removed from his command of the NVA (poor health may have also been a factor in this demotion). Though he remained defense minister until 1982, Giap was increasingly on the sidelines of decision making. However, it was his strategy that led to peace talks that brought about the withdrawal of American forces in 1973. In 1975 Giap rejoiced as North Vietnamese forces took control of the South and reunified the country as the Republic of Vietnam.

In 1992 Giap was awarded the Gold Star Order, Vietnam's highest honor, for his contributions to the "revolutionary cause of party and nation." Still living as of the mid-2000s, Giap remains a hero in his native land. His writings, especially *People's War, People's Army* (1962), are considered a definitive source of information on guerrilla warfare during the Vietnam War. Though he had no formal military training, Giap is assured a place as one of the most successful military strategists of the twentieth century.

Sources

Currey, Cecil B. "Senior General Vo Nguyen Giap Remembers." *Journal of Third World Studies,* Fall 2003.

Currey, Cecil B. *Victory at Any Cost: The Genius of Viet Nam's Gen. Vo Nguyen Giap.* Washington and London: Brassey's, 1997.

Macdonald, Peter. *Giap: The Victor in Vietnam.* New York: W.W. Norton, 1993.

"Vo Nguyen Giap." *CNN Cold War.* http://www.cnn.com/SPECIALS/cold.war/episodes/11/interviews/giap/ (April 10, 2006).

William C. Westmoreland (1914-2005)
U.S. Commander in Vietnam, 1964-1968

William Childs Westmoreland was born on March 26, 1914, in Spartanburg, South Carolina. He enjoyed a privileged childhood. His father, John Ripley Westmoreland, managed a textile plant and later became a banker, and his mother, "Mimi" Childs Westmoreland, came from a proud and well-off Southern family. Though he was never an especially brilliant student, Westmoreland was a natural leader from an early age. He excelled in Boy Scouts as a troop leader and was elected president of his high school class. His parents wanted him to be a doctor or a lawyer, but a high school trip to a scouting jamboree in England convinced the young man that he wanted to be a soldier and travel the world. He parlayed his family connections into an appointment to the U.S. Military Academy at West Point and began his illustrious career in the Army.

Westmoreland thrived in the military and he wholeheartedly embraced West Point's motto, "Duty, Honor, Country." He was the highest-ranking officer in his senior class and upon graduation in 1936 he received the "Pershing Sword," a prestigious award granted to the graduate showing the highest standards for military discipline. Over the next several years Westmoreland developed his skills as a specialist in field artillery, training in Oklahoma and Hawaii before being stationed in Fort Bragg, North Carolina.

Tested in War

Early in World War II, Westmoreland—now a major and commander of the U.S. Army's 34th Field Artillery unit—was called to lead his troops in battle in North Africa. During his tour there he distinguished himself for his willingness to place himself and his men in danger in order to secure advantage, and his unit was part of a successful effort to drive German troops out of North Africa. In 1944 Westmoreland was made executive officer of the Ninth Division

Artillery stationed in England, and in the weeks after the D-Day Invasion of France, he helped American forces drive the German army eastward toward eventual defeat. "Westy," as he became known, was well-liked by both his soldiers and his superior officers, including General Dwight D. Eisenhower.

Over the course of the two decades following World War II, Westmoreland developed a portfolio of experiences that equipped him for leadership at the highest levels of the military. He went to jump school to learn to be a paratrooper, and later commanded airborne divisions both during the Korean War in 1952 and during peacetime in the late 1950s. He spent a year in the Advanced Management Program at Harvard in 1954, and learned the ropes of the Army bureaucracy in several different assignments, including a stint as secretary under Army Chief of Staff Maxwell Taylor. He also spent three years as superintendent at the U.S. Military Academy at West Point. By 1964 he had earned the rank of general and stood prepared for the greatest challenge of his career: Vietnam.

A Fight That Can't Be Won?

When Westmoreland was placed in charge of Military Assistance Command, Vietnam (MACV), in June 1964, he had every intention of adding to the United States' distinguished record of victory in wartime. As commander of all U.S. Army forces in Vietnam, he immediately set out to train the South Vietnamese army (the Army of the Republic of Vietnam, or ARVN) so that it could stop the advances made by the Viet Cong within South Vietnam and defeat North Vietnamese forces on the field of battle. When ARVN forces proved inadequate, Westmoreland became an early and committed advocate for the use of American ground troops in Vietnam. He firmly believed that it was America's job to stop the spread of Communism, and he urged that American military forces be used to strike at North Vietnam "surely, swiftly, and powerfully ... with sufficient force to hurt." Westmoreland could not have anticipated how difficult it would be for him to achieve these military objectives.

During the first year of his command Westmoreland was a popular figure, both in Vietnam and back in the United States. He was known for his frequent trips to the frontlines to boost the morale of his soldiers, and he promoted the use of "search and destroy" missions to knock out enemy positions without costly losses of American soldiers. In 1965 *Time* magazine named the handsome, strong-jawed soldier its "Man of the Year." Even the most pessimistic critics of American military efforts in Vietnam had to acknowledge that when Westmoreland entered a battle on his terms, American troops were never defeated. Westmoreland thus concluded that with more combat troops, he could lead America to victory. Yet for all the talk of American triumphs and the war's devastating impact on the enemy, the end of the war came no closer.

Through 1966 and 1967, Westmoreland successfully petitioned Washington D.C. for more U.S. troops in Vietnam. But Communist attacks on American and South Vietnamese positions continued unabated, and though American troops won every conventional battle, the real war was being fought in guerrilla attacks that U.S. soldiers were ill-equipped to counter.

As American losses mounted in 1967, President Lyndon B. Johnson brought Westmoreland home to participate in a public relations tour to reassure the American people. Westmoreland predicted imminent victory, telling reporters that he could see "the light at the end of the tunnel." Just a few months later, in January of 1968, North Vietnamese and Viet Cong forces launched the Tet Offensive, a massive and well-coordinated attack on positions throughout Vietnam.

In military terms, Tet was a disaster for the Communists, who lost huge numbers of soldiers and were forced to relinquish most of the territory captured in Tet's opening days. But in public relations terms Tet was a great victory for North Vietnam and its Viet Cong allies. Reporters and anti-war protestors mocked Westmoreland's earlier assurances of eminent victory. In addition, the general's post-Tet calls for more U.S. troops and an expansion of military operations outside of South Vietnam were flatly denied by President Lyndon B. Johnson, whose presidency was already reeling from the economic and political costs of the war. Instead, Johnson relieved Westmoreland of command in Vietnam and brought him back to Washington D.C. to serve as chief of staff for the U.S. Army.

The Lessons of Vietnam

Throughout his long and difficult tenure in Vietnam, Westmoreland had been a good soldier: he never publicly criticized his superior officers nor his civilian commanders, including the president. He faithfully executed his orders, even when he believed that the clear path to victory was blocked by poor decision-making at high levels. Only later, after he retired, did he offer his own detailed assessment of flawed U.S. policies in Vietnam. In his 1976 memoir, *A Soldier Reports,* and in numerous public speeches, Westmoreland defended his conduct of the war and rebuked Washington lawmakers for not giving him the military resources that he believed would have won the war. Westmoreland also accused the press of failing to understand events within Vietnam and of using the news to promote an anti-war political agenda. His theory that military victory could have been achieved had it not been for civilian meddling—expressed in his accusation that the Army had been sent to fight with "one hand behind its back"—became one of the major interpretations used to explain the eventual American defeat in the Vietnam War.

Westmoreland served as Army Chief of Staff until 1972, when he retired. He made an unsuccessful bid for the office of governor of South Carolina in 1974, then faded for a time from the public eye. In 1982 CBS News ran a television program accusing Westmoreland of participating in a conspiracy to mislead the public about enemy troop strength in Vietnam. Westmoreland sued CBS for libel. The two sides eventually reached an out-of-court settlement, with both camps claiming victory (CBS News did issue an apology to Westmoreland for some aspects of its report). Westmoreland's impassioned defense of American military actions in Vietnam made him a favorite of conservatives, and he was widely consulted by those within the administration of President Ronald Reagan. Westmoreland eventually retired to his home in Charleston, South Carolina. He died in a nursing home on July 18, 2005.

Sources

Borklund, C. W. *Military Leaders Since World War II.* New York: Facts on File, 1992.

"General William Westmoreland." *The Economist,* July 30, 2005.

Furgurson, Ernest. *Westmoreland: The Inevitable General.* Boston: Little, Brown, 1968.

"William Westmoreland: The Eagle Scout." *U.S. News & World Report,* March 16, 1998.

Westmoreland, William C. *A Soldier Reports.* Garden City, NY: Doubleday, 1976.

Zaffiri, Samuel. *Westmoreland: A Biography of General William C. Westmoreland.* New York: Morrow, 1994.

PRIMARY SOURCES

Declaration of Independence of the Democratic Republic of Vietnam

At the end of World War II (1939-45), Viet Minh leader Ho Chi Minh decided that the time had come to end his country's long history of subjugation at the feet of foreign powers. On September 2, 1945, he issued this "Declaration of Independence." Clearly modeled after the one proclaimed by the United States when it asserted its independence from England in the eighteenth century, Ho Chi Minh's document recounted a long list of abuses committed by France during its years of colonial rule over Vietnam. It also appealed to the world to support his country's claim to independence. Following is the full text of the Declaration.

"All men are created equal. They are endowed by their Creator with certain unalienable Rights; among these are Life, Liberty, and the pursuit of Happiness."

This immortal statement was made in the Declaration of Independence of the United States of America in 1776. In a broader sense, this means: All the peoples on the earth are equal from birth, all the peoples have a right to live, to be happy and free.

The Declaration of the French Revolution made in 1791 on the Rights of Man and of the Citizen also states: "All men are born free and with equal rights, and must always remain free and have equal rights."

These are undeniable truths.

Nevertheless, for more than eighty years, the French imperialists, abusing the standard of Liberty, Equality, and Fraternity, have violated our Fatherland and oppressed our fellow citizens. They have acted contrary to the ideals of humanity and justice.

In the field of politics, they have deprived our people of every democratic liberty.

They have enforced inhuman laws; they have set up three distinct political regimes in the North, the Center, and the South of Vietnam in order to wreck our national unity and prevent our people from being united.

They have built more prisons than schools. They have mercilessly slain our patriots; they have drowned our uprisings in rivers of blood.

They have fettered public opinion; they have practiced obscurantism against our people.

To weaken our race they have forced us to use opium and alcohol.

In the field of economics, they have fleeced us to the backbone, impoverished our people and devastated our land.

They have robbed us of our rice fields, our mines, our forests, and our raw materials. They have monopolized the issuing of bank notes and the export trade.

They have invented numerous unjustifiable taxes and reduced our people, especially our peasantry, to a state of extreme poverty.

They have hampered the prospering of our national bourgeoisie; they have mercilessly exploited our workers.

In the autumn of 1940, when the Japanese fascists violated Indochina's territory to establish new bases in their fight against the Allies, the French imperialists went down on their bended knees and handed over our country to them.

Thus, from that date, our people were subjected to the double yoke of the French and the Japanese. Their sufferings and miseries increased. The result was that, from the end of last year to the beginning of this year, from Quang Tri Province to the North of Vietnam, more than two million of our fellow citizens died from starvation. On March 9 [1945], the French troops were disarmed by the Japanese. The French colonialists either fled or surrendered, showing that not only were they incapable of "protecting" us, but that, in the span of five years, they had twice sold our country to the Japanese.

On several occasions before March 9, the Vietminh League urged the French to ally themselves with it against the Japanese. Instead of agreeing to this proposal, the French colonialists so intensified their terrorist activities against the Vietminh members that before fleeing they massacred a great number of our political prisoners detained at Yen Bay and Caobang.

Notwithstanding all this, our fellow citizens have always manifested toward the French a tolerant and humane attitude. Even after the Japanese putsch of March 1945, the Vietminh League helped many Frenchmen to cross the frontier, rescued some of them from Japanese jails, and protected French lives and property.

From the autumn of 1940, our country had in fact ceased to be a French colony and had become a Japanese possession.

After the Japanese had surrendered to the Allies, our whole people rose to regain our national sovereignty and to found the Democratic Republic of Vietnam.

The truth is that we have wrested our independence from the Japanese and not from the French.

The French have fled, the Japanese have capitulated, Emperor Bao Dai has abdicated. Our people have broken the chains which for nearly a century have fettered them and have won independence for the Fatherland. Our people at the same time have overthrown the monarchic regime that has reigned supreme for dozens of centuries. In its place has been established the present Democratic Republic.

For these reasons, we, members of the Provisional Government, representing the whole Vietnamese people, declare that from now on we break off all relations of a colonial character with France; we repeal all the international obligations that France has so far subscribed to on behalf of Vietnam, and we abolish all the special rights the French have unlawfully acquired in our Fatherland.

The whole Vietnamese people, animated by a common purpose, are determined to fight to the bitter end against any attempt by the French colonialists to reconquer their country.

We are convinced that the Allied nations, which at Teheran and San Francisco have acknowledged the principles of self-determination and equality of nations, will not refuse to acknowledge the independence of Vietnam.

A people who have courageously opposed French domination for more than eighty years, a people who have fought side by side with the Allies against the fascists during these last years, such a people must be free and independent.

For these reasons, we, members of the Provisional Government of the Democratic Republic of Vietnam, solemnly declare to the world that Vietnam has the right to be a free and independent country—and in fact it is so already. The entire Vietnamese people are determined to mobilize all their physical and mental strength, to sacrifice their lives and property in order to safe guard their independence and liberty.

Source: Ho Chi Minh. "Declaration of Independence of the Democratic Republic of Vietnam," September 2, 1945. Reprinted in *Selected Writings*. Hanoi: Foreign Languages Publishing House, 1977. Available online at http://www.vietnamembassy-usa.org/learn_about_vietnam/politics/dec_of_independence.

President Eisenhower Explains the "Domino Theory"

The foundation of American foreign policy in the early years of the Cold War was the conviction that Communism had to be checked wherever it threatened to spread. The first expression of this mandate was President Harry S. Truman's "Truman Policy," announced in 1948. Six years later, in an April 7, 1954, press conference, President Dwight D. Eisenhower explained his thoughts on this policy, which drove American actions in Southeast Asia in the years ahead.

Q. Robert Richards, Copley Press: Mr. President, would you mind commenting on the strategic importance of Indochina to the free world? I think there has been, across the country, some lack of understanding on just what it means to us.

A. THE PRESIDENT. You have, of course, both the specific and the general when you talk about such things.

First of all, you have the specific value of a locality in its production of materials that the world needs.

Then you have the possibility that many human beings pass under a dictatorship that is inimical to the free world.

Finally, you have broader considerations that might follow what you would call the "falling domino" principle. You have a row of dominoes set up, you knock over the first one, and what will happen to the last one is the certainty that it will go over very quickly. So you could have a beginning of a disintegration that would have the most profound influences.

Now, with respect to the first one, two of the items from this particular area that the world uses are tin and tungsten. They are very important. There are others, of course, the rubber plantations and so on.

Then with respect to more people passing under this domination, Asia, after all, has already lost some 450 million of its peoples to the Communist dictatorship, and we simply can't afford greater losses.

But when we come to the possible sequence of events, the loss of Indochina, of Burma, of Thailand, of the Peninsula, and Indonesia following, now you begin to talk about areas that not only multiply the disadvantages that you would suffer through loss of materials, sources of materials, but now you are talking really about millions and millions and millions of people.

Finally, the geographical position achieved thereby does many things. It turns the so-called island defensive chain of Japan, Formosa, of the Philippines and to the southward; it moves in to threaten Australia and New Zealand.

It takes away, in its economic aspects, that region that Japan must have as a trading area or Japan, in turn, will have only one place in the world to go—that is, toward the Communist areas in order to live.

So, the possible consequences of the loss are just incalculable to the free world.

Source: Eisenhower, Dwight D. Press Conference, April 7, 1954. *Public Papers of the Presidents of the United States: Dwight D. Eisenhower, 1954.* Washington, DC: Office of the Federal Register, 1960.

Program of the South Vietnam National Liberation Front

The 1954 Geneva Accords ended French colonial rule in Vietnam and divided the country into two separate states: Communist North Vietnam and pro-Western South Vietnam. Once France withdrew from the region, the United States took up the job of supporting anti-Communist factions within South Vietnam. It was not an easy job, for there were substantial numbers of people within South Vietnam who longed to rid their country of Western influences and seize power from the wealthy landowners who were supported by the West. After 1960, those anti-American, pro-Communist sympathizers found leadership from a group called Mat Tran Dan oc Giai Phong Mien Nam, or the National Liberation Front (NLF).

The NLF was the latest and most powerful incarnation of several nationalist movements to emerge in Vietnam since 1941. In that year, many Vietnamese joined a group called the Viet Minh, which sought independence from all colonial rule. After World War II, this movement continued to resist French rule and became increasingly dominated by Communists. When the NLF was born in 1960, the Communist government in Hanoi immediately lent covert support to its efforts to overthrow the rulers of South Vietnam. However, the NLF—known to Americans as the Viet Cong—did not openly proclaim its Communist orientation; eager to appeal to a wider cross-section of the populace, its leadership instead emphasized its desire for national unification and independence. Following are excerpts from the founding charter of the NLF, dated December 20, 1960:

Since the French colonialists invaded our country, our people have unremittingly struggled for national independence and freedom. In 1945, our compatriots throughout the country rose up, overthrew the Japanese and French and seized power, and afterwards heroically carried out a resistance war for nine years, defeated the French aggressors and the U.S. interventionists, and brought our people's valiant resistance war to a glorious victory.

At the Geneva Conference the French imperialists had, in July 1954, to undertake to withdraw their troops from Vietnam. The participating countries to the Conference solemnly declared their recognition of the sovereignty, independence, unity and territorial integrity of Vietnam.

Since then we should have been able to enjoy peace, and join the people throughout the country in building an independent, democratic, unified, prosperous and strong Vietnam.

Reprinted with permission from A Vietcong Memoir, Copyright © 1985 Truong Nhu Tang, David Chanoff, and Doan Van Toai.

However, the American imperialists, who had in the past helped the French colonialists to massacre our people, have now plotted to partition our country permanently, enslave its southern part through a disguised colonial regime and turn it into a military base in preparation for aggressive war in Southeast Asia. They have brought the Ngo Dinh Diem clique—their stooges—to power under the signboard of a fake independent state, and use their "aid" policy and advisers' machine to control all the military, economic, political and cultural branches in South Vietnam.

The aggressors and traitors have set up the most dictatorial and cruel rule in Vietnam's history. They repress and persecute all democratic and patriotic movements, abolish all human liberties. They monopolize all branches of economy, strangle industry, agriculture and trade, ruthlessly exploit all popular strata. They use every device of mind poisoning, obscurantism and deprivation in an attempt to quell the patriotism of our people. They feverishly increase their military forces, build military bases, use the army as an instrument for repressing the people and for war preparations in accordance with U.S. imperialists' policy.

For more than six years, countless crimes have been perpetrated by the U.S.-Diem dictatorial and cruel rule: terrorizing gunshots have never ceased to resound throughout South Vietnam; tens of thousands of patriots have been shot, beheaded, disemboweled with liver plucked out; hundreds of thousands of people have been tortured, and thrown into jail where they died a slow death; countless people have been victims of arson, house removal and usurpation of land, and drafted for forced labor or press-ganged into the army; innumerable families are in distress or torn away as a result of the policy of concentrating people in "prosperity zones" and "resettlement centers," of exacting rents and taxes, terror, arrest, plunder, ransom, widespread unemployment and poverty, which are seriously threatening the life of all popular strata.

There must be peace! There must be independence! There must be democracy! There must be enough food and clothing! There must be peaceful reunification of the fatherland!

That is our most earnest and pressing aspiration. It has become an iron will, and a prodigious strength urging our people to unite and resolutely rise up so as to overthrow the cruel rule of the U.S. imperialists and their stooges, and to save our homes and our country.

In view of the supreme interests of the fatherland, with the firmness to struggle to the end for the people's legitimate aspirations and in accordance with the progressive trend in the world, the South Vietnam National Liberation Front comes into being.

The South Vietnam National Liberation Front undertakes to unite people from all walks of life, social classes, nationalities, political parties, organizations, religious communities, and patriotic personalities in South Vietnam, without distinction of political tendencies, in order to struggle for the overthrow of the rule of the U.S. imperialists and their henchmen and for the realization of independence, democracy, improvement of living conditions, peace and neutrality in South Vietnam pending peaceful reunification of the fatherland.

The program of the South Vietnam National Liberation Front comprises the following 10 points:

I. To Overthrow the Disguised Colonial Regime of the U.S. Imperialists and the Dictatorial Ngo Dinh Diem Administration—Lackey of the United States—and to Form National Democratic Coalition Administration ...

II. To Bring into Being a Broad and Progressive Democracy ...

III. To Build an Independent and Sovereign Economy and Improve the People's Living Conditions ...

IV. To Carry Out Land-Rent Reduction and to Advance Toward the Settlement of the Agrarian Problem so as to Ensure Land to the Tillers ...

V. To Build a National and Democratic Education and Culture ...

VI. To Build an Army for the Defense of the Fatherland and the People ...

VII. To Guarantee the Right of Equality Between Nationalities, and Between Men and Women; to Protect the Legitimate Rights of Foreign Residents in Vietnam and Vietnamese Living Abroad ...

VIII. To Carry Out a Foreign Policy of Peace and Neutrality ...

IX. To Establish Normal Relations Between the Two Zones and Advance Toward Peaceful Reunification of the Fatherland ...

X. To Oppose Aggressive War; Actively Defend World Peace ...

Compatriots throughout the country!

All Vietnamese patriots!

Following nearly a century of struggle and nine years of resistance our people who have shed so much blood and laid down many lives are determined not to be enslaved again!

For peace, independence, freedom and the unity of our fatherland, for the destiny of our people, for the sake of our lives and future and the future of our descendants.

Let all of us rise up!

Let all of us unite!

Let us close our ranks and march forward to fight under the banner of the South Vietnam National Liberation Front to overthrow the cruel domination of the U.S. imperialists and the Ngo Dinh Diem clique, their henchmen, in order to save our country and our homes.

We will surely win because the union of our people is an invincible force, because justice is on our side, and obsolete colonialism is now disintegrating and heading for total collapse. In the world, the movement for peace, democracy and national independence is expanding widely and strongly, and is winning more and more successes. This situation is very favorable to our struggle for national salvation.

The U.S. imperialists and their henchmen will certainly be defeated!

The cause of national liberation in South Vietnam will certainly triumph!

Let us unite, be confident and struggle heroically! Let us go forward and win a glorious victory for our people and our fatherland!

Source: Tang, Truong Nhu, with David Chanoff and Doan Van Toai. *A Vietcong Memoir.* New York: Harcourt Brace Jovanovich, 1985.

The 1964 Gulf of Tonkin Resolution

During the early 1960s, Viet Cong forces in South Vietnam made steady progress in undermin-ing the national government of South Vietnam, in large measure because of guerrilla strikes that were funded and supported by the government of North Vietnam. American strategists became convinced that the United States needed to step up its support for the South Vietnamese govern-ment and its army. However, President Lyndon B. Johnson knew that convincing Congress to support direct American intervention in support of South Vietnam would be a challenging task.

In the summer of 1964, though, the task of securing Congressional approval for an expansion of U.S. military involvement in Vietnam unexpectedly became easier. On July 31, 1964, a U.S. naval warship patrolling the waters of the Gulf of Tonkin, off the coast of North Vietnam, reported that it had been fired upon by North Vietnamese gunboats. Three days later, during a heavy storm, American warships in the Gulf reported that they were fired upon again. Most his-torians believe that this second attack was actually a false report conjured up by anxious and inexperienced radar and sonar operators. Nonetheless, after reports of the second attack reached the White House, Johnson asked Congress for the authority to commit U.S. forces in the region. In the first document excerpted below, Johnson asks for broad war-making powers from Con-gress. The second document is the text of the Congressional resolution which granted Johnson the authority he requested to expand U.S. military involvement in Vietnam.

Presidenťs Message to Congress, August 5, 1964

To the Congress of the United States:

Last night I announced to the American people that the North Viet-namese regime had conducted further deliberate attacks against U.S. naval vessels operating in international waters, and I had therefore directed air action against gunboats and supporting facilities used in these hostile opera-tions. This air action has now been carried out with substantial damage to the boats and facilities. Two U.S. aircraft were lost in the action.

After consultation with the leaders of both parties in the Congress, I fur-ther announced a decision to ask the Congress for a resolution expressing the unity and determination of the United States in supporting freedom and in protecting peace in southeast Asia.

These latest actions of the North Vietnamese regime has given a new and grave turn to the already serious situation in southeast Asia. Our commitments in that area are well known to the Congress. They were first made in 1954 by President Eisenhower. They were further defined in the Southeast Asia Collective Defense Treaty approved by the Senate in February 1955.

This treaty with its accompanying protocol obligates the United States and other members to act in accordance with their constitutional processes to meet Communist aggression against any of the parties or protocol states.

Our policy in southeast Asia has been consistent and unchanged since 1954. I summarized it on June 2 in four simple propositions:

1. America keeps her word. Here as elsewhere, we must and shall honor our commitments.

2. The issue is the future of southeast Asia as a whole. A threat to any nation in that region is a threat to all, and a threat to us.

3. Our purpose is peace. We have no military, political, or territorial ambitions in the area.

4. This is not just a jungle war, but a struggle for freedom on every front of human activity. Our military and economic assistance to South Vietnam and Laos in particular has the purpose of helping these countries to repel aggression and strengthen their independence.

The threat to the free nations of southeast Asia has long been clear. The North Vietnamese regime has constantly sought to take over South Vietnam and Laos. This Communist regime has violated the Geneva accords for Vietnam. It has systematically conducted a campaign of subversion, which includes the direction, training, and supply of personnel and arms for the conduct of guerrilla warfare in South Vietnamese territory. In Laos, the North Vietnamese regime has maintained military forces, used Laotian territory for infiltration into South Vietnam, and most recently carried out combat operations—all in direct violation of the Geneva Agreements of 1962.

In recent months, the actions of the North Vietnamese regime have become steadily more threatening.... [*Johnson details evidence of earlier North Vietnamese aggression against American personnel.*]

As President of the United States I have concluded that I should now ask the Congress, on its part, to join in affirming the national determination that all such attacks will be met, and that the United States will continue in its basic policy of assisting the free nations of the area to defend their freedom.

187

As I have repeatedly made clear, the United States intends no rashness, and seeks no wider war. We must make it clear to all that the United States is united in its determination to bring about the end of Communist subversion and aggression in the area. We seek the full and effective restoration of the international agreements signed in Geneva in 1954, with respect to South Vietnam, and again in Geneva in 1962, with respect to Laos....

The events of this week would in any event have made the passage of a congressional resolution essential. But there is an additional reason for doing so at a time when we are entering on three months of political campaigning. Hostile nations must understand that in such a period the United States will continue to protect its national interests, and that in these matters there is no division among us....

Joint Resolution of Congress, August 7, 1964

Resolved by the Senate and House of Representatives of the United States of America in Congress assembled,

That the Congress approves and supports the determination of the President, as Commander in Chief, to take all necessary measures to repel any armed attack against the forces of the United States and to prevent further aggression.

Sec. 2. The United States regards as vital to its national interest and to world peace the maintenance of international peace and security in southeast Asia. Consonant with the Constitution of the United States and the Charter of the United Nations and in accordance with its obligations under the Southeast Asia Collective Defense Treaty, the United States is, therefore, prepared, as the President determines, to take all necessary steps, including the use of armed force, to assist any member or protocol state of the Southeast Asia Collective Defense Treaty requesting assistance in defense of its freedom.

Sec. 3. This resolution shall expire when the President shall determine that the peace and security of the area is reasonably assured by international conditions created by action of the United Nations or otherwise, except that it may be terminated earlier by concurrent resolution of the Congress.

Source: Johnson, Lyndon B. Speech to Congress, August 5, 1964. *Public Papers of the Presidents of the United States, Lyndon B. Johnson, 1963-64.*Washington, DC: Office of the Federal Register, 1965; "Joint Resolution of Congress H.J. RES1145 August 7, 1964." *Department of State Bulletin*, August 24, 1964. Available online at the Avalon Project, Yale Law School, http:/www.yale.edu/lawweb/avalon/tonkin-g.htm.

America's Policy of "Sustained Reprisal" in Vietnam

The Gulf of Tonkin Resolution of 1964 provided the Johnson White House and American military strategists with authorization to use force in defense of South Vietnam. But there was great debate about how exactly American forces could best be used to help stop Viet Cong attacks and punish North Vietnam for its aggression against South Vietnam.

President Lyndon B. Johnson and others within his administration believed that without North Vietnamese support, the Viet Cong could not continue their insurgency against the South Vietnamese government. They were divided, however, on how best to counter the Communist attacks. Some within the administration wanted to commit ground troops and open an all-out assault; others believed that America should avoid sending ground troops to fight in Southeast Asia. In the end, the military policy that was chosen was one articulated by National Security Advisor McGeorge Bundy. The following 1965 document contains excerpts from Bundy's explanation of his proposed policy of "sustained reprisal."

I. INTRODUCTORY

We believe that the best available way of increasing our chance of success in Vietnam is the development and execution of a policy of sustained reprisal against North Vietnam—a policy in which air and naval action against the North is justified by and related to the whole Viet Cong campaign of violence and terror in the South.

While we believe that the risks of such a policy are acceptable, we emphasize that its costs are real. It implies significant U.S. air losses even if no full air war is joined, and it seems likely that it would eventually require an extensive and costly effort against the whole air defense system of North Vietnam. U.S. casualties would be higher—and more visible to American feelings—than those sustained in the struggle in South Vietnam.

Yet measured against the costs of defeat in Vietnam, this program seems cheap. And even if it fails to turn the tide—as it may—the value of the effort seems to us to exceed its cost.

II. OUTLINE OF THE POLICY

1. In partnership with the Government of Vietnam, we should develop and exercise the option to retaliate against any VC act of violence to persons or property.

2. In practice, we may wish at the outset to relate our reprisals to those acts of relatively high visibility such as the Pleiku incident. Later, we might retaliate against the assassination of a province chief, but not necessarily the murder of a hamlet official; we might retaliate against a grenade thrown into a crowded cafe in Saigon, but not necessarily to a shot fired into a small shop in the countryside.

3. Once a program of reprisals is clearly underway, it should not be necessary to connect each specific act against North Vietnam to a particular outrage in the South. It should be possible, for example, to publish weekly lists of outrages in the South and to have it clearly understood that these outrages are the cause of such action against the North as may be occurring in the current period…. We must keep it clear at every stage both to Hanoi and to the world, that our reprisals will be reduced or stopped when outrages in the South are reduced or stopped—and that we are not attempting to destroy or conquer North Vietnam.

4. In the early stages of such a course, we should take the appropriate occasion to make clear our firm intent to undertake reprisals on any further acts, major or minor, that appear to us and the GVN [Government of South Vietnam] as indicating Hanoi's support. We would announce that our two governments have been patient and forbearing in the hope that Hanoi would come to its senses without the necessity of our having to take further action; but the outrages continue and now we must react against those who are responsible; we will not provoke; we will not use our force indiscriminately; but we can no longer sit by in the face of repeated acts of terror and violence for which the DRV [Democratic Republic of Vietnam] is responsible.

5. Having once made this announcement, we should execute our reprisal policy with as low a level of public noise as possible. It is to our interest that our acts should be seen—but we do not wish to boast about them in ways that make it hard for Hanoi to shift its ground. We should instead direct maximum attention to the continuing acts of violence which are the cause of our continuing reprisals.

6. This reprisal policy should begin at a low level. Its level of force and pressure should be increased only gradually—and as indicated above it should be decreased if VC terror visibly decreases. The object would not be to "win" an air war against Hanoi, but rather to influence the course of the struggle in the South.

7. At the same time it should be recognized that in order to maintain the power of reprisal without risk of excessive loss, an "air war" may in fact be necessary....

III. EXPECTED EFFECT OF SUSTAINED REPRISAL POLICY

We emphasize that our primary target in advocating a reprisal policy is the improvement of the situation in South Vietnam. Action against the North is usually urged as a means of affecting the will of Hanoi to direct and support the VC. We consider this an important but longer-range purpose. The immediate and critical targets are in the South—in the minds of the South Vietnamese and in the minds of the Viet Cong cadres....

We cannot assert that a policy of sustained reprisal will succeed in changing the course of the contest in Vietnam. It may fail, and we cannot estimate the odds of success with any accuracy—they may be somewhere between 25% and 75%. What we can say is that even if it fails, the policy will be worth it. At a minimum it will damp down the charge that we did not do all that we could have done, and this charge will be important in many countries, including our own. Beyond that, a reprisal policy—to the extent that it demonstrates U.S. willingness to employ this new norm in counter-insurgency—will set a higher price for the future upon all adventures of guerrilla warfare, and it should therefore somewhat increase our ability to deter such adventures. We must recognize, however, that that ability will be gravely weakened if there is failure for any reason in Vietnam.

Source: Bundy, McGeorge. Memorandum on Proposed Vietnam Policy of "Sustained Reprisal." *Foreign Relations of the United States, 1964-1968. Volume II, Vietnam January-June 1965.* Washington, DC: U.S. Government Printing Office, 1996.

Lyndon Johnson Speaks of "Peace without Conquest"

In February of 1965 President Johnson initiated an aerial bombing campaign called Operation Rolling Thunder against North Vietnamese targets. But his military advisors warned him that without more American troops on the ground in South Vietnam, the United States would not make much progress in its efforts to stop North Vietnamese and Viet Cong attacks. President Johnson responded with a campaign to convince the American public of the need for ground troops in South Vietnam. In excerpts from this speech, delivered on the campus of Johns Hopkins University on April 7, 1965, President Johnson offers his reasons why America should support an expansion of the U.S. war effort.

I have come here to review once again with my own people the views of the American Government.

Tonight Americans and Asians are dying for a world where each people may choose its own path to change.

This is the principle for which our ancestors fought in the valleys of Pennsylvania. It is the principle for which our sons fight tonight in the jungles of Viet-Nam.

Viet-Nam is far away from this quiet campus. We have no territory there, nor do we seek any. The war is dirty and brutal and difficult. And some 400 young men, born into an America that is bursting with opportunity and promise, have ended their lives on Viet-Nam's steaming soil.

Why must we take this painful road?

Why must this Nation hazard its ease, and its interest, and its power for the sake of a people so far away?

We fight because we must fight if we are to live in a world where every country can shape its own destiny. And only in such a world will our own freedom be finally secure.

This kind of world will never be built by bombs or bullets. Yet the infirmities of man are such that force must often precede reason, and the waste of war, the works of peace.

We wish that this were not so. But we must deal with the world as it is, if it is ever to be as we wish.

THE NATURE OF THE CONFLICT

The world as it is in Asia is not a serene or peaceful place.

The first reality is that North Viet-Nam has attacked the independent nation of South Viet-Nam. Its object is total conquest.

Of course, some of the people of South Viet-Nam are participating in attack on their own government. But trained men and supplies, orders and arms, flow in a constant stream from north to south.

This support is the heartbeat of the war.

And it is a war of unparalleled brutality. Simple farmers are the targets of assassination and kidnapping. Women and children are strangled in the night because their men are loyal to their government. And helpless villages are ravaged by sneak attacks. Large-scale raids are conducted on towns, and terror strikes in the heart of cities.

The confused nature of this conflict cannot mask the fact that it is the new face of an old enemy.

Over this war—and all Asia—is another reality: the deepening shadow of Communist China. The rulers in Hanoi are urged on by Peking. This is a regime which has destroyed freedom in Tibet, which has attacked India, and has been condemned by the United Nations for aggression in Korea. It is a nation which is helping the forces of violence in almost every continent. The contest in Viet-Nam is part of a wider pattern of aggressive purposes.

WHY ARE WE IN VIET-NAM ?

Why are these realities our concern? Why are we in South Viet-Nam?

We are there because we have a promise to keep. Since 1954 every American President has offered support to the people of South Viet-Nam. We have helped to build, and we have helped to defend. Thus, over many years, we have made a national pledge to help South Viet-Nam defend its independence.

And I intend to keep that promise.

To dishonor that pledge, to abandon this small and brave nation to its enemies, and to the terror that must follow, would be an unforgivable wrong.

We are also there to strengthen world order. Around the globe, from Berlin to Thailand, are people whose well-being rests, in part, on the belief that they can count on us if they are attacked. To leave Viet-Nam to its fate would shake the confidence of all these people in the value of an American commitment and in the value of America's word. The result would be increased unrest and instability, and even wider war.

We are also there because there are great stakes in the balance. Let no one think for a moment that retreat from Viet-Nam would bring an end to conflict. The battle would be renewed in one country and then another. The central lesson of our time is that the appetite of aggression is never satisfied. To withdraw from one battlefield means only to prepare for the next. We must say in southeast Asia—as we did in Europe—in the words of the Bible: "Hitherto shalt thou come, but no further."

There are those who say that all our effort there will be futile—that China's power is such that it is bound to dominate all southeast Asia. But there is no end to that argument until all of the nations of Asia are swallowed up.

There are those who wonder why we have a responsibility there. Well, we have it there for the same reason that we have a responsibility for the defense of Europe. World War II was fought in both Europe and Asia, and when it ended we found ourselves with continued responsibility for the defense of freedom.

OUR OBJECTIVE IN VIET-NAM

Our objective is the independence of South Viet-Nam, and its freedom from attack. We want nothing for ourselves—only that the people of South Viet-Nam be allowed to guide their own country in their own way.

We will do everything necessary to reach that objective. And we will do only what is absolutely necessary.

In recent months attacks on South Viet-Nam were stepped up. Thus, it became necessary for us to increase our response and to make attacks by air. This is not a change of purpose. It is a change in what we believe that purpose requires.

We do this in order to slow down aggression.

We do this to increase the confidence of the brave people of South Viet-Nam who have bravely borne this brutal battle for so many years with so many casualties.

And we do this to convince the leaders of North Viet-Nam—and all who seek to share their conquest—of a very simple fact: We will not be defeated. We will not grow tired.

We will not withdraw, either openly or under the cloak of a meaningless agreement.

We know that air attacks alone will not accomplish all of these purposes. But it is our best and prayerful judgment that they are a necessary part of the surest road to peace.

We hope that peace will come swiftly. But that is in the hands of others besides ourselves. And we must be prepared for a long continued conflict. It will require patience as well as bravery, the will to endure as well as the will to resist.

I wish it were possible to convince others with words of what we now find it necessary to say with guns and planes: Armed hostility is futile. Our resources are equal to any challenge. Because we fight for values and we fight for principles, rather than territory or colonies, our patience and our determination are unending.

Once this is clear, then it should also be clear that the only path for reasonable men is the path of peaceful settlement.

Such peace demands an independent South Viet-Nam—securely guaranteed and able to shape its own relationships to all others—free from outside interference—tied to no alliance—a military base for no other country.

These are the essentials of any final settlement.

We will never be second in the search for such a peaceful settlement in Viet-Nam....

CONCLUSION

We often say how impressive power is. But I do not find it impressive at all. The guns and the bombs, the rockets and the warships, are all symbols of human failure. They are necessary symbols. They protect what we cherish. But they are witness to human folly.

A dam built across a great river is impressive.

In the countryside where I was born, and where I live, I have seen the night illuminated, and the kitchens warmed, and the homes heated, where once the cheerless night and the ceaseless cold held sway. And all this happened because electricity came to our area along the humming wires of the REA [Rural Electrification Administration]. Electrification of the countryside—yes, that, too, is impressive.

A rich harvest in a hungry land is impressive.

The sight of healthy children in a classroom is impressive.

These—not mighty arms—are the achievements which the American Nation believes to be impressive.

And, if we are steadfast, the time may come when all other nations will also find it so.

Every night before I turn out the lights to sleep I ask myself this question: Have I done everything that I can do to unite this country? Have I done everything I can to help unite the world, to try to bring peace and hope to all the peoples of the world? Have I done enough?

Ask yourselves that question in your homes—and in this hall tonight. Have we, each of us, all done all we could? Have we done enough?

We may well be living in the time foretold many years ago when it was said: "I call heaven and earth to record this day against you, that I have set before you life and death, blessing and cursing: therefore choose life, that both thou and thy seed may live."

This generation of the world must choose: destroy or build, kill or aid, hate or understand.

We can do all these things on a scale never dreamed of before.

Well, we will choose life. In so doing we will prevail over the enemies within man, and over the natural enemies of all mankind.

Source: Johnson, Lyndon B. Address at Johns Hopkins University, April 7, 1965. *Public Papers of the Presidents of the United States: Lyndon B. Johnson, 1965.*Volume I, Washington, D. C.: Office of the Federal Register, 1966.

The SNCC Speaks Out on Vietnam

Founded in 1960, The Student Nonviolent Coordinating Committee—best known as SNCC, or "snick"—was one of the most important groups advocating nonviolent protest in support of the civil rights movement. In the early years of the Vietnam War, SNCC and other civil rights groups believed that it was not in their interests to add their voices to others that were decrying American involvement and actions in the war. They were concerned that if they spoke out against the war, they would alienate people who might be won over to the civil rights cause. But as it became increasingly clear that a disproportionate percentage of the American foot soldiers fighting and dying in Vietnam were black, SNCC's leadership decided that it was time to point out that black soldiers were dying on foreign soil—yet were still denied basic rights in their native country.

Early in the position paper, the SNCC refers to the case of Samuel Younge (though the paper misspells his last name) to bolster its arguments. Samuel Younge was a black civil rights activist who was shot in the back and killed by a white gas station owner in Tuskegee, Alabama, on January 3, 1966, after an argument over segregated bathrooms.

The following is the complete text of SNCC's position paper, released on January 6, 1966, outlining its stand on the Vietnam War.

The Student Nonviolent Coordinating Committee has a right and a responsibility to dissent with United States foreign policy on any issue when it sees fit. The Student Nonviolent Coordinating Committee now states its opposition to the United States' involvement in Vietnam on these grounds:

We believe the United States government has been deceptive in its claims of concern for the freedom of the Vietnamese people, just as the government has been deceptive in claiming concern for the freedom of colored people in other countries such as the Dominican Republic, the Congo, South Africa, Rhodesia, and in the United States itself.

We, the Student Nonviolent Coordinating Committee, have been involved in the black peoples' struggle for liberation and self-determination in this country for the past five years. Our work, particularly in the South, has taught us that the United States government has never guaranteed the

"SNCC Position Paper on Vietnam" reprinted from "Takin' It to the Streets": A Sixties Reader, 2nd ed. (2003) with permission of Oxford University Press, Inc.

freedom of oppressed citizens, and is not yet truly determined to end the rule of terror and oppression within its own borders.

We ourselves have often been victims of violence and confinement executed by United States governmental officials. We recall the numerous persons who have been murdered in the South because of their efforts to secure their civil and human rights, and whose murderers have been allowed to escape penalty for their crimes.

The murder of Samuel Young in Tuskegee, Alabama, is no different than the murder of peasants in Vietnam, for both Young and the Vietnamese sought, and are seeking, to secure the rights guaranteed them by law. In each case, the United States government bears a great part of the responsibility for these deaths.

Samuel Young was murdered because United States law is not being enforced. Vietnamese are murdered because the United States is pursuing an aggressive policy in violation of international law. The United States is no respecter of persons or law when such persons or laws run counter to its needs or desires.

We recall the indifference, suspicion and outright hostility with which our reports of violence have been met in the past by government officials.

We know that for the most part, elections in this country, in the North as well as the South, are not free. We have seen that the 1965 Voting Rights Act and the 1966 Civil Rights Act have not yet been implemented with full federal power and sincerity.

We question, then, the ability and even the desire of the United States government to guarantee free elections abroad. We maintain that our country's cry of "preserve freedom in the world" is a hypocritical mask, behind which it squashes liberation movements which are not bound, and refuse to be bound, by the expediencies of United States cold war policies.

We are in sympathy with, and support, the men in this country who are unwilling to respond to a military draft which would compel them to contribute their lives to United States aggression in Vietnam in the name of the "freedom" we find so false in this country.

We recoil with horror at the inconsistency of a supposedly "free" society where responsibility to freedom is equated with the responsibility to lend oneself to military aggression. We take note of the fact that 16% of the draftees from this country are Negroes called on to stifle the liberation of Vietnam, to preserve a "democracy" which does not exist for them at home.

We ask, where is the draft for the freedom fight in the United States?

We therefore encourage those Americans who prefer to use their energy in building democratic forms within this country. We believe that work in the civil rights movement and with other human relations organizations is a valid alternative to the draft. We urge all Americans to seek this alternative, knowing full well that it may cost them their lives—as painfully as in Vietnam.

Source: Bloom, Alexander, and Wini Brienes. *"Takin' It to the Streets": A Sixties Reader.* 2nd ed. New York: Oxford University Press, 2003.

A North Vietnamese Soldier Recounts the 1968 Tet Offensive

Beginning on January 30, 1968, the North Vietnamese Army, working in conjunction with the South Vietnamese National Liberation Front, launched a massive attack on targets across South Vietnam. This month-long attack, called the Tet Offensive after the name for the Vietnamese New Year celebration, was the largest and most concentrated North Vietnamese attack of the entire Vietnam War. It failed in its ultimate purpose: to strike a mortal blow against Saigon and spark a popular uprising against the South Vietnamese government. The offensive took place, however, at a time when many American military strategists were publicly proclaiming that the United States was nearing victory in Vietnam. Tet showed the world that the war was far from over.

In the following excerpt, North Vietnamese Army soldier Tuan Van Van tells of his role in an attack on a U.S. marine base near Cam Lo in South Vietnam's Quang Tri Province.

Around midnight we moved as close as possible to the American perimeter. We just wore shorts and covered our bodies with dirt for camouflage. Uniforms can snag on barbed wire so we wore as little as possible. When everyone was in position we all dug foxholes and waited. Some guys were even able to sleep. However, many of the men in my company had, like me, just come from the North and had no combat experience. We were too excited to rest. Some guys were so eager they couldn't stop talking. At one point the deputy battalion commander came to me and whispered, "Damn it, get your troops to shut up. They're going to give away our position."

As we waited, small munitions teams crawled forward to place explosives under the barbed wire and other obstacles around the perimeter. One of my platoons was responsible for doing that in our area. A second platoon was prepared to attack the bunkers just inside the perimeter where the Americans were on guard. Then a third platoon would rush in and try to spread out deeper inside the base.

We did a lot of careful planning before the battle. Weeks before, as part of a small reconnaissance team, we had crawled and cut our way through the mines and barbed wire to get a close look at the base. We drew maps of the layout, including the positions of all the bunkers and buildings so our mortar men could preplan their targets. We were especially determined to hit the communications center. In preparing our troops, we made sure they understood the importance of fighting as close to the enemy as possible. As much as possible we wanted to take the battle right into the enemy bunkers and grab the Americans by the belt buckle. If we merely fired from a distance they could destroy us with artillery from Camp Carroll or from offshore destroyers.

We launched the attack at five A.M. First we fired a flare. That was the signal to detonate the dynamite that blasted holes in the perimeter. At the same time our mortar men and machine gunners began firing into the base at their preplanned targets. Within seconds we blew a bugle and whistles to signal our troops to advance. All four hundred of us moved forward screaming, "Attack! Attack! Attack!"

Just five minutes after we began to move, artillery fire started falling. Fortunately, by that time most of us had penetrated the perimeter and the shells landed behind us. With a few other men I raced through the opening and tried to make it to the communications center. It was very dark and incredibly chaotic. It was nearly impossible to see where you were going or what you were firing at. Bullets were flying in every direction.

We knew we couldn't maintain a dragged-out battle. Enemy forces throughout the area were very strong and the base itself had an enormous amount of firepower. So we just destroyed as much as we could and gave the signal to withdraw. We were in and out, all well before daybreak.

We had about seventy men wounded and twenty killed. I have no idea how many died on the other side. Most of our casualties were hit by artillery fire during our withdrawal. These great losses were always the hardest part of the war to endure and they still are. So many died without an opportunity to see their country reunited and at peace. My first battle, it turned out, was just one of hundreds of attacks that took place that morning all over the South. At the time, though, I had no idea of the scale of the Tet Offensive. People with much higher rank coordinated it all. For me it was only the first of many battles that would continue until 1975.

Source: Appy, Christian G. *Patriots: The Vietnam War Remembered from All Sides.* New York: Viking, 2003.

Lyndon Johnson Reacts to Tet

In early 1968, after nearly three years of continuously escalating military involvement in the Vietnam War, many analysts and American citizens concluded that the United States had become mired in a bloody stalemate. The Tet Offensive of January and February 1968, during which North Vietnamese forces pushed deep into South Vietnam before finally being repulsed, illustrated just how distant victory was for American and South Vietnamese forces. In the following nationally televised speech, delivered on March 31, 1968, President Lyndon B. Johnson explained a change in direction in American military strategy. He then concluded this historic address with the stunning announcement that he would not seek re-election later in the year.

Good evening, my fellow Americans:

Tonight I want to speak to you of peace in Vietnam and Southeast Asia.

No other question so preoccupies our people. No other dream so absorbs the 250 million human beings who live in that part of the world. No other goal motivates American policy in Southeast Asia.

For years, representatives of our Government and others have traveled the world—seeking to find a basis for peace talks.

Since last September, they have carried the offer that I made public at San Antonio. That offer was this:

That the United States would stop its bombardment of North Vietnam when that would lead promptly to productive discussions—and that we would assume that North Vietnam would not take military advantage of our restraint.

Hanoi denounced this offer, both privately and publicly. Even while the search for peace was going on, North Vietnam rushed their preparations for a savage assault on the people, the government, and the allies of South Vietnam.

Their attack—during the Tet holidays—failed to achieve its principal objectives.

It did not collapse the elected government of South Vietnam or shatter its army—as the Communists had hoped. It did not produce a "general uprising" among the people of the cities as they had predicted. The Communists were unable to maintain control of any of the more than 30 cities that they attacked. And they took very heavy casualties.

202

But they did compel the South Vietnamese and their allies to move certain forces from the countryside into the cities. They caused widespread disruption and suffering. Their attacks, and the battles that followed, made refugees of half a million human beings. The Communists may renew their attack any day. They are, it appears, trying to make 1968 the year of decision in South Vietnam—the year that brings, if not final victory or defeat, at least a turning point in the struggle.

This much is clear:

If they do mount another round of heavy attacks, they will not succeed in destroying the fighting power of South Vietnam and its allies. But tragically, this is also clear: Many men—on both sides of the struggle—will be lost. A nation that has already suffered 20 years of warfare will suffer once again. Armies on both sides will take new casualties. And the war will go on.

There is no need for this to be so.

There is no need to delay the talks that could bring an end to this long and this bloody war.

Tonight, I renew the offer I made last August—to stop the bombardment of North Vietnam. We ask that talks begin promptly, that they be serious talks on the substance of peace. We assume that during those talks Hanoi will not take advantage of our restraint.

We are prepared to move immediately toward peace through negotiations.

So, tonight, in the hope that this action will lead to early talks, I am taking the first step to deescalate the conflict. We are reducing—substantially reducing—the present level of hostilities. And we are doing so unilaterally, and at once.

Tonight, I have ordered our aircraft and our naval vessels to make no attacks on North Vietnam, except in the area north of the demilitarized zone where the continuing enemy buildup directly threatens allied forward positions and where the movements of their troops and supplies are clearly related to that threat.

The area in which we are stopping our attacks includes almost 90 percent of North Vietnam's population, and most of its territory. Thus there will be no attacks around the principal populated areas, or in the food-producing areas of North Vietnam.

Even this very limited bombing of the North could come to an early end—if our restraint is matched by restraint in Hanoi. But I cannot in good conscience stop all bombing so long as to do so would immediately and directly endanger the lives of our men and our allies. Whether a complete bombing halt becomes possible in the future will be determined by events.

Our purpose in this action is to bring about a reduction in the level of violence that now exists. It is to save the lives of brave men—and to save the lives of innocent women and children. It is to permit the contending forces to move closer to a political settlement.

And tonight, I call upon the United Kingdom and I call upon the Soviet Union—as cochairmen of the Geneva Conferences, and as permanent members of the United Nations Security Council—to do all they can to move from the unilateral act of deescalation that I have just announced toward genuine peace in Southeast Asia.

Now, as in the past, the United States is ready to send its representatives to any forum, at any time, to discuss the means of bringing this ugly war to an end.

I am designating one of our most distinguished Americans, Ambassador Averell Harriman, as my personal representative for such talks. In addition, I have asked Ambassador Llewellyn Thompson, who returned from Moscow for consultation, to be available to join Ambassador Harriman at Geneva or any other suitable place—just as soon as Hanoi agrees to a conference.

I call upon President Ho Chi Minh to respond positively, and favorably, to this new step toward peace. But if peace does not come now through negotiations, it will come when Hanoi understands that our common resolve is unshakable, and our common strength is invincible.

Tonight, we and the other allied nations are contributing 600,000 fighting men to assist 700,000 South Vietnamese troops in defending their little country. Our presence there has always rested on this basic belief: The main burden of preserving their freedom must be carried out by them—by the South Vietnamese themselves.

We and our allies can only help to provide a shield behind which the people of South Vietnam can survive and can grow and develop. On their efforts—on their determination and resourcefulness—the outcome will ultimately depend. That small, beleaguered nation has suffered terrible punishment for more than 20 years.

I pay tribute once again tonight to the great courage and endurance of its people. South Vietnam supports armed forces tonight of almost 700,000 men—and I call your attention to the fact that this is the equivalent of more than 10 million in our own population. Its people maintain their firm determination to be free of domination by the North.

There has been substantial progress, I think, in building a durable government during these last 3 years. The South Vietnam of 1965 could not have survived the enemy's Tet offensive of 1968. The elected government of South Vietnam survived that attack—and is rapidly repairing the devastation that it wrought.

The South Vietnamese know that further efforts are going to be required:

—to expand their own armed forces,

—to move back into the countryside as quickly as possible,

—to increase their taxes,

—to select the very best men that they have for civil and military responsibility,

—to achieve a new unity within their constitutional government, and

—to include in the national effort all those groups who wish to preserve South Vietnam's control over its own destiny.

Last week President Thieu ordered the mobilization of 135,000 additional South Vietnamese. He plans to reach—as soon as possible—a total military strength of more than 800,000 men. To achieve this, the Government of South Vietnam started the drafting of 19-year-olds on March 1st. On May 1st, the Government will begin the drafting of 18-year-olds. Last month, 10,000 men volunteered for military service—that was two and a half times the number of volunteers during the same month last year. Since the middle of January, more than 48,000 South Vietnamese have joined the armed forces—and nearly half of them volunteered to do so.

All men in the South Vietnamese armed forces have had their tours of duty extended for the duration of the war, and reserves are now being called up for immediate active duty.

President Thieu told his people last week:

"We must make greater efforts and accept more sacrifices because, as I have said many times, this is our country. The existence of our nation is at stake, and this is mainly a Vietnamese responsibility."

He warned his people that a major national effort is required to root out corruption and incompetence at all levels of government. We applaud this evidence of determination on the part of South Vietnam. Our first priority will be to support their effort.

We shall accelerate the reequipment of South Vietnam's armed forces—in order to meet the enemy's increased firepower. This will enable them progressively to undertake a larger share of combat operations against the Communist invaders.

On many occasions I have told the American people that we would send to Vietnam those forces that are required to accomplish our mission there. So, with that as our guide, we have previously authorized a force level of approximately 525,000.

Some weeks ago—to help meet the enemy's new offensive—we sent to Vietnam about 11,000 additional Marine and airborne troops. They were deployed by air in 48 hours, on an emergency basis. But the artillery, tank, aircraft, medical, and other units that were needed to work with and to support these infantry troops in combat could not then accompany them by air on that short notice.

In order that these forces may reach maximum combat effectiveness, the Joint Chiefs of Staff have recommended to me that we should prepare to send—during the next 5 months—support troops totaling approximately 13,500 men. A portion of these men will be made available from our active forces. The balance will come from reserve component units which will be called up for service.

The actions that we have taken since the beginning of the year:

—to reequip the South Vietnamese forces,

—to meet our responsibilities in Korea, as well as our responsibilities in Vietnam,

—to meet price increases and the cost of activating and deploying reserve forces,

—to replace helicopters and provide the other military supplies we need, all of these actions are going to require additional expenditures.

The tentative estimate of those additional expenditures is $2.5 billion in this fiscal year, and $2.6 billion in the next fiscal year. These projected increases in expenditures for our national security will bring into sharper focus the nation's need for immediate action: action to protect the prosperity of the American people and to protect the strength and the stability of our American dollar.

On many occasions I have pointed out that, without a tax bill or decreased expenditures, next year's deficit would again be around $20 billion. I have emphasized the need to set strict priorities in our spending. I have stressed that failure to act and to act promptly and decisively would raise very strong doubts throughout the world about America's willingness to keep its financial house in order.

Yet Congress has not acted. And tonight we face the sharpest financial threat in the postwar era—a threat to the dollar's role as the keystone of international trade and finance in the world. Last week, at the monetary conference in Stockholm, the major industrial countries decided to take a big step toward creating a new international monetary asset that will strengthen the international monetary system. I am very proud of the very able work done by Secretary Fowler and Chairman Martin of the Federal Reserve Board.

But to make this system work the United States must bring its balance of payments to—or very close to—equilibrium. We must have a responsible fiscal policy in this country. The passage of a tax bill now, together with expenditure control that the Congress may desire and dictate, is absolutely necessary to protect this Nation's security, to continue our prosperity, and to meet the needs of our people....

These times call for prudence in this land of plenty. I believe that we have the character to provide it, and tonight I plead with the Congress and with the people to act promptly to serve the national interest, and thereby serve all of our people.

Now let me give you my estimate of the chances for peace:

—the peace that will one day stop the bloodshed in South Vietnam,

—that will permit all the Vietnamese people to rebuild and develop their land,

—that will permit us to turn more fully to our own tasks here at home.

I cannot promise that the initiative that I have announced tonight will be completely successful in achieving peace any more than the 30 others that we have undertaken and agreed to in recent years. But it is our fervent hope that North Vietnam, after years of fighting that have left the issue unresolved, will now cease its efforts to achieve a military victory and will join with us in moving toward the peace table. And there may come a time when South Vietnamese—on both sides—are able to work out a way to settle their own differences by free political choice rather than by war.

As Hanoi considers its course, it should be in no doubt of our intentions. It must not miscalculate the pressures within our democracy in this election year. We have no intention of widening this war. But the United States will never accept a fake solution to this long and arduous struggle and call it peace.

No one can foretell the precise terms of an eventual settlement. Our objective in South Vietnam has never been the annihilation of the enemy. It has been to bring about a recognition in Hanoi that its objective—taking over the South by force—could not be achieved. We think that peace can be based on the Geneva Accords of 1954—under political conditions that permit the South Vietnamese—all the South Vietnamese—to chart their course free of any outside domination or interference, from us or from anyone else.

So tonight I reaffirm the pledge that we made at Manila—that we are prepared to withdraw our forces from South Vietnam as the other side withdraws its forces to the north, stops the infiltration, and the level of violence thus subsides. Our goal of peace and self-determination in Vietnam is directly related to the future of all of Southeast Asia—where much has happened to inspire confidence during the past 10 years. We have done all that we knew how to do to contribute and to help build that confidence.

A number of its nations have shown what can be accomplished under conditions of security. Since 1966, Indonesia, the fifth largest nation in all the world, with a population of more than 100 million people, has had a government that is dedicated to peace with its neighbors and improved conditions for its own people. Political and economic cooperation between nations has grown rapidly.

I think every American can take a great deal of pride in the role that we have played in bringing this about in Southeast Asia. We can rightly judge— as responsible Southeast Asians themselves do—that the progress of the past 3 years would have been far less likely—if not completely impossible—if America's sons and others had not made their stand in Vietnam.

At Johns Hopkins University, about 3 years ago, I announced that the United States would take part in the great work of developing Southeast Asia, including the Mekong Valley, for all the people of that region. Our determination to help build a better land—a better land for men on both sides of the present conflict—has not diminished in the least. Indeed, the ravages of war, I think, have made it more urgent than ever.

So, I repeat on behalf of the United States again tonight what I said at Johns Hopkins—that North Vietnam could take its place in this common effort just as soon as peace comes.

Over time, a wider framework of peace and security in Southeast Asia may become possible. The new cooperation of the nations of the area could be a foundation-stone. Certainly friendship with the nations of such a Southeast Asia is what the United States seeks—and that is all that the United States seeks.

One day, my fellow citizens, there will be peace in Southeast Asia.

It will come because the people of Southeast Asia want it—those whose armies are at war tonight, and those who, though threatened, have thus far been spared. Peace will come because Asians were willing to work for it—and to sacrifice for it—and to die by the thousands for it.

But let it never be forgotten: Peace will come also because America sent her sons to help secure it. It has not been easy—far from it. During the past 4½ years, it has been my fate and my responsibility to be Commander in Chief. I have lived—daily and nightly—with the cost of this war. I know the pain that it has inflicted. I know, perhaps better than anyone, the misgivings that it has aroused.

Throughout this entire, long period, I have been sustained by a single principle: that what we are doing now, in Vietnam, is vital not only to the security of Southeast Asia, but it is vital to the security of every American. Surely we have treaties which we must respect. Surely we have commitments that we are going to keep. Resolutions of the Congress testify to the need to resist aggression in the world and in Southeast Asia.

But the heart of our involvement in South Vietnam—under three different presidents, three separate administrations—has always been America's own security. And the larger purpose of our involvement has always been to help the nations of Southeast Asia become independent and stand alone, self-sustaining, as members of a great world community—at peace with themselves, and at peace with all others.

With such an Asia, our country—and the world—will be far more secure than it is tonight. I believe that a peaceful Asia is far nearer to reality because of what America has done in Vietnam. I believe that the men who endure the dangers of battle—fighting there for us tonight—are helping the entire world avoid far greater conflicts, far wider wars, far more destruction, than this one.

The peace that will bring them home someday will come. Tonight I have offered the first in what I hope will be a series of mutual moves toward peace. I pray that it will not be rejected by the leaders of North Vietnam. I pray that they will accept it as a means by which the sacrifices of their own people may be ended. And I ask your help and your support, my fellow citizens, for this effort to reach across the battlefield toward an early peace.

Finally, my fellow Americans, let me say this:

Of those to whom much is given, much is asked. I cannot say and no man could say that no more will be asked of us. Yet, I believe that now, no less than when the decade began, this generation of Americans is willing to "pay any price, bear any burden, meet any hardship, support any friend, oppose any foe to assure the survival and the success of liberty."

Since those words were spoken by John F. Kennedy, the people of America have kept that compact with mankind's noblest cause. And we shall continue to keep it.

Yet, I believe that we must always be mindful of this one thing, whatever the trials and the tests ahead. The ultimate strength of our country and our cause will lie not in powerful weapons or infinite resources or boundless wealth, but will lie in the unity of our people.

This I believe very deeply.

Throughout my entire public career I have followed the personal philosophy that I am a free man, an American, a public servant, and a member of my party, in that order always and only. For 37 years in the service of our Nation, first as a Congressman, as a Senator, and as Vice President, and now as your President, I have put the unity of the people first. I have put it ahead of any divisive partisanship.

And in these times as in times before, it is true that a house divided against itself by the spirit of faction, of party, of region, of religion, of race, is a house that cannot stand.

There is division in the American house now. There is divisiveness among us all tonight. And holding the trust that is mine, as President of all the people, I cannot disregard the peril to the progress of the American people and the hope and the prospect of peace for all peoples. So, I would ask all

Americans, whatever their personal interests or concern, to guard against divisiveness and all its ugly consequences.

Fifty-two months and 10 days ago, in a moment of tragedy and trauma, the duties of this office fell upon me. I asked then for your help and God's, that we might continue America on its course, binding up our wounds, healing our history, moving forward in new unity, to clear the American agenda and to keep the American commitment for all of our people.

United we have kept that commitment. United we have enlarged that commitment.

Through all time to come, I think America will be a stronger nation, a more just society, and a land of greater opportunity and fulfillment because of what we have all done together in these years of unparalleled achievement.

Our reward will come in the life of freedom, peace, and hope that our children will enjoy through ages ahead. What we won when all of our people united must not now be lost in suspicion, distrust, selfishness, and politics among any of our people.

Believing this as I do, I have concluded that I should not permit the Presidency to become involved in the partisan divisions that are developing in this political year.

With America's sons in the fields far away, with America's future under challenge right here at home, with our hopes and the world's hopes for peace in the balance every day, I do not believe that I should devote an hour or a day of my time to any personal partisan causes or to any duties other than the awesome duties of this office—the Presidency of your country.

Accordingly, I shall not seek, and I will not accept, the nomination of my party for another term as your President.

But let men everywhere know, however, that a strong, a confident, and a vigilant America stands ready tonight to seek an honorable peace—and stands ready tonight to defend an honored cause—whatever the price, whatever the burden, whatever the sacrifice that duty may require.

Thank you for listening.

Good night and God bless all of you.

Source: Johnson, Lyndon B. Nationally televised speech of March 31, 1968. *Public Papers of the Presidents of the United States: Lyndon B. Johnson, 1968-69*. Washington, DC: Office of the Federal Register, 1970.

American Soldiers Write Home from Vietnam

American soldiers were sent to Vietnam beginning in 1960. Ground troops began arriving in Vietnam in 1965, and on April 30, 1969, the number of American soldiers deployed in Vietnam reached a wartime high of 543,400. From that point forward, troop levels were steadily brought down, and the last U.S. troops left the country in the spring of 1973. The soldiers who served in Vietnam represented a diverse cross section of America, and their opinions about their experiences in Vietnam were equally diverse. In the letters reproduced here, three Americans—Hiram D. "Butch" Strickland of North Carolina; David L. Glading of New Jersey; and Charlie B. Dickey of Washington—wrote home to tell their loved ones about why they fought, what they saw, and what they hoped to find waiting at home for them when they finished their tours. Private Strickland did not return home; his letter was found among his belongings after he was killed on February 1, 1966. Sergeant Glading and Sergeant Dickey both survived the war.

From Hiram D. Strickland:

Dear Folks,

I'm writing this letter as my last one. You've probably already received word that I'm dead and that the government wishes to express its deepest regret.

Believe me, I didn't want to die, but I know it was part of my job. I want my country to live for billions and billions of years to come.

I want it to stand as a light to all people oppressed and guide them to the same freedom we know. If we can stand and fight for freedom, then I think we have done the job God set down for us. It's up to every American to fight for the freedom we hold so dear. If we don't, the smells of free air could become dark and damp as in a prison cell.

We won't be able to look at ourselves in a mirror, much less at our sons and daughters, because we know we have failed our God, country, and our future generations.

I can hold my head high because I fought, whether it be in heaven or hell. Besides, the saying goes, "One more GI from Vietnam, St. Peter; I've served my time in hell."

From Letters From Vietnam, edited by Bill Adler, copyright © 2003 by Bill Adler. Used by permission of Presidio Press, an imprint of The Ballantine Publishing Group, a division of Random House, Inc.

I fought for Sandy, Nell, Gale [his sisters], Mom, Dad. But when the twins and Sandy's kids get old enough, they'll probably have to fight, too. Tell them to go proudly and without fear of death because it is worth keeping the land free.

I remember the story from Mr. Williams' [Thomas Williams, a teacher at Strickland's high school] English classes when I was a freshman that said, "The cowards die a thousand times, the brave die but once."

Don't mourn me, Mother, for I am happy I have died fighting my country's enemies, and I will live forever in people's minds. I've done what I've always dreamed of. Don't mourn me, for I have died a soldier of the United States of America.

God bless you all and take care. I'll be seeing you in heaven.
Your loving son and brother,
Butch

From David L. Glading:

18 Nov 69
Kathy,

I was reading the paper and feel kinda down because of the demonstration in Washington, DC. I guess I'm proud to be an American and proud of my country. It's still number one to me, right or wrong. Although I can't agree completely with the way the war is going, I don't agree on just up and leaving because then the whole purpose, the very reason all of these men have died for, is lost. People in the states need to have an enemy invade them, have them have to see homes burned, their fathers killed or taken away, living in a bunker with bugs and insects just to be able to live through mortar or artillery fire, having GIs come during the day and VC come at night. No one can understand unless they have been here. The demonstrations help the enemy more than anything else. The protests are a slap in the face to most of the guys over here. They are sent here to fight and possibly die protecting America and the other free nations. Their own people through the protesting are prolonging the war longer, thus more GIs get killed. The VC want to see the U.S. get on its knees. I don't.

I went down the road yesterday afternoon to get a few things and my two little girl friends were there. They were about 100 ft away from me and just ran all the way to me. Big smiles on their faces and just saying "Dabid" and a bunch of other Vietnamese I couldn't understand. I gave them a few cans of C-rations. They picked me some berries and gave them to me to eat plus picked a bunch of flowers and put them in my hat. They like to look at the pictures in my wallet.

From Charlie B. Dickey:

1 June 1969
Dearest Jamie,

I'm sitting in my hootch right now, it is just starting to rain, from the looks of the clouds and the wind it's gonna be a real big one.

It was really hot today, well over 100 degrees, so hot you just don't feel like moving. Sweat just rolls off of you, like being in a sauna bath. No kidding! In fact it is just like that! Even the air burns your lungs.

My Wife, one can never realize how dear freedom is until you taste the bitterness of a war meant to protect freedom. People may scorn and protest but know that we fight for all of you who wish to be free. I know now what it means to have real freedom.

My Dearest, I must close for now, be good, be safe, remember I love you.
Your Devoted Husband,
Charlie

Source: Adler, Bill, ed. *Letters to Vietnam.* New York: Ballantine Books, 2003.

An American Witness to the My Lai Massacre

On March 16, 1968, a group of U.S. infantrymen out on patrol near the village of My Lai sys-
tematically slaughtered more than 100 unarmed Vietnamese civilians, mostly women and chil-
dren (estimates of the total number of Vietnamese murdered vary from 128 to more than 500).
For more than a year after the incident, military personnel kept the incident—later known as
the My Lai Massacre—a secret. Eventually, however, an investigation was launched. This inves-
tigation led to the court martial and murder conviction of one officer, Lieutenant William Calley.
But 24 other officers and enlisted men charged in the case, including Company C Captain Ernest
Medina, who is mentioned in the excerpt below, never received prison sentences; they were either
acquitted or had charges dropped on technicalities. Calley was sentenced to life in prison for his
war crimes. But his case became so heavily tangled in national politics that he gained his release
from prison in late 1975.

Larry Colburn was a door gunner on an American observation chopper out on patrol near My
Lai when the massacre took place. In the following interview excerpt, he recounts his feelings
when he and the rest of the helicopter crew, which was led by pilot Hugh C. Thompson Jr., came
upon the nightmarish scene.

We weren't pacifists. We did our job and when we had to kill people we did. But we didn't do it for sport. We didn't randomly shoot people. In our gun company it was very important to capture weapons, not just to legitimize your kill, but psychologically it was easier when you could say, "If I didn't do that, he was going to shoot me."

We flew an OH-23—a little gasoline-engine bubble helicopter. We were aerial scouts—a new concept. Instead of just sending assault helicopters they'd use our small aircraft as bait and have a couple gunships cover us. Basically we'd go out and try to get into trouble. We'd fly real low and if we encountered anything we'd mark it with smoke, return fire, and let the gunships work out. We also went on "snatch missions," kidnapping draft-age males to take back for interrogation. We did that a lot in 1968.

On March 16, we came on station a little after seven A.M. The only briefing I got was that they were going to put a company on the ground to sweep through this village. Normally we'd go in beforehand to see if we could find enemy posi-

From PATRIOTS: THE VIETNAM WAR REMEMBERED FROM ALL SIDES by Christian G. Appy, copyright © 2003 Christian G. Appy. Used by permission of Viking Penguin, a division of Penguin Group (USA) Inc.

tions or entice people to shoot at us. It was clear and warm and the fog was lifting off the rice paddies. On our first pass we saw a man in uniform carrying a carbine and a pack coming out of a tree line. Thompson said, "Who wants him?" I said, "I'll take him." So he aimed the air craft at him and got it down low and started toward the suspect. He was obviously Viet Cong. He was armed, evading, and headed for the next tree line. I couldn't hit him to save my life. We worked that area a little more but that was the only armed Vietnamese I saw that day.

After that we just started working the perimeter of My Lai-4, -5, and -6 [separate sub-hamlets or small villages] and I remember seeing the American troops come in on slicks [helicopters]. We got ahead of them to see if they were going to encounter anything and we still didn't receive fire. It was market day and we saw a lot of women and children leaving the hamlet. They were moving down the road carrying empty baskets. As we went further around the perimeter we saw a few wounded women in the rice fields south of My Lai-4. We marked their bodies with smoke grenades expecting that medics would give them medical assistance.

When we came back to the road we started seeing bodies, the same people that were walking to the market. They hadn't even gotten off the road. They were in piles, dead. We started going through all the scenarios of what might have happened. Was it artillery? Gunships? Viet Cong? The American soldiers on the ground were just walking around in a real nonchalant sweep. No one was crouching, ducking, or hiding.

Then we saw a young girl about twenty years old lying in the grass. We could see that she was unarmed and wounded in the chest. We marked her with smoke because the squad was not too far away. The smoke was green meaning it's safe to approach. Red would have meant the opposite. We were hovering six feet off the ground not more than twenty feet away when Captain Medina came over, kicked her, and finished her off. He did it right in front of us. When we saw Medina do that, it all clicked. It was our guys doing the killing.

The bodies we marked with smoke—you find yourself feeling that you indirectly killed them. I'll never forget one lady who was hiding in the grass. She was crouched in a fetal position. I motioned to her—stay down, be quiet, stay there. We flew off on more reconnaissance. We came back later and she was in the same position, right where I'd told her to stay. But someone had come up behind her and literally blown her brains out. I'll never forget that look of bewilderment on her face.

216

Around ten A.M. Thompson spotted a group of women and children running toward a bunker northeast of My Lai-4 followed by a group of U.S. soldiers. When we got overhead, Andreotta spotted some faces peeking out of an earthen bunker. Thompson knew that in a matter of seconds they were going to die so he landed the aircraft in between the advancing American troops and the bunker. He went over and talked to a Lieutenant Brooks. Thompson said, "These are civilians. How do we get them out of the bunker?" Brooks said, "I'll get them out with hand grenades." The veins were sticking out on Thompson's neck and I thought they were actually going to fight. Thompson came back and said to Andreotta and me, "If they open up on these people when I'm getting them out of the bunker, shoot 'em." Then he walked away leaving us standing there looking at each other. Thompson went over to the bunker and motioned for the people to come out. There were nine or ten of them.

We had a staredown going with the American soldiers. About half of them were sitting down, smoking and joking. I remember looking at one fellow and waving. He waved back and that's when I knew we were okay, that these guys weren't going to do anything to us. No one pointed weapons at us and we didn't point any weapons at them.

Thompson called Dan Millians, a gunship pilot friend of his, and said, "Danny, I've got a little problem down here, can you help out?" Millians said sure and did something unheard of. You don't land a gunship to use it as a medevac, but he did. He got those people a couple miles away and let 'em go. I think he had to make two trips.

We flew over the ditch where more than a hundred Vietnamese had been killed. Andreotta saw movement so Thompson landed again. Andreotta went directly into that ditch. He literally had to wade waist deep through people to get to a little child. I stood there in the open. Glenn came over and handed me the child, but the ditch was so full of bodies and blood he couldn't get out. I gave him the butt of my rifle and pulled him out. We took the little one to an orphanage. We didn't know if he was a little boy or little girl. Just a cute little child. I felt for broken bones or bullet holes and he appeared to be fine. He wasn't crying, but he had this blank stare on his face and he was covered with blood.

The only thing I remember feeling back then was that these guys were really out for revenge. They'd lost men to booby traps and snipers and they were ready to engage. They were briefed the night before and I've heard it was said that they were going to go in there to waste everything. They didn't capture any weapons. They didn't kill any draft-age males. I've seen the list of dead and there were a hundred and twenty some humans under the age of five. It's something I've struggled with my whole life, how people can do that. I know what it's like to seek revenge, but we would look for a worthy opponent. These were elders, mothers, children, and babies. The fact that VC camped out there at night is no justification for killing everyone in the hamlet.

Compare it to a little town in the United States. We're at war with someone on our own soil. They came into a town and rape the women, kill the babies, kill everyone. How would we feel? And it wasn't just murdering civilians. They were butchering people. The only thing they didn't do is cook 'em and eat 'em. How do you get that far over the edge?

Source: Appy, Christian G. *Patriots: The Vietnam War Remembered from All Sides.* New York: Viking, 2003.

Richard Nixon Explains "Vietnamization"

Less than a year after being elected on a pledge to end the war in Vietnam, President Richard Nixon announced a major shift in U.S. policy and troop commitments in Vietnam. In this November 3, 1969, speech to the American public he provides his perspective on the war and touts his plans to bring peace to Southeast Asia. The centerpiece of this plan, he explained, was a policy of "Vietnamization"—a strategy to gradually wean South Vietnam off its dependence on America's military and help it take the lead in the fight against North Vietnam and its Viet Cong allies.

In the months and years following this speech, Nixon did gradually remove all American ground troops from Vietnam. But he also approved major incursions into Laos and Cambodia during this same period, and the total number of American soldiers who died in Vietnam under the Nixon administration was nearly as great as the number who died while Lyndon B. Johnson was in the White House.

Good evening, my fellow Americans.

Tonight I want to talk to you on a subject of deep concern to all Americans and to many people in all parts of the world — the war in Vietnam.

I believe that one of the reasons for the deep division about Vietnam is that many Americans have lost confidence in what their Government has told them about our policy. The American people cannot and should not be asked to support a policy which involves the overriding issues of war and peace unless they know the truth about that policy.

Tonight, therefore, I would like to answer some of the questions that I know are on the minds of many of you listening to me. How and why did America get involved in Vietnam in the first place? How has this administration changed the policy of the previous administration? What has really happened in the negotiations in Paris and on the battlefront in Vietnam? What choices do we have if we are to end the war? What are the prospects for peace? Now, let me begin by describing the situation I found when I was inaugurated on January 20:

The war had been going on for four years. 31,000 Americans had been killed in action. The training program for the South Vietnamese was behind schedule; 540,000 Americans were in Vietnam with no plans to reduce the number. No progress had been made at the negotiations in Paris and the United States had not put forth a comprehensive peace proposal. The war was causing deep division at home and criticism from many of our friends as well as our enemies abroad.

In view of these circumstances there were some who urged that I end the war at once by ordering the immediate withdrawal of all American forces. From a political standpoint this would have been a popular and easy course to follow. After all, we became involved in the war while my predecessor was in office. I could blame the defeat which would be the result of my action on him and come out as the peacemaker. Some put it to me quite bluntly: This was the only way to avoid allowing Johnson's war to become Nixon's war.

But I had a greater obligation than to think only of the years of my administration and of the next election. I had to think of the effect of my decision on the next generation and on the future of peace and freedom in America and in the world.

Let us all understand that the question before us is not whether some Americans are for peace and some Americans are against peace. The question at issue is not whether Johnson's war becomes Nixon's war. The great question is: How can we win America's peace?

Well, let us turn now to the fundamental issue. Why and how did the United States become involved in Vietnam in the first place? Fifteen years ago North Vietnam, with the logistical support of communist China and the Soviet Union, launched a campaign to impose a communist government on South Vietnam by instigating and supporting a revolution.

In response to the request of the Government of South Vietnam, President Eisenhower sent economic aid and military equipment to assist the people of South Vietnam in their efforts to prevent a communist takeover. Seven years ago, President Kennedy sent 16,000 military personnel to Vietnam as combat advisers. Four years ago, President Johnson sent American combat forces to South Vietnam.

Now, many believe that President Johnson's decision to send American combat forces to South Vietnam was wrong. And many others—I among them—have been strongly critical of the way the war has been conducted.

But the question facing us today is: Now that we are in the war, what is the best way to end it?

In January I could only conclude that the precipitate withdrawal of American forces from Vietnam would be a disaster not only for South Vietnam but for the United States and for the cause of peace.

For the South Vietnamese, our precipitate withdrawal would inevitably allow the Communists to repeat the massacres which followed their takeover in the North 15 years before; They then murdered more than 50,000 people and hundreds of thousands more died in slave labor camps.

We saw a prelude of what would happen in South Vietnam when the Communists entered the city of Hue last year. During their brief rule there, there was a bloody reign of terror in which 3,000 civilians were clubbed, shot to death, and buried in mass graves.

With the sudden collapse of our support, these atrocities of Hue would become the nightmare of the entire nation—and particularly for the million and a half Catholic refugees who fled to South Vietnam when the Communists took over in the North.

For the United States, this first defeat in our nation's history would result in a collapse of confidence in American leadership, not only in Asia but throughout the world.

Three American presidents have recognized the great stakes involved in Vietnam and understood what had to be done.

In 1963, President Kennedy, with his characteristic eloquence and clarity, said:

> ...we want to see a stable government there, carrying on a struggle to maintain its national independence. We believe strongly in that. We are not going to withdraw from that effort. In my opinion, for us to withdraw from that effort would mean a collapse not only of South Vietnam, but Southeast Asia. So we are going to stay there.

President Eisenhower and President Johnson expressed the same conclusion during their terms of office.

For the future of peace, precipitate withdrawal would thus be a disaster of immense magnitude. A nation cannot remain great if it betrays its allies and lets down its friends. Our defeat and humiliation in South Vietnam without question would promote recklessness in the councils of those great powers who have not yet abandoned their goals of world conquest. This would spark violence wherever our commitments help maintain the peace—in the Middle East, in Berlin, eventually even in the Western Hemisphere. Ultimately, this would cost more lives. It would not bring peace; it would bring more war.

For these reasons, I rejected the recommendation that I should end the war by immediately withdrawing all of our forces. I chose instead to change American policy on both the negotiating front and battlefront. In order to end a war fought on many fronts, I initiated a pursuit for peace on many fronts. In a television speech on May 14, in a speech before the United Nations, and on a number of other occasions I set forth our peace proposals in great detail.

We have offered the complete withdrawal of all outside forces within one year.

We have proposed a cease-fire under international supervision.

We have offered free elections under international supervision with the Communists participating in the organization and conduct of the elections as an organized political force. And the Saigon Government has pledged to accept the result of the elections.

We have not put forth our proposals on a take-it-or-leave-it basis. We have indicated that we are willing to discuss the proposals that have been put forth by the other side. We have declared that anything is negotiable except the right of the people of South Vietnam to determine their own future. At the Paris peace conference, Ambassador Lodge has demonstrated our flexibility and good faith in 40 public meetings.

Hanoi has refused even to discuss our proposals. They demand our unconditional acceptance of their terms, which are that we withdraw all American forces immediately and unconditionally and that we overthrow the Government of South Vietnam as we leave.

We have not limited our peace initiatives to public forums and public statements. I recognized, in January, that a long and bitter war like this usually cannot be settled in a public forum. That is why in addition to the public statements and negotiation I have explored every possible private avenue that might lead to a settlement.

Tonight I am taking the unprecedented step of disclosing to you some of our other initiatives for peace—initiatives we undertook privately and secretly because we thought we thereby might open a door which publicly would be closed.

I did not wait for my inauguration to begin my quest for peace. Soon after my election, through an individual who is directly in contact on a personal basis with the leaders of North Vietnam, I made two private offers for a rapid, comprehensive settlement. Hanoi's replies called in effect for our surrender before negotiations.

Since the Soviet Union furnishes most of the military equipment for North Vietnam, Secretary of State Rogers, my Assistant for National Security Affairs, Dr. Kissinger, Ambassador Lodge, and I, personally, have met on a number of occasions with representatives of the Soviet Government to enlist their assistance in getting meaningful negotiations started. In addition, we have had extended discussions directed toward that same end with representatives of other governments which have diplomatic relations with North Vietnam. None of these initiatives have to date produced results.

In mid-July, I became convinced that it was necessary to make a major move to break the deadlock in the Paris talks. I spoke directly in this office, where I am now sitting, with an individual who had known Ho Chi Minh on a personal basis for 25 years. Through him I sent a letter to Ho Chi Minh. I did this outside of the usual diplomatic channels with the hope that with the necessity of making statements for propaganda removed, there might be constructive progress toward bringing the war to an end. Let me read from that letter to you now:

Dear Mr. President:

> I realize that it is difficult to communicate meaningfully across the gulf of four years of war. But precisely because of this gulf, I wanted to take this opportunity to reaffirm in all solemnity my desire to work for a just peace. I deeply believe that the war in Vietnam has gone on too long and delay in bringing it to an end can benefit no one — least of all the people of Vietnam.... The time has come to move forward at the conference table toward an early resolution of this tragic war. You will find us forthcoming and open-minded in a common effort to bring the blessings of peace to the brave people of Vietnam. Let history record that at this critical juncture, both sides turned their face toward peace rather than toward conflict and war.

223

I received Ho Chi Minh's reply on August 30, three days before his death. It simply reiterated the public position North Vietnam had taken at Paris and flatly rejected my initiative. The full text of both letters is being released to the press.

In addition to the public meetings that I have referred to, Ambassador Lodge has met with Vietnam's chief negotiator in Paris in 11 private sessions. We have taken other significant initiatives which must remain secret to keep open some channels of communication which may still prove to be productive. But the effect of all the public, private and secret negotiations which have been undertaken since the bombing halt a year ago and since this administration came into office on January 20 can be summed up in one sentence: No progress whatever has been made except agreement on the shape of the bargaining table.

Well now, who is at fault?

It has become clear that the obstacle in negotiating an end to the war is not the President of the United States. It is not the South Vietnamese Government. The obstacle is the other side's absolute refusal to show the least willingness to join us in seeking a just peace. And it will not do so while it is convinced that all it has to do is to wait for our next concession, and our next concession after that one, until it gets everything it wants.

There can now be no longer any question that progress in negotiation depends only on Hanoi's deciding to negotiate, to negotiate seriously.

I realize that this report on our efforts on the diplomatic front is discouraging to the American people, but the American people are entitled to know the truth—the bad news as well as the good news—where the lives of our young men are involved.

Now let me turn, however, to a more encouraging report on another front. At the time we launched our search for peace I recognized we might not succeed in bringing an end to the war through negotiation. I, therefore, put into effect another plan to bring peace—a plan which will bring the war to an end regardless of what happens on the negotiating front.

It is in line with a major shift in U.S. foreign policy which I described in my press conference at Guam on July 25. Let me briefly explain what has been described as the Nixon Doctrine—policy which not only will help end the war in Vietnam, but which is an essential element of our program to prevent future Vietnams.

We Americans are a do-it-yourself people. We are an impatient people. Instead of teaching someone else to do a job, we like to do it ourselves. And this trait has been carried over into our foreign policy. In Korea and again in Vietnam, the United States furnished most of the money, most of the arms, and most of the men to help the people of those countries defend their freedom against Communist aggression.

Before any American troops were committed to Vietnam, a leader of another Asian country expressed this opinion to me when I was traveling in Asia as a private citizen. He said: "When you are trying to assist another nation defend its freedom, U.S. policy should be to help them fight the war but not to fight the war for them."

Well, in accordance with this wise counsel, I laid down in Guam three principles as guidelines for future American policy toward Asia:

First, the United States will keep all of its treaty commitments.

Second, we shall provide a shield if a nuclear power threatens the freedom of a nation allied with us or of a nation whose survival we consider vital to our security.

Third, in cases involving other types of aggression, we shall furnish military and economic assistance when requested in accordance with our treaty commitments. But we shall look to the nation directly threatened to assume the primary responsibility of providing the manpower for its defense.

After I announced this policy, I found that the leaders of the Philippines, Thailand, Vietnam, South Korea, and other nations which might be threatened by Communist aggression welcomed this new direction in American foreign policy.

The defense of freedom is everybody's business—not just America's business. And it is particularly the responsibility of the people whose freedom is threatened. In the previous administration, we Americanized the war in Vietnam. In this administration, we are Vietnamizing the search for peace.

The policy of the previous administration not only resulted in our assuming the primary responsibility for fighting the war, but even more significantly did not adequately stress the goal of strengthening the South Vietnamese so that they could defend themselves when we left.

The Vietnamization plan was launched following Secretary Laird's visit to Vietnam in March. Under the plan, I ordered first a substantial increase in the training and equipment of South Vietnamese forces.

In July, on my visit to Vietnam, I changed General Abrams' orders so that they were consistent with the objectives of our new policies. Under the new orders, the primary mission of our troops is to enable the South Vietnamese forces to assume the full responsibility for the security of South Vietnam. Our air operations have been reduced by over 20 percent. And now we have begun to see the results of this long overdue change in American policy in Vietnam.

After five years of Americans going into Vietnam, we are finally bringing American men home. By December 15, over 60,000 men will have been withdrawn from South Vietnam, including 20 percent of all of our combat forces. The South Vietnamese have continued to gain in strength. As a result they have been able to take over combat responsibilities from our American troops.

Two other significant developments have occurred since this administration took office.

Enemy infiltration, infiltration which is essential if they are to launch a major attack, over the last three months is less than 20 percent of what it was over the same period last year. Most important—United States casualties have declined during the last two months to the lowest point in three years.

Let me now turn to our program for the future. We have adopted a plan which we have worked out in cooperation with the South Vietnamese for the complete withdrawal of all U.S. combat ground forces, and their replacement by South Vietnamese forces on an orderly scheduled timetable. This withdrawal will be made from strength and not from weakness. As South Vietnamese forces become stronger, the rate of American withdrawal can become greater.

I have not and do not intend to announce the timetable for our program. And there are obvious reasons for this decision which I am sure you will understand. As I have indicated on several occasions, the rate of withdrawal will depend on developments on three fronts.

One of these is the progress which can be or might be made in the Paris talks. An announcement of a fixed timetable for our withdrawal would completely remove any incentive for the enemy to negotiate an agreement. They would simply wait until our forces had withdrawn and then move in.

The other two factors on which we will base our withdrawal decisions are the level of enemy activity and the progress of the training programs of the South Vietnamese forces. And I am glad to be able to report tonight progress on both of these fronts has been greater than we anticipated when we started the program in June for withdrawal. As a result, our timetable for withdrawal is more optimistic now than when we made our first estimates in June. Now, this clearly demonstrates why it is not wise to be frozen in on a fixed timetable. We must retain the flexibility to base each withdrawal decision on the situation as it is at that time rather than on estimates that are no longer valid.

Along with this optimistic estimate, I must—in all candor—leave one note of caution. If the level of enemy activity significantly increases we might have to adjust our timetable accordingly.

However, I want the record to be completely clear on one point.

At the time of the bombing halt just a year ago, there was some confusion as to whether there was an understanding on the part of the enemy that if we stopped the bombing of North Vietnam they would stop the shelling of cities in South Vietnam. I want to be sure that there is no misunderstanding on the part of the enemy with regard to our withdrawal program.

We have noted the reduced level of infiltration, the reduction of our casualties, and are basing our withdrawal decisions partially on those factors. If the level of infiltration or our casualties increase while we are trying to scale down the fighting, it will be the result of a conscious decision by the enemy.

Hanoi could make no greater mistake than to assume that an increase in violence will be to its advantage. If I conclude that increased enemy action jeopardizes our remaining forces in Vietnam, I shall not hesitate to take strong and effective measures to deal with that situation.

This is not a threat. This is a statement of policy, which as commander in chief of our armed forces, I am making in meeting my responsibility for the protection of American fighting men wherever they may be.

My fellow Americans, I am sure you can recognize from what I have said that we really only have two choices open to us if we want to end this war. I can order an immediate, precipitate withdrawal of all Americans from Vietnam without regard to the effects of that action. Or we can persist in our search for a just peace through a negotiated settlement if possible, or through continued implementation of our plan for Vietnamization if necessary, a plan in which we will withdraw all of our forces from Vietnam on a schedule in accordance with our program, as the South Vietnamese become strong enough to defend their own freedom.

I have chosen this second course. It is not the easy way. It is the right way. It is a plan which will end the war and serve the cause of peace—not just in Vietnam but in the Pacific and in the world.

In speaking of the consequences of a precipitate withdrawal, I mentioned that our allies would lose confidence in America. Far more dangerous, we would lose confidence in ourselves. Oh, the immediate reaction would be a sense of relief that our men were coming home. But as we saw the consequences of what we had done, inevitable remorse and divisive recrimination would scar our spirit as a people.

We have faced other crises in our history and have become stronger by rejecting the easy way out and taking the right way in meeting our challenges. Our greatness as a nation has been our capacity to do what had to be done when we knew our course was right.

I recognize that some of my fellow citizens disagree with the plan for peace I have chosen. Honest and patriotic Americans have reached different conclusions as to how peace should be achieved.

In San Francisco a few weeks ago, I saw demonstrators carrying signs reading: "Lose in Vietnam, bring the boys home." Well, one of the strengths of our free society is that any American has a right to reach that conclusion and to advocate that point of view. But as president of the United States, I would be untrue to my oath of office if I allowed the policy of this nation to be dictated by the minority who hold that point of view and who try to impose it on the nation by mounting demonstrations in the street.

For almost 200 years, the policy of this nation has been made under our Constitution by those leaders in the Congress and the White House elected by all of the people. If a vocal minority, however fervent its cause, prevails over reason and the will of the majority, this nation has no future as a free society.

And now I would like to address a word, if I may, to the young people of this nation who are particularly concerned, and I understand why they are concerned, about this war.

I respect your idealism. I share your concern for peace. I want peace as much as you do. There are powerful personal reasons I want to end this war.

This week I will have to sign 83 letters to mothers, fathers, wives and loved ones of men who have given their lives for America in Vietnam. It is very little satisfaction to me that this is only one-third as many letters as I signed the first week in office. There is nothing I want more than to see the day come when I do not have to write any of those letters.

I want to end the war to save the lives of those brave young men in Vietnam.

But I want to end it in a way which will increase the chance that their younger brothers and their sons will not have to fight in some future Vietnam someplace in the world.

And I want to end the war for another reason. I want to end it so that the energy and dedication of you, our young people, now too often directed into bitter hatred against those responsible for the war, can be turned to the great challenges of peace, a better life for all Americans, a better life for all people on this Earth.

I have chosen a plan for peace. I believe it will succeed. If it does succeed, what the critics say now won't matter. If it does not succeed, anything I say then won't matter.

I know it may not be fashionable to speak of patriotism or national destiny these days. But I feel it is appropriate to do so on this occasion.

Two hundred years ago this nation was weak and poor. But even then, America was the hope of millions in the world. Today we have become the strongest and richest nation in the world. And the wheel of destiny has turned so that any hope the world has for the survival of peace and freedom will be determined by whether the American people have the moral stamina and the courage to meet the challenge of free world leadership.

Let historians not record that when America was the most powerful nation in the world we passed on the other side of the road and allowed the last hopes for peace and freedom of millions of people to be suffocated by the forces of totalitarianism.

And so tonight—to you, the great silent majority of my fellow Americans—I ask for your support. I pledged in my campaign for the presidency to end the war in a way that we could win the peace. I have initiated a plan of action which will enable me to keep that pledge. The more support I can have from the American people, the sooner that pledge can be redeemed; for the more divided we are at home, the less likely the enemy is to negotiate at Paris.

Let us be united for peace. Let us also be united against defeat. Because let us understand: North Vietnam cannot defeat or humiliate the United States. Only Americans can do that.

Fifty years ago, in this room and at this very desk, President Woodrow Wilson spoke words which caught the imagination of a war-weary world. He said: "This is the war to end war." His dream for peace after World War I was shattered on the hard realities of great power politics, and Woodrow Wilson died a broken man.

Tonight I do not tell you that the war in Vietnam is the war to end wars. But I do say this: I have initiated a plan which will end this war in a way that will bring us closer to that great goal to which Woodrow Wilson and every American president in our history has been dedicated—the goal of a just and lasting peace.

As president I hold the responsibility for choosing the best path to that goal and then leading the nation along it. I pledge to you tonight that I shall meet this responsibility with all of the strength and wisdom I can command in accordance with our hopes, mindful of your concerns, sustained by your prayers.

Thank you and good night.

Source: Nixon, Richard M. Address to the Nation on the War in Vietnam, November 3, 1969. *Public Papers of the Presidents of the United States: Richard M. Nixon, 1969.* Washington, DC: Office of the Federal Register, 1971.

The Paris Peace Accords

The Agreement on Ending the War and Restoring Peace in Vietnam, which brought an end to U.S. military involvement in Vietnam, was signed on January 27, 1973. Signatories to this treaty, widely known as the Paris Peace Accords, included not only the United States and North Vietnam, but also the Republic of South Vietnam (the national government of South Vietnamese President Nguyen Van Thieu), and the Provisional Revolutionary Government or PRG. North Vietnam had created the PRG in 1969 as a way to force the enemy (and the world) to recognize the Viet Cong political leadership as a legitimate entity. This strategy was ultimately successful, for the United States reluctantly agreed to give the PRG the same level of recognition as the Thieu government in the Accords.

Though President Nixon declared that the agreement allowed the U.S. to achieve "peace with honor," Thieu and other South Vietnamese politicians accused the United States of forcing them to accept a deeply flawed treaty. They publicly warned of future invasions from North Vietnam, once the United States had departed. That prediction came true in early 1975, when a massive military invasion led to the reunification of Vietnam under Communist rule. Following are excerpts from the text of the January 1973 Accords.

Article 1

...The United States and all other countries respect the independence, sovereignty, unity, and territorial integrity of Viet-Nam as recognized by the 1954 Geneva Agreements on Viet-Nam....

Article 2

A cease fire shall be observed throughout South Viet-Nam as of 2400 hours G.M.T., on January 27, 1973. At the same hour, the United States will stop all its military activities against the territory of the Democratic Republic of Viet-Nam by ground, air and naval forces, wherever they may be based, and end the mining of the territorial waters, ports, harbors, and waterways of the Democratic Republic of Viet-Nam. The United States will remove, permanently deactivate or destroy all the mines in the territorial waters, ports, harbors, and waterways of North Viet-Nam as soon as this Agreement goes into effect. The complete cessation of hostilities mentioned in this Article shall be durable and without limit of time....

Article 4

The United States will not continue its military involvement or intervene in the internal affairs of South Viet-Nam.

231

Article 5

Within sixty days of the signing of this Agreement, there will be a total withdrawal from South Viet-Nam of troops, military advisers, and military personnel including technical military personnel and military personnel associated with the pacification program, armaments, munitions, and war material of the United States and those of the other foreign countries mentioned in Article 3(a). Advisers from the above-mentioned countries to all paramilitary organizations and the police force will also be withdrawn within the same period of time.

Article 6

The dismantlement of all military bases in South Viet-Nam of the United States and of the other foreign countries mentioned in Article 3(a) shall be completed within sixty days of the signing of this Agreement.

Article 7

From the enforcement of the cease-fire to the formation of the government provided for in Article 9(b) and 14 of this Agreement, the two South Vietnamese parties shall not accept the introduction of troops, military advisers, and military personnel including technical military personnel, armaments, munitions, and war material into South Viet-Nam....

Article 8

(a) The return of captured military personnel and foreign civilians of the parties shall be carried out simultaneously with and completed not later than the same day as the troop withdrawal mentioned in Article 5. The parties shall exchange complete lists of the above-mentioned captured military personnel and foreign civilians on the day of the signing of this Agreement.

(b) The Parties shall help each other to get information about those military personnel and foreign civilians of the parties missing in action, to determine the location and take care of the graves of the dead so as to facilitate the exhumation and repatriation of the remains, and to take any such other measures as may be required to get information about those still considered missing in action.

(c) The question of the return of Vietnamese civilian personnel captured and detained in South Viet-Nam will be resolved by the two South Vietnamese parties on the basis of the principles of Article 21(b) of the Agreement on the Cessation of Hostilities in Viet-Nam of July 20, 1954. The two

South Vietnamese parties will do so in a spirit of national reconciliation and concord, with a view to ending hatred and enmity, in order to ease suffering and to reunite families. The two South Vietnamese parties will do their utmost to resolve this question within ninety days after the cease-fire comes into effect....

Article 11

Immediately after the cease-fire, the two South Vietnamese parties will: achieve national reconciliation and concord, end hatred and enmity, prohibit all acts of reprisal and discrimination against individuals or organizations that have collaborated with one side or the other; ensure the democratic liberties of the people: personal freedom, freedom of speech, freedom of the press, freedom of meeting, freedom of organization, freedom of political activities, freedom of belief, freedom of movement, freedom of residence, freedom of work, right to property ownership, and right to free enterprise....

Chapter V: The Reunification of Viet-Nam and The Relationship Between North and South Viet-Nam

Article 15

The reunification of Viet-Nam shall be carried out step by step through peaceful means on the basis of discussions and agreements between North and South Viet-Nam, without coercion or annexation by either party, and without foreign interference. The time for reunification will be agreed upon by North and South Viet-Nam. Pending reunification:

(a) The military demarcation line between the two zones at the 17th parallel is only provisional and not a political or territorial boundary, as provided for in paragraph 6 of the Final Declaration of the 1954 Geneva Conference.

(b) North and South Viet-Nam shall respect the Demilitarized Zone on either side of the Provisional Military Demarcation Line.

(c) North and South Viet-Nam shall promptly start negotiations with a view to reestablishing normal relations in various fields. Among the questions to be negotiated are the modalities of civilian movement across the Provisional Military Demarcation Line.

(d) North and South Viet-Nam shall not join any military alliance or military bloc and shall not allow foreign powers to maintain military bases, troops, military advisers, and military personnel on their respective territories, as stipulated in the 1954 Geneva Agreements on Viet-Nam....

Article 21

The United States anticipates that this Agreement will usher in an era of reconciliation with the Democratic Republic of Viet-Nam as with all the peoples of Indochina. In pursuance of its traditional policy, the United States will contribute to healing the wounds of war and to postwar reconstruction of the Democratic Republic of Viet-Nam and throughout Indochina.

Article 22

The ending of the war, the restoration of peace in Viet-Nam, and the strict implementation of this Agreement will create conditions for establishing a new, equal and mutually beneficial relationship between the United States and the Democratic Republic of Viet-Nam on the basis of respect of each other's independence and sovereignty, and non-interference in each other's internal affairs. At the same time this will ensure stable peace in Viet-Nam and contribute to the preservation of lasting peace in Indochina and Southeast Asia....

The Return of Captured Military Personnel and Foreign Civilians

Article 1

The parties signatory to the Agreement shall return the captured military personnel of the parties mentioned in Article 8(a) of the Agreement as follows: all captured military personnel of the United States and those of the other foreign countries mentioned in Article 3(a) of the Agreement shall be returned to United States authorities; all captured Vietnamese military personnel, whether belonging to regular or irregular armed forces, shall be returned to the two South Vietnamese parties; they shall be returned to that South Vietnamese party under whose command they served.

Article 2

All captured civilians who are nationals of the United States or of any other foreign countries mentioned in Article 3(a) of the Agreement shall be returned to United States authorities. All other captured foreign civilians shall be returned to the authorities of their country of nationality by any one of the parties willing and able to do so.

Article 3

The parties shall today exchange complete lists of captured persons mentioned in Articles 1 and 2 of this Protocol.

Article 4

(a) The return of all captured persons mentioned in Articles 1 and 2 of this Protocol shall be completed within sixty days of the signing of the Agreement at a rate no slower than the rate of withdrawal from South Viet-Nam of United States forces and those of the other foreign countries mentioned in Article 5 of the Agreement.

(b) Persons who are seriously ill, wounded or maimed, old persons and women shall be returned first. The remainder shall be returned either by returning all from one detention place after another or in order of their dates of capture, beginning with those who have been held the longest....

With Regard to Dead and Missing Persons

Article 10

(a) The Four-Party Joint Military Commission shall ensure joint action by the parties in implementing Article 8 (b) of the Agreement. When the Four-Party Joint Military Commission has ended its activities, a Four-Party Joint Military team shall be maintained to carry on this task.

(b) With regard to Vietnamese civilian personnel dead or missing in South Viet-Nam, the two South Vietnamese parties shall help each other to obtain information about missing persons, determine the location and take care of the graves of the dead, in a spirit of national reconciliation and concord, in keeping with the people's aspirations....

Source: Agreement on Ending the War and Restoring Peace in Vietnam, January 27, 1973. *Department of State Bulletin*, February 12, 1973.

The Vietnam Veterans Memorial

When the Vietnam Veterans Memorial was first built in Washington, D.C., in the early 1980s, it was enormously controversial. Critics claimed that the design, created by a young Chinese-American art student named Maya Lin, was disrespectful and inappropriate. They argued that "the Wall," which called for a black V-shaped wall of polished granite engraved with the names of all dead or missing-in-action Americans, was no more than a "black gash of shame." Criticism was so strong and sustained that it was agreed that the memorial area would also include a statue of three young American soldiers.

During and after the dedication of the Vietnam Veterans Memorial in November 1982, however, anger over Lin's design almost completely disappeared. "Veterans and their relatives found the Memorial a powerful and apt remembrance of their friends and loved ones," wrote Stewart O'Nan in The Vietnam Reader. *Today, the Vietnam Veterans Memorial ranks as one of the most revered and respected monuments in the entire United States, and it perennially ranks as the most heavily visited Park Service site in the nation's capital.*

African-American poet Yusef Komunyakaa was born on April 29, 1947, in Bogalusa, Lousiana. He enlisted in the U.S. Army in 1965 and earned a Bronze Star in Vietnam before leaving the army in the early 1970s. He also started his writing career in Vietnam, as a correspondent and editor of The Southern Cross, *a military newspaper. Since returning to the United States, he has become one of the nation's most respected poets. A Pulitzer Prize winner and professor of creative writing at Princeton University, he has produced ten volumes of poetry over the years, including the 1988 work* Dien Cai Dau. *In this poetry collection, Komunyakaa chronicles his Vietnam experiences and postwar emotions in verse. "Facing It," which is reprinted below, explores the poet's feelings upon visiting the Vietnam Veterans Memorial.*

> Facing It
> My black face fades,
> hiding inside the black granite.
> I said I wouldn't,
> dammit: No tears.
> I'm stone. I'm flesh.
> My clouded reflection eyes me
> like a bird of prey, the profile of night

Yusef Komunyakaa, "Facing It" from Dien Cai Dau © 1988 by Yusef Komunyakaa and reprinted by permission of Wesleyan University Press. www.wesleyan.edu/wespress.

slanted against morning. I turn
this way—the stone lets me go.
I turn that way—I'm inside
The Vietnam Veterans Memorial
again, depending on the light
to make a difference.
I go down the 58,022 names,
half-expecting to find
my own in letters like smoke.
I touch the name Andrew Johnson;
I see the booby trap's white flash.
Names shimmer on a woman's blouse
but when she walks away
the names stay on the wall.
Brushstrokes flash, a red bird's
wings cutting across my stare.
The sky. A plane in the sky.
A white vet's image floats
closer to me, then his pale eyes
look through mine. I'm a window.
He's lost his right arm
inside the stone. In the black mirror
a woman's trying to erase names:
No, she's brushing a boy's hair.

Source: Komunyakaa, Yusef. "Facing It." From *Dien Cai Dau.* Middletown, CT: Wesleyan University Press, 1988.

IMPORTANT PEOPLE, PLACES, AND TERMS

Abrams, Jr., Creighton (1914-1974)
U.S. Army General, commander of U.S. forces in Vietnam from 1968 to 1972.

ARVN
The Army of the Republic of Vietnam, the main military force of South Vietnam.

Ball, George (1909-1994)
United States Undersecretary of State, 1961-1966.

Colonialism
Political and military control over one country by another; often used in reference to the eighteenth through twentieth centuries, when European powers built worldwide empires based on this practice.

Communism
A political system in which the state controls all economic activity. In practice, Communist governments also establish single-party rule and place significant limits on personal freedom and individual rights.

Demilitarized Zone (DMZ)
A five-mile wide buffer zone between North and South Vietnam, established in 1954 by the Geneva Accords.

Democratic Republic of Vietnam
Official name for North Vietnam from 1945 until 1975, when South Vietnam was conquered and the reunified country was renamed the Socialist Republic of Vietnam.

Dien Bien Phu
Village in northern Vietnam that was the site of a pivotal 1954 battle between French and allied troops and Viet Minh guerrillas; the decisive

Viet Minh victory helped convince France to give up its colonial claims on Vietnam.

Domino Theory

The belief that if a nation "turns" Communist, neighboring nations will be at much greater risk of also falling to Communism.

Eisenhower, Dwight D. (1890-1969)

President of the United States, 1953-1961.

French Indochina

See Indochina

Guerilla War

A form of warfare conducted by loosely organized, irregular troops and often consisting of harassment, sneak attacks, sabotage, and other non-traditional forms of warfare.

Hanoi

The capital of North Vietnam during the war, and today the capital of the Socialist Republic of Vietnam; also sometimes used as a shorthand reference to the ruling government.

Hawks

American lawmakers and citizens who supported U.S. military intervention in Vietnam.

Ho Chi Minh (1890-1969)

Communist revolutionary and President of North Vietnam, 1945-1969.

Ho Chi Minh Trail

A long network of roads, pathways, rivers, and other routes that ran through Cambodia and Laos, this trail was used by North Vietnam throughout the war to ferry supplies and reinforcements to Viet Cong guerrillas operating in South Vietnam.

Indochina

The region consisting of Vietnam, Laos, and Cambodia which fell under French colonial rule in the nineteenth century. Also known as French Indochina.

Johnson, Lyndon B. (1908-1973)

President of the United States, 1963-1969.

Kennedy, John F. (1917-1963)
President of the United States, 1961-1963.

Kissinger, Henry (1923-)
U.S. National Security Advisor, 1969-1975, and Secretary of State, 1973-1977.

Lao Dong
Name for the ruling Communist organization in North Vietnam; also known as the Vietnam Workers Party.

McNamara, Robert (1916-)
U.S. Secretary of Defense, 1961-1967.

National Liberation Front (NLF)
Southern Vietnamese Communist and nationalist political group formed in 1960 and dedicated to unifying Vietnam under Communist leadership; commonly referred to as the Viet Cong.

Nationalism
An ideology emphasizing loyalty and devotion to a nation or homeland, and the importance of common cultural and ethnic bonds.

Ngo Dinh Diem (1901-1963)
Premier/President of South Vietnam, 1954-1963.

Nguyen Van Theiu (1923-2001)
President of South Vietnam, 1967-1975.

Nixon, Richard M. (1913-1994)
President of the United States, 1969-1974.

NLF
See National Liberation Front (NLF)

North Vietnamese Army (NVA)
Also known as the People's Army of Vietnam (PAVN), this was the main military force of Communist North Vietnam.

NVA
See North Vietnamese Army (NVA)

Pham Van Dong (1906-2000)
Premier of North Vietnam, 1955-1975, and of the Socialist Republic of Vietnam, 1975-1986.

Provisional Revolutionary Government (PRG)
Established by the Communist leadership of North Vietnam in 1969 as its legal voice in South Vietnam, this entity was portrayed as the legitimate government of South Vietnam by North Vietnam and other socialist nations until reunification in 1975.

Republic of Vietnam
Official name of South Vietnam from 1955 until 1975, when Communist forces conquered the country.

Saigon
The capital of South Vietnam; also sometimes used as a shorthand reference to the ruling government of South Vietnam; renamed Ho Chi Minh City after it was occupied by Communist forces in 1975.

Socialist Republic of Vietnam
Official name given to Vietnam after it was reunified in 1975 under Communist rule.

State of Vietnam
Official name of South Vietnam from 1946 to 1955, when it was renamed the Republic of Vietnam.

Viet Cong
The term that the United States and South Vietnam used to refer to the fighting forces of the National Liberation Front, a Communist-backed political group that fought against the government of South Vietnam.

Viet Minh
The abbreviated term for the Vietnam Do Lap Dong Minh Hoi, or League for the Independence of Vietnam, a group of Vietnamese nationalists who fought against French colonial rule from World War II to the signing of the Geneva Accords in 1954.

Vo Nguyen Giap (1912-)
North Vietnamese senior general, 1946-1972, and minister of national defense, 1946-1982.

Westmoreland, William (1914-2005)
U.S. Army General, commander of U.S. forces in Vietnam, 1964-1968.

CHRONOLOGY

c. 208 B.C.E.

Chinese troops invade the northern half of present-day Vietnam, naming it "Nam Viet," or "land of the southern Viets." *See p. 6.*

111 C.E.

Chinese emperor Wu-ti conquers Nam Viet (which at the time includes only the northern half of the country) and makes it a province of China. *See p. 6.*

938

A Vietnamese army led by Ngo Quyen secures independence for Vietnam by defeating Chinese forces in the decisive naval battle of Bach Dang. *See p. 7.*

1428

China recognizes Vietnamese independence.

1627

Jesuit priest Alexander de Rhodes becomes the first Frenchmen to enter Vietnam; his arrival marks the beginning of a new era of Catholic missionary work and French influence over Vietnamese economics and politics. *See p. 7.*

1858

France establishes a military base at the coastal city of Danang in Vietnam. *See p. 8.*

1887

France formally establishes French Indochina, comprised of Vietnam and Cambodia; Laos is folded into the empire six years later.

c. 1920

The Vietnam Quoc Dan Dang (VNQDD, or Vietnamese Nationalist Party) is established; it works for independence until 1930, when the group is crushed after a failed military uprising. *See p. 11.*

1930

Ho Chi Minh and others form the Indochinese Communist Party (ICP), the first Communist organization in Vietnam. *See p. 11.*

1932

Bao Dai returns from France to reign as emperor of Vietnam under the French.

1939

France is drawn into World War II. *See p. 12.*

1941

Japan takes control of Vietnam and the rest of Indochina, but allows France to continue its colonial administration of the region. *See p. 12.*

Ho Chi Minh and other ICP members—including Vo Nguyen Giap and Pham Van Dong—form the Vietnam Doc Lap Dong Minh Hoi (the League for the Independence of Vietnam), better known as the Viet Minh. *See p. 12.*

1944

The Viet Minh organizes its own army under the command of Vo Nguyen Giap and begins to secure control of several provinces in northern Vietnam. *See p. 13.*

1945

The United States bombs Japanese targets in Vietnam in order to support the Viet Minh. *See p. 13.*

August 29 - The Viet Minh declare the creation of the Democratic Republic of Vietnam (DRV). *See p. 13.*

September 23 - French troops (supported by British forces) regain control of Saigon. *See p. 14.*

1946

Open war begins between French colonial forces and the Viet Minh. *See p. 14.*

1949

Communists seize power in China and openly support the Viet Minh, which in turn more openly acknowledges its Communist ties. *See p. 15.*

1950

The United States sends $10 million to support French efforts against the Viet Minh, beginning a 25-year U.S. commitment in Vietnam. *See p. 15.*

The United States forms the Military Assistance Advisory Group (MAAG) to provide military advice to French forces in Vietnam.

January 14 - Ho Chi Minh announces that the Democratic Republic of Vietnam is the sole, legitimate government in Vietnam; this government is recognized by China and the Soviet Union.

1954

March 13 - The pivotal battle of Dien Bien Phu begins, with the Viet Minh laying siege to a strategically vital French stronghold. *See p. 16.*

April 7 - President Dwight D. Eisenhower articulates the domino theory as a guide for U.S. actions in Southeast Asia. *See p. 24.*

May 7 – The French commanders at Dien Bien Phu surrender to the Viet Minh after more than 50 days of fighting. *See p. 17.*

June 16 - Emperor Bao Dai appoints Ngo Dinh Diem as the prime minister of the State of Vietnam (South Vietnam). *See p. 23.*

July 20 - The Geneva Accords end French colonial rule over Vietnam and provide for the temporary partition of Vietnam along the 17th Parallel into northern and southern halves. *See p. 20.*

1955

January – First U.S. military supplies are delivered to Saigon.

October 23 - Ngo Dinh Diem becomes president of the newly named Republic of Vietnam (RVN). One day later, President Dwight Eisenhower pledges support for the Diem regime. *See p. 25.*

October 26 – Diem formally names South Vietnam the Republic of Vietnam (RVN). *See p. 25.*

1956

U.S. support allows Diem to remove political and military challengers within South Vietnam, and to avoid the 1956 elections that would surely have reunified Vietnam under the Communist rule of Ho Chi Minh. *See p. 26.*

1959

Students at the University of Michigan form the Students for a Democratic Society (SDS). *See p. 101.*

May - The North Vietnamese Army begins building a supply route from North Vietnam into South Vietnam via neighboring Cambodia and Laos; this route becomes an early version of the Ho Chi Minh Trail. *See p. 28.*

1960

September - The Lao Dong party announces its goal to liberate South Vietnam from the Diem government and reunify the country. *See p. 28.*

November 8 - John F. Kennedy is elected president of the United States.

December 20 - The National Liberation Front (NLF) political group is founded in Hanoi to coordinate the Communist war effort in the South. The NFL organizes its own army, called the People's Liberation Armed Force (PLAF) or Viet Cong (VC). *See p. 28.*

1961

February - President John F. Kennedy sends supplies, equipment, and military advisors to support the South Vietnamese government. *See p. 30.*

1962

February 6 - President Kennedy creates the Military Assistance Command, Vietnam (MACV) to oversee U.S. military assistance to South Vietnam. *See p. 30.*

1963

January 2 - American military advisors lose confidence in the existing command of the South Vietnam Army after it performs poorly in the Battle of Ap Bac. *See p. 30.*

May 8 - South Vietnamese police shoot and kill unarmed Buddhists protesting government discrimination against the nation's Buddhist population. *See p. 31.*

June 11 – Domestic unrest in South Vietnam intensifies as an elderly Buddhist monk named Thich Quang Duc douses himself with gasoline and burns himself to death in the middle of a busy street in Saigon; other Buddhist suicide protests follow in the ensuing weeks. *See p. 31.*

November 1 – South Vietnamese President Ngo Dinh Diem and his brother, Nhu, are captured and killed in a coup d'etat. *See p. 32.*

November 22 - Lyndon B. Johnson assumes the presidency of the United States following the assassination of President John F. Kennedy. *See p. 32.*

1964

January – President Johnson approves covert operations against North Vietnam. *See p. 36.*

August 4 – Erroneous reports of a second North Vietnamese attack on the naval destroyer U.S.S. *Maddox* in the Gulf of Tonkin convince the Johnson administration of the need to expand U.S. military operations in Vietnam. *See p. 36.*

August 7 - Congress passes House Joint Resolution 1145, otherwise known as the Gulf of Tonkin Resolution, authorizing the U.S. president to use American forces to resist Communist aggression in Vietnam. *See p. 37.*

November 3 - President Johnson defeats Republican presidential nominee Barry Goldwater to retain the presidency. *See p. 37.*

1965

February 13 - President Johnson authorizes Operation Rolling Thunder, a strategy of gradually escalating bombing missions against enemy targets in North Vietnam. *See p. 38.*

March 8 - 3,500 American soldiers land on the beach in Danang, becoming the first armed U.S. combat troops to enter Vietnam. *See p. 41.*

March 24 – An influential antiwar "teach-in" is held at the University of Michigan; this early antiwar demonstration is soon eclipsed by numerous other protests of far greater size. *See p. 102.*

April 6 - President Johnson authorizes U.S. ground troops for offensive operations in Vietnam.

April 17 - The March on Washington to End the War in Vietnam, the first major antiwar rally in the United States, attracts a crowd of 15,000 to 25,000 protestors. *See p. 102.*

June – Generals Nguyen Van Thieu and Nguyen Cao Ky take control of South Vietnam's national government. *See p. 42.*

November 16 – After weeks of fighting, American forces defeat Viet Cong forces in the Battle of Ia Drang, one of the rare direct military clashes of the war.

December – U.S. troop levels in Vietnam reach 184,000.

1966

January 31 - After a weeklong pause, President Johnson restarts the bombing of North Vietnam.

Following Buddhist demonstrations, the South Vietnamese government seizes control of local government in the cities of Hue and Danang.

December – U.S. troop levels in Vietnam reach 389,000.

1967

February 22 – American forces launch Operation Junction City, the largest U.S. military offensive of the war; the offensive continues until mid-May.

April 15 - A crowd of 125,000 antiwar protestors in New York City and a group of 70,000 in San Francisco gather to peacefully call for an end to the war. *See p. 103.*

September 3 - Nguyen Van Thieu is "elected" president of the South Vietnamese government in rigged elections. *See p. 42.*

October 21-23 - The National Mobilization Committee to End the War (or MOBE for short) organizes a peaceful antiwar march that attracts as many as 250,000 people in Washington, D.C. *See p. 104.*

Vietnam veterans form their own antiwar group called the Vietnam Veterans against the War (VVAW). *See p. 110.*

December – U.S. troop levels in Vietnam increase to 463,000.

1968

January 31 - The North Vietnamese launch the Tet Offensive against cities and villages throughout South Vietnam. *See p. 49.*

February 27 - CBS News anchorman Walter Cronkite declares on national television that it seems "more certain than ever that the bloody experience of Vietnam is to end in a stalemate." *See p. 54.*

March 1 – U.S. Secretary of Defense Robert McNamara is replaced by Clark Clifford. *See p. 55.*

March 2 – American Marines retake the city of Hue from Communist forces after weeks of street-to-street combat. *See p. 51.*

March 16 – American troops murder hundreds of unarmed Vietnamese civilians in the My Lai massacre. *See p. 88.*

March 31 - President Johnson announces that he will not seek reelection and that he will call a halt to the bombing in Vietnam. *See p. 57.*

April 4 - Civil rights leader Martin Luther King Jr. is assassinated in Memphis, Tennessee. *See p. 62.*

April 16 – Pentagon officials begin publicly discussing a shift toward "Vietnamization" of the war in Vietnam. *See p. 60.*

May 13 - Official delegations from the United States, North Vietnam, and South Vietnam begin official peace negotiations in Paris. *See p. 74.*

June 5 - Democratic presidential hopeful Robert F. Kennedy is shot and killed by an assassin in Los Angeles. *See p. 62.*

August 26-29 – Clashes between city police and antiwar protestors cast a shadow over the National Democratic Nominating Convention in Chicago. *See p. 62; p. 107.*

October - Operation Rolling Thunder, the American air bombing campaign against North Vietnam, draws to a close.

November 4 - Republican Richard M. Nixon is elected president. *See p. 63.*

1969

March 18 - President Nixon authorizes Operation MENU, a secret bombing campaign against Communist forces within Cambodia. *See p. 64.*

April 9 – American troop levels in Vietnam reach their war-time high of 543,400 troops.

May 9 - A New York Times reporter reveals the secret bombing raids on Cambodia; President Nixon retaliates by ordering wiretaps on the phones of those suspected of leaking the story. *See p. 64.*

June 8 - President Nixon announces his intention to withdraw 25,000 American combat troops from Vietnam. *See p. 65.*

August - National Security Advisor Henry Kissinger begins secret meetings with North Vietnamese lead negotiator Le Duc Tho. *See p. 74.*

September 3 - Ho Chi Minh dies.

October 15 - Moratorium Day, organized by antiwar protest groups, is observed by hundreds of thousands of people who turn out for demonstrations in Boston, Massachusetts, and New York City. *See p. 109.*

November 3 - President Nixon explains his administration's approach to "Vietnamization" in a televised address to the nation. *See p. 65; p. 109.*

1970

April 30 - President Nixon informs the American people that he has sent U.S. troops into neutral Cambodia in order to enhance security in South Vietnam. News of this perceived expansion of the war sparks massive antiwar protests across the United States. *See p. 71; p. 109.*

May 4 - Ohio National Guard troops open fire on unarmed antiwar protestors at Kent State University, killing four students and wounding nine others. *See p. 71; p. 109.*

May-June - As many as four million students across the United States participate in antiwar protests at 1,300 universities. Of the total, 536 campuses close temporarily, and 51 of them close for the rest of the academic term. *See p. 71; p. 109*

June 24 – The U.S. Senate repeals the 1964 Gulf of Tonkin Resolution. *See p. 71.*

June 30 – American forces withdraw from Cambodia. *See p. 71.*

November – The number of U.S. troops deployed in Vietnam drops to 334,000.

1971

February – South Vietnamese forces supported by American airpower enter Laos, only to be soundly defeated by Communist forces. *See p. 73.*

April – Leaders of Vietnam Veterans Against the War launch "Operation Dewey Canyon III," an antiwar demonstration, in Washington, D.C. During this time VVAW spokesman John Kerry and other Vietnam veterans testify before Congress about their perceptions of the war in Vietnam. *See p. 111.*

June 13 - The New York Times publishes a series of secret government documents about the Vietnam War known as the "Pentagon Papers."

December – U.S. troop levels in Vietnam drop to 157,000.

1972

January 25 - Nixon announces the existence of the secret talks between the United States and North Vietnam, and expresses a new willingness to withdraw U.S. forces after free elections in Vietnam. *See p. 74.*

February 21 - Nixon becomes the first U.S. president to visit Communist China. *See p. 74.*

Spring - North Vietnam launches the Easter Offensive, a failed attempt to bring about the collapse of the government in Saigon. *See p. 76.*

May 1972 - Nixon visits the Soviet Union. *See p. 74.*

May 8-October 23 - Linebacker I, one of the most concentrated and effective American bombing campaigns of the entire Vietnam War, is carried out against North Vietnamese targets. *See p. 77.*

October 26 - Henry Kissinger emerges from Paris peace negotiations to announce the imminent end of the war. *See p. 77.*

November 7 - Nixon wins reelection to a second term as president of the United States. *See p. 77.*

December 18 - The Peace Talks in Paris end without an agreement and Nixon orders another round of bombing. Officially called Linebacker II, the bombings are nicknamed the "Christmas Bombings" by peace activists. *See p. 78.*

1973

January 27 - Delegates from the United States, North Vietnam, the Thieu government in South Vietnam, and the People's Revolutionary Government sign the Agreement on Ending the War and Restoring Peace in Vietnam, otherwise known as the Paris Accords. *See p. 78.*

February – American prisoners of war (POWs) begin returning home. *See p. 79.*

March 29 - Following the departure of the last American troops, only 240 American personnel remain in South Vietnam, primarily at the American embassy in Saigon. *See p. 79.*

June 19 – The Case-Church Amendment is passed, preventing any further U.S. military involvement in Southeast Asia.

August – American bombing missions over Cambodia come to an end. *See p. 81.*

November 7 - Congress enacts the War Powers Act to limit the power of a president to wage war. *See p. 81.*

The draft is eliminated and the U.S. military becomes an all-volunteer armed forces.

1974

February 6 - Congress votes to begin impeachment proceedings against President Nixon, forcing him to release volumes of secret tape recordings of conversations in the White House that reveal his involvement in the Watergate scandal.

August 9 - President Nixon resigns as a result of the Watergate scandal; his vice president, Gerald Ford, assumes the duties of the office. *See p. 81.*

September 16 – President Ford offers clemency to Vietnam-era draft evaders and military deserters.

December – North Vietnam brazenly breaks the terms of the Paris accords with attacks on Phuoc Long and other South Vietnamese positions. *See p. 81.*

1975

March 10 – The North Vietnamese Army begins its final decisive offensive into the South. *See p. 82.*

March 10 - Congress denies President Ford's requested aid package for the beleaguered South Vietnamese. *See p. 82.*

April 16 - President Ford urges all Americans remaining in South Vietnam to leave the country.

April 17 – Khmer Rouge troops under the command of Pol Pot seize the Cambodian capital of Phnom Penh, ushering in a murderous four-year reign that claims the lives of between one and two million Cambodians. *See p. 122*

April 21 - South Vietnamese President Thieu resigns; vice President Tran Van Huong takes his place as Communists overrun most of the last remaining South Vietnamese defenses. *See p. 83.*

April 27 – North Vietnamese Army forces encircle Saigon. *See p. 83.*

April 28 - Tran Van Huong turns over the presidency of South Vietnam to General Duong Van Minh. *See p. 83.*

April 29 - U.S. Ambassador Graham Martin orders the evacuation of the U.S. embassy in Saigon. *See p. 83.*

April 30 - North Vietnamese troops take control of Saigon, ending the war. *See p. 83.*

December 3 – Communists take control of Laos and rename the war-torn nation the People's Democratic Republic of Laos. *See p. 122.*

1976

July – Communist leaders announce that Vietnam will henceforth be known as the Socialist Republic of Vietnam; Saigon is renamed Ho Chi Minh City.

1977

U.S. begins talks to consider official U.S. recognition of Vietnam.

1978

December – Vietnam launches an invasion of neighboring Cambodia, quickly ousting the murderous Khmer Rouge regime headed by Pol Pot. *See p. 123.*

1982

The Vietnam Veterans Memorial ("The Wall") is formally dedicated in Washington, D.C.

1988

The United States and Vietnam conduct the first joint field investigations of American MIA (missing in action) soldiers from the Vietnam War.

1989

Vietnam withdraws from Cambodia.

1991

Nearing collapse, the Soviet Union ends direct financial aid to Vietnam. *See p. 125.*

The United States opens limited diplomatic relations with Vietnam.

1994

February 3 – The United States lifts its thirty-year-old trade embargo against Vietnam.

1995

July – Full diplomatic relations are established between the United States and Vietnam. *See p. 125.*

2000

November 16-19 – U.S. President Bill Clinton pays a three-day official visit to Vietnam.

2004

The first American commercial airline flight since the end of the Vietnam War lands in Ho Chi Minh City.

2005

June 19 – Vietnamese Prime Minister Phan Van Khai makes the first visit to the United States by a Vietnamese leader since the end of the war.

SOURCES FOR FURTHER STUDY

Appy, Christian G. *Patriots: The Vietnam War Remembered from All Sides.* New York: Viking, 2003. In compiling this collection of stories and anecdotes about all areas of the Vietnam conflict, Appy interviewed more than 350 people. A valuable collection of first-hand accounts.

Caputo, Philip. *10,000 Days of Thunder: A History of the Vietnam War.* New York: Atheneum, 2005. This lavishly illustrated work, written by an award-winning journalist and Vietnam War veteran, brings together a string of short chapters discussing key events, weapons, and people involved in the war.

Karnow, Stanley. *Vietnam: A History.* Rev. ed. New York: Penguin Books, 1991. Probably the most famous general history of the Vietnam conflict. Karnow experienced Vietnam firsthand as a journalist, and he provides a readable, insightful, and exciting account of the war.

Kissinger, Henry. *Ending the Vietnam War: A History of American's Involvement In and Extrication from the Vietnam War.* Rev. ed. New York: Simon & Schuster, 2003. A condensed and updated version of several other books by the former Secretary of State, this volume offers Kissinger's distinct account of the Vietnam conflict and the central role he played in it.

Marrin, Albert. *America and Vietnam: The Elephant and the Tiger.* New York: Viking, 1992. An excellent introduction to the Vietnam War, Marrin's work covers the various political, social, and economic aspects of the war.

Myers, Walter Dean. *A Place Called Heartbreak: A Story of Vietnam.* Austin, TX: Raintree Steck-Vaughn, 1993. Myers has written several novels about Vietnam and his story-telling flair is evident in this nonfiction account of the exploits of Major Fred Cherry, a fighter pilot who was shot down over Vietnam and held in a North Vietnamese prison for over seven years.

Neu, E. Charles, ed. *After Vietnam: Legacies of a Lost War.* Baltimore and London: Johns Hopkins University Press, 2000. This collection of lectures delivered at Johns Hopkins University in 1998 offers young readers a glimpse into the major issues that remain alive for academic scholars of the Vietnam War. Each of the five authors approach the topic in a slightly different way, and offer interesting perspectives on the war and its legacy.

Wormser, Richard. *Three Faces of Vietnam*. New York: F. Watts, 1993. Wormser uses three different perspectives—that of an American soldier, a Vietnamese civilian, and an American antiwar protestor—to reveal different ideas about the meaning of the war in Vietnam.

BIBLIOGRAPHY

Books and Periodicals

Adler, Bill, ed. *Letters From Vietnam*. New York. Ballantine Books, 2003.

Anderson, David L. *The Columbia Guide to the Vietnam War*. New York: Columbia University Press, 2002.

Appy, Christian G. *Patriots: The Vietnam War Remembered from All Sides*. New York: Viking, 2003.

Balogh, Brian. "From Metaphor to Quagmire: The Domestic Legacy of the Vietnam War." In *After Vietnam: Legacies of a Lost War*. Edited by Charles E. Neu. Baltimore and London: Johns Hopkins University Press, 2000.

Berman, Larry. *No Peace, No Honor: Nixon, Kissinger, and Betrayal in Vietnam*. New York: Free Press, 2001.

Boettcher, Thomas D. *Vietnam: The Valor and the Sorrow*. Boston and Toronto: Little, Brown, 1985.

Buzzanco, Robert. *Vietnam and the Transformation of American Life*. Malden, MA: Blackwell, 1999.

Caputo, Philip. *A Rumor of War*. New York: Henry Holt, 1996.

Caputo, Philip. *10,000 Days of Thunder: A History of the Vietnam War*. New York: Atheneum, 2005.

DeGroot, Gerard J. *A Noble Cause?: America and the Vietnam War*. New York: Pearson Education, 2000.

Dorland, Gil. *Legacy of Discord: Voices of the Vietnam War Era*. Washington, DC: Brassey's, 2001.

Doyle, Edward, and Stephen Weiss. *A Collision of Cultures: The Americans in Vietnam, 1954-1973*. Boston: Boston Publishing Company, 1984.

Duiker, William J. *Ho Chi Minh*. New York: Hyperion, 2000.

Dunn, John M. *A History of U.S. Involvement*. San Diego, CA: Lucent Books, 2001.

Dunnigan, F. James, and Nofi, A. Albert. *Dirty Little Secrets of the Vietnam War*. New York. St. Martin's Press, 1999.

FitzGerald, Frances. *Fire in the Lake: The Vietnamese and the Americans in Vietnam*. Boston: Little, Brown, 1972.

Gardner, Lloyd C. *Pay Any Price: Lyndon Johnson and the Wars for Vietnam*. Chicago: Ivan R. Dee, 1995.

Gibson, James William. *The Perfect War: The War We Couldn't Lose and How We Did.* Boston: Atlantic Monthly Press, 1986.

Gilbert, Marc Jason, ed. *Why the North Won the Vietnam War.* New York: Palgrave, 2002.

Hay, Jeff, ed. *Richard M. Nixon.* San Diego, CA: Greenhaven Press, 2001.

Hearden, Patrick J. *The Tragedy of Vietnam.* 2nd ed. New York: Pearson Longman, 2005.

Herring, George C. *America's Longest War: The United States and Vietnam, 1950-1975.* 3rd ed. New York: McGraw-Hill, 1996.

Jorgenson, Kregg P. J. *Acceptable Loss.* New York: Ivy Books, 1991.

Karnow, Stanley. *Vietnam: A History.* Rev. ed. New York: Penguin Books, 1991.

Kissinger, Henry. *Ending the Vietnam War: A History of American's Involvement In and Extrication from the Vietnam War.* Rev. ed. New York: Simon & Schuster, 2003.

Lee, J. Edward, and H. C. "Toby" Haynsworth. *Nixon, Ford and the Abandonment of South Vietnam.* Jefferson, NC, and London: McFarland, 2002.

Marrin, Albert. *America and Vietnam: The Elephant and the Tiger.* New York: Viking, 1992.

McMahon, J. Robert, ed. *Major Problems in the History of the Vietnam War.* Lexington, Massachusetts and Toronto: D.C. Heath, 1990.

Moore, Norton John, ed. *The Vietnam Debate: A Fresh Look at the Arguments.* Lanham, MD, and London: University Press of America, 1990.

Moss, George Donelson. *Vietnam: An American Ordeal.* 3rd ed. Upper Saddle River, NJ: Prentice Hall, 1998.

Neu, E. Charles, ed. *After Vietnam: Legacies of a Lost War.* Baltimore and London: Johns Hopkins University Press, 2000.

O'Nan, Stewart, ed. *The Vietnam Reader.* New York: Anchor Books, 1998.

Palmer, Bruce, Jr. *The 25-Year War: America's Military Role in Vietnam.* Lexington, KY: University Press of Kentucky, 1984.

Pratt, Clark John, compiler. *Vietnam Voices: Perspectives on the War Years 1941-1982.* New York: Viking, 1984.

Prochnau, William. *Once Upon a Distant War.* New York: Times Books, 1995.

Schell, Jonathan. *The Real War.* New York: Pantheon, 1987.

Schulzinger, Robert D. *A Time for War: The United States and Vietnam, 1941-1975.* New York: Oxford University Press, 1997.

Shawcross, William. *Sideshow: Kissinger, Nixon, and the Destruction of Cambodia.* Rev. ed. New York: Cooper Square Press, 1987.

Sheehan, Neil. *A Bright Shining Lie.* New York: Vintage Books, 1988.

Summers, Harry G., Jr. *Historical Atlas of the Vietnam War.* Boston: Houghton Mifflin, 1995.

Truong Nhu Tang, with David Chanoff and Doan Van Toai. *A Vietcong Memoir.* San Diego, New York, and London: Harcourt Brace Jovanovich, 1985.

Tucker, Spencer C. *Encyclopedia of the Vietnam War: A Political, Social, and Military History.* 3 vols. Santa Barbara, CA: ABC-CLIO, 1998.

Tucker, Spencer C. *Vietnam.* Lexington, KY: University Press of Kentucky, 1999.

Vandiver, E. Frank. *Shadows of Vietnam: Lyndon Johnson's Wars.* College Station: Texas A&M University Press, 1997.

Wolff, Tobias. "After the Crusade." *Time,* April 24, 1995.

Wormser, Richard. *Three Faces of Vietnam*. New York: F. Watts, 1993.

Young, Marilyn B., John J. Fitzgerald, and A. Tom Grunfeld.*The Vietnam War: A History in Documents*. New York: Oxford University Press, 2002.

Online

Battlefield Vietnam. http://www.pbs.org/battlefieldvietnam

Country Studies. "A Country Study: Vietnam." http://lcweb2.loc.gov/frd/cs/vntoc.html

The History Place Presents the Vietnam War. http://www.historyplace.com/unitedstates/vietnam/

Vietnam Online. http://www.pbs.org/wgbh/amex/vietnam

Vietnam War. http://www.vietnampix.com

The Wars for Vietnam. http://vietnam.vassar.edu

DVD and VHS

Dear America: Letters Home from Vietnam. VHS. New York: HBO, 1987.

The Fall of Saigon. DVD. Boston: WGBH, 2006.

The Fog of War. DVD. Culver City, CA: Columbia TriStar Home Entertainment, 2003.

The Long Way Home Project. 4 vols. VHS. Castle Rock, CO: Flickers Films, 2002.

Vietnam: A Television History. 4 vols. DVD. Boston: WGBH, 2004.

PHOTO CREDITS

INDEX

(ill.) denotes illustration

A

Abrams, Creighton, 60, 65, 117, 226
Abu Ghraib prison, Iraq, 118
Agent Orange, 46, 116, 119
Agreement on Ending the War and Restoring
     Peace in Vietnam. *See* Paris Peace Accords
Al Qaeda, 116
American Friends Service Committee, 100
An Xa, 165
Annam Province, 8
anti-Semitism, 143
antiballistic missile systems, 150
antiwar movement, 4, 43-44, 47-48, 56, 61,
     65, 69, 93, 119, 141, 161, 197-99, 228
     criticism of, 104-105, 107, 108, 110, 213
     Democratic National Convention
          (Chicago, 1968), 62, 63 (ill.), 107-108
     dissolution of, 107, 108, 110-11
     influence of, 99-100
     Kent State shootings, 71, 109, 162
     legacy of, 111-12
     origins and growth of, 100-01, 102,
          103-104
     reaction to Tet Offensive, 106-107, 172
Ap Bac, 30
Apocalypse Now, 120
Arab-Israeli War, 145
Army of the Republic of Vietnam (ARVN),
     26, 34, 41, 42, 65, 81, 171

     performance of, 30, 52, 60, 68, 73, 76,
          82, 87-89
ARVN. *See* Army of the Republic of Vietnam
atrocities, 51, 88-89, 111, 116, 215-18
attrition, 44, 90, 91-92
Au Lac, 6
Ayers, B. Drummond, Jr., 93

B

Bach Dang, Battle of, 7
Ball, George, 38-39
          biography, 129-32
Balogh, Brian, 119
Bao Dai, 14, 20, 23, 25, 155, 156, 179
Battle for Hue. *See* Hue, Battle for
Battle of Bach Dang. *See* Bach Dang, Battle of
Battle of Hamburger Hill. *See* Hamburger
     Hill, Battle of
Bay of Pigs invasion, 150
Bernstein, Carl, 163
Bien Hoa, 38
Binh Xuyen, 23
Binh Zuyen, 156
Black Panthers, 107
body counts, 45, 91-92, 116, 151
          See also Vietnam War, casualties in
Buddhist Crisis, 31-32, 157
Bundy, McGeorge, 38, 131, 189-91
Bundy, William, 87
Bush, George H.W., 115, 125
Bush, George W., 116, 119

C

C. Turner Joy, 36
CALCAV. *See* Clergy and Laity Concerned about Vietnam (CALCAV)
Calley, William, 88, 89, 215
Cam Lo, 200
Cambodia, 122-23
    secret bombing of, 64
    U.S. invasion of, 69-71, 109, 146, 162, 219
Can Lao, 26
Canton, China, 134
Cao Dai, 12, 23, 156
Cao T'o, 6
Caputo, Philip, 88
Carter, Jimmy, 132, 147
Castro, Fidel, 150
Catholic Peace Fellowship, 103
Catholics, Vietnamese, 8, 23, 156
Catton, Philip, 155
Central Intelligence Agency (CIA). *See* U.S. Central Intelligence Agency (CIA)
China, 65, 86, 112, 144, 193
    diplomatic relations with United States, 74, 76, 145, 162
    rule over Vietnam, 6-7
    support for North Vietnam, 42, 77, 135, 220
    support for Viet Minh, 14-15, 19
Christmas bombings, 78, 146, 162
CIA. *See* U.S. Central Intelligence Agency (CIA)
Cimino, Michael, 120
City College of New York, 143
civil rights movement, 62, 93, 100-101, 112, 119, 197, 199
Civil Rights Act of 1964, 33, 140
Civil Rights Act of 1966, 198
Clean Air Act of 1965, 33
Cleary, Gottlieb, Steen and Ball, 130
Cleary, John, 70 (ill.)

Clergy and Laity Concerned about Vietnam (CALCAV), 103
Clifford, Clark, 55
Clinton, Bill, 115, 119, 125
Cochin China, 8-9, 14
Colburn, Larry, 215-18
Cold War, 34, 101, 119, 130, 144, 150, 162, 180
Columbia University, 106
Coming Home, 120
Committee to Re-Elect the President (CREEP), 162
communism
    fall of, 115, 124
    U.S. efforts to contain, 15, 19, 24, 30, 34, 35, 67, 86, 114, 136, 141, 144, 160, 171
    Vietnamese, 6, 11, 15, 28, 97, 137, 154-55, 165
Confucianism, 7
Confucius, 7
Conrad, Joseph, 120
Convoy of Tears, 82
Coppola, Francis Ford, 120
Cox, Archibald, 163
CREEP. *See* Committee to Re-Elect the President (CREEP)
Cronkite, Walter, 4, 49, 54, 107
Cuban Missile Crisis, 130, 150

D

Daley, Richard, 62, 107
Danang, 8, 41, 83
De Niro, Robert, 120
Deer Hunter, The, 120
DeGroot, Gerard J., 100
Demilitarized Zone (DMZ), 28, 233
Democratic Kampuchea. *See* Cambodia
Democratic National Convention (Chicago, 1968), 62, 63 (ill.), 107-108
Democratic Party, 108, 139, 142, 162

Democratic Republic of Vietnam (DRV), 13,
    19-20, 135, 136, 177, 179
    See also North Vietnam; Vietnam
détente, 76, 162
DeVoto, Bernard, 129
Dickey, Charlie B., 212, 214
Diem, Ngo Dinh. *See* Ngo Dinh Diem
Dien Bien Phu, siege of, 15-17, 16 (ill.), 167
Dien Cai Dau, 236
*Discipline of Power: Essentials of a Modern
    World Structure, The,* (Ball) 132
DMZ. *See* Demilitarized Zone (DMZ)
domino theory, 24, 32, 33, 114, 131, 150,
    152, 180
Douglas, Helen Gahagan, 160
Downs, Fred, 113
Doyle, Edward, 96
draft resistors, 93
DRV. *See* Democratic Republic of Vietnam
    (DRV)
Duke University, 159
Dulles, John Foster, 25 (ill.)
Duong Van ("Big") Minh, 42, 83, 158

E

Easter Offensive, 169
Eisenhower, Dwight D., 25, 25 (ill.), 26, 62,
    85, 144, 160, 171, 187, 220, 221
    and domino theory, 24, 180-81
El Salvador, 115
Ending the Vietnam War (Kissinger), 27, 47, 60
environmental movement, 119
ExCom, 130

F

"Facing It," 236-37
Fallows, James, 152
Farm Credit Administration, 129
Federal Reserve Board, 207
Fellowship of Reconciliation, 100
films, 120-21, 152

Fire in the Lake, 5
First Blood, 120
Fishburne, Laurence, 121 (ill.)
FitzGerald, Frances, 5
Fitzgerald, John J., 90-91
Fleischer, Ann, 145
Fog of War, The, 152
Fonda, Jane, 120
Ford, Gerald R., 81, 145, 147, 163
Ford Motor Company, 149
fragging, 94
France, 19-20
    colonial rule in Vietnam, 5-6, 7-10, 13-
        14, 133, 135, 154, 155, 165-67, 177-
        78, 179, 182
    See also French-Viet Minh conflict
free speech movement, 101
free-fire zones, 46
French Indochina, 8
French Revolution, Declaration of, 177
French-Viet Minh conflict, 14-17, 19-20,
    135-36, 155, 166-67
    See also France, colonial rule in Vietnam
Frost, David, 163
Fulbright, J. William, 96
Full Metal Jacket, 121

G

Geneva Peace Accords of 1954, 5, 19-20, 22,
    26, 136, 155, 167, 182, 187, 188, 208,
    231, 233
Georgetown University, 147
Gia Long, 7
Giap, Vo Nguyen. *See* Vo Nguyen Giap
Gibson, James William, 96
Glading, David L., 212, 213-14
Gold Star Order, 169
Goldwater, Barry, 37
Goldwater-Nichols Defense Reorganization
    Act of 1986, 117
Gorbachev, Mikhail, 152

Great Depression, 129, 139, 159

Great Society programs, 3, 33, 86, 101, 105, 140

Greenway, H.D.S., 4

guerilla warfare, 44-45, 90, 135, 168, 172, 187, 191

Gulf of Tonkin Resolution, 36-38, 71, 100, 102, 141, 151, 186-88

H

Haiphong Harbor, 77

Haldeman, Robert, 67

Hamburger Hill, 121

Hamburger Hill, Battle of, 60

Harriman, Averell, 204

Harvard University, 143, 148, 171

Hearden, Patrick J., 46, 125

Heart of Darkness, The, 120

Herring, George C., 47

Hiss, Alger, 160

Hitler, Adolf, 143

Ho Chi Minh, 11 (ill.), 11-12, 15 (ill.), 17, 20, 22, 26, 28, 34, 42, 46, 67, 97, 155, 156, 165, 166, 167, 177, 204, 223-24
    biography, 133-37
    issues Vietnamese Declaration of Independence, 5, 13, 135, 177-79

Ho Chi Minh Campaign, 82

Ho Chi Minh City, 83, 137

Ho Chi Minh Trail, 28, 39, 40 (ill.), 41, 69, 75, 81

Hoa Hao, 12, 23, 156

Hoffman, Abbie, 107

Holocaust, 143

Hopkins, Welly, 138

House Un-American Activities Committee (HUAC). *See* U.S. House of Representatives, Un-American Activities Committee (HUAC)

HUAC. *See* U.S. House of Representatives, Un-American Activities Committee (HUAC)

Hue, 4, 31, 51-52, 83, 89, 154, 165, 221

Humphrey, Hubert H., 62, 63, 108, 142, 161

Hussein, Saddam, 115, 116

I

Ia Drang, 46

ICP. *See* Indochinese Communist Party (ICP)

In Retrospect: The Tragedy and Lessons of Vietnam (McNamara), 33, 55, 151, 152

India, 193

Indochina, 6, 180

Indochina War. *See* French-Viet Minh conflict

Indochinese Communist Party (ICP), 11-12, 134, 166

Indonesia, 208

Iran, 132

Iran-Contra affair, 115

Iraq War, 115-16, 118

Irvin, John, 121

J

Jackson State University, 109

Japan, 12, 13, 135, 148-49, 166, 178, 181

Jim Crow laws, 139

Johns Hopkins University, 192

Johnson, Claudia Alta "Lady Bird" Taylor, 139

Johnson, Lucy Baines, 139

Johnson, Lynda Bird, 139

Johnson, Lyndon B., 5, 32, 35 (ill.), 36, 43 (ill.), 44, 48, 52 (ill.), 56 (ill.), 65, 86, 87 (ill.), 100, 101, 131-32, 136, 144, 150, 151, 161, 172, 189, 219, 220, 221
    and peace negotiations, 47, 59-60
    biography, 138-42
    decides not to seek reelection, 54-57, 99, 105-107, 112, 202, 211
    escalates U.S. involvement in Vietnam, 37, 39
    Great Society programs, 3, 33, 86, 101, 105, 140

Gulf of Tonkin Resolution, 37, 186-88
    reacts to Tet Offensive, 57, 202-11
    speech at Johns Hopkins University, 43,
        192-96, 208
    views of antiwar movement, 104-105
Johnson, Sam Ealy, Jr., 138

K

Karnow, Stanley, 20
Kennedy, John F., 19, 29, 30, 32, 41, 62, 86,
    101, 130, 140, 144, 149, 150, 151, 160,
    210, 220, 221
Kennedy, Robert F., 56, 62, 107
Kennedy-Nixon debates, 160
Kent State University shootings, 71, 109, 162
Kerry, John, 111
Khmer Rouge, 69, 70, 122-23
kill ratio, 91
King, Martin Luther, Jr., 62, 99, 103, 107
Kissinger Associates, 147
Kissinger, Henry, 27, 60, 63, 64, 70, 77, 79
    (ill.), 161, 223
    and peace negotiations, 47, 74
    biography, 143-47
Kleberg, Richard, 138-39
Komunyakaa, Yusef, 236-37
Korea, 193
Korean War, 19, 171
Krulack, Victor, 29
Kubrick, Stanley, 121
Ky, Nguyen Cao. See Nguyen Cao Ky

L

Lao Dong, 22, 28
Lao People's Democratic Republic. See Laos
Laos, 122, 187, 188
    invasion of, 75, 146, 219
Le Duc Tho, 74, 79 (ill.), 146, 147
League for the Independence of Vietnam. See
    Viet Minh
LeMay, Curtis, 148-49

Lend-Lease Administration, 129
Lenin, Vladimir, 134, 165
Lin, Maya, 236
Lincoln, Abraham, 142
Lodge, Henry Cabot, 32, 157-58, 222, 223,
    224
Lon Nol, 69, 70

M

MAAG. See U.S. Military Assistance Advisory
    Group (MAAG)
MACV. See U.S. Military Assistance
    Command, Vietnam (MACV)
Maddox, 36
mandarinate system, 7, 154
Mao Zedong, 136
March on Washington to End the War in
    Vietnam, 102-03
Martin, Graham, 83
Marx, Karl, 134, 165
Mat Tran Dan Toc Giai Mien Nam. See
    National Liberation Front (NLF)
McCain, John, 119
McCarthy, Eugene, 56, 61, 106
McGovern, George, 77, 162
McNamara, Mary Craig, 148
McNamara, Robert S., 33, 35 (ill.), 38, 44,
    54-55, 90, 130, 131
    biography, 148-53
Medicaid, 33, 140
Medicare, 33, 140
Medina, Ernest, 215, 216
Mendenhall, Joseph, 29
Military Assistance Advisory Group (MAAG).
    See U.S. Military Assistance Advisory
    Group (MAAG)
Military Assistance Command, Vietnam. See
    U.S. Military Assistance Command,
    Vietnam (MACV)
Millians, Dan, 217

Minh, Duong Van ("Big"). *See* Duong Van
    ("Big") Minh
Missing in Action, 121
MOBE. *See* National Mobilization Committee
    to End the War in Vietnam (MOBE)
Moratorium Day, 109
Morris, Errol, 152
mutual assured destruction, 149
My Lai massacre, 88-89, 116, 215-18

N

napalm, 46, 116
NASA. *See* National Aeronautics and Space
    Administration (NASA)
National Aeronautics and Space
    Administration (NASA), 139
National Council for Reconciliation, 78
National Emergency Committee of Clergy
    Concerned about Vietnam, 103
National Liberation Front (NLF), 28, 74,
    136, 168, 200
       founding charter of, 182-85
       See also Provisional Revolutionary
          Government (PRG); Viet Cong
National Mobilization Committee to End the
    War in Vietnam (MOBE), 103-104, 109
National Youth Administration (NYA), 139
nationalism, Vietnamese, 6, 10, 12, 97, 114,
    135, 137, 151, 155, 165, 166, 182
NATO. *See* North Atlantic Treaty
    Organization (NATO)
Navarre, Henri, 15-16
Nazi Party, 143
New Deal programs, 129, 139
New York Times, 64
Ngo Dinh Diem, 25 (ill.), 34, 136, 167, 183,
    184
       biography, 154-58
       fall of, 30-32
       government of, 26-27
       rise to power, 23, 25
       U.S. support for, 29, 30

Ngo Dinh Kha, 154
Ngo Dinh Khoi, 155
Ngo Dinh Nhu, 26, 29, 156, 158
Ngo Quyen, 7
Nguyen Ai Quoc. *See* Ho Chi Minh
Nguyen Cao Ky, 42, 43 (ill.), 79, 87
Nguyen dynasty, 7, 10, 14
Nguyen Khanh, 42
Nguyen Ngoc Loan, 54 (ill.)
Nguyen Sinh Cung. *See* Ho Chi Minh
Nguyen Tat Thanh. *See* Ho Chi Minh
Nguyen Van Thieu, 42, 43 (ill.), 49, 53, 68,
    74, 87 (ill.), 87, 146, 205-206, 231
       and Paris Peace Accords, 77-78, 79, 80
       fall of, 81-83
Nhu, Madame, 32, 156, 157, 158
Nhu, Ngo Dinh. *See* Ngo Dinh Nhu
Nicaragua, 115
Nixon doctrine, 224-25
Nixon, Julie, 159
Nixon, Patricia, 159
Nixon Presidential Library and Birthplace, 164
Nixon, Richard M., 60, 66 (ill.), 140, 142, 231
       biography, 159-64
       diplomacy of, 74, 145
       invasion of Cambodia, 64, 69-71
       letter to Ho Chi Minh, 223-24
       "madman" strategy, 67
       peace negotiations, 108-109, 145
       presidential campaigns of, 62-63, 77
       resignation of, 81
       "Silent Majority" speech, 109, 219-30
       Vietnamization plan, 59, 65-68, 219,
          227-28
       withdraws U.S. combat troops from
          Vietnam, 78, 99, 109-10, 132
Nixon, Thelma "Pat" Ryan, 159
NLF. *See* National Liberation Front (NLF)
Nobel Peace Prize, 147
Norris, Chuck, 121
North Atlantic Treaty Organization (NATO),
    115

North Vietnam, 42, 136, 141, 155, 192, 210, 220, 231
  advantages and disadvantages in Vietnam War, 85, 97-98
  assessment of war effort, 96-98
  atrocities committed by, 88, 89
  invasion of Cambodia, 122-23
  peace negotiations, 74, 77, 78, 79
  strategy in Vietnam War, 168-69
  Tet Offensive, 3-4, 48, 49-52, 50 (ill.), 89, 105, 142, 168, 172, 200-201, 202, 205
  U.S. bombing of, 38, 39, 46, 60, 64, 77, 78, 90, 110, 136-37, 141, 146, 151, 162, 189, 192, 194, 202, 203
  victory in Vietnam War, 81-83
  See also North Vietnamese Army (NVA)
North Vietnamese Army (NVA), 41, 49, 59, 69, 70, 76, 81, 89, 98, 168
  Ho Chi Minh Campaign, 82, 83
  recollections of soldiers, 200-201
  See also North Vietnam
Northwestern University, 129
nuclear weapons, 149-50
Nuclear Weapons and Foreign Policy (Kissinger), 144
NYA. *See* National Youth Administration

O

Office of Strategic Services (OSS). *See* U.S. Office of Strategic Services (OSS)
Ohio National Guard, 71, 109
Operation Dewey Canyon III, 111
Operation Linebacker, 77, 78, 146
Operation Ranch Hand, 46
Operation Rolling Thunder, 38, 39, 41, 46, 136-37, 192
OSS. *See* U.S. Office of Strategic Services (OSS)
O'Nan, Stewart, 236

P

pacification, 60, 68, 157

Paris Peace Accords, 67, 77-80, 146-47, 162
  text of, 231-35
Past Has Another Pattern, The (Ball), 132
Pathet Lao, 75, 122
Peace Corps, 101
Pentagon Papers, 65, 162
People's Army of Vietnam (PAVN), 135
People's Liberation Armed Force (PLAF). *See* Viet Cong
People's War: People's Army (Vo Nguyen Giap), 98, 169
Pershing Sword, 170
Persian Gulf War, 115, 118
Personalism, 157
Pham Van Dong, 12, 124, 166
Phan Boi Chau, 10-11
Phuoc Long, 81
Platoon, 121
Pleiku incident, 39, 190
poetry, 236
Pol Pot, 122
"Port Huron Statement, The," 101
Potter, Paul, 102-03
POW. *See* prisoners of war (POW)
PRG. *See* Provisional Revolutionary Government (PRG)
Princeton University, 236
prisoners of war (POW), 77, 79, 80 (ill.), 121, 231, 234-35
Provisional Revolutionary Government (PRG), 74, 78, 231
Pulitzer Prize, 236

Q

Quang Ngai Province, 88
Quang Thai, 165
Quang Tri Province, 200
Quoc Hoc, 154

R

REA. *See* Rural Electrification Administration (REA)

Reagan, Ronald, 24, 114 (ill.), 114-15, 118, 147, 152, 163, 173
Red River Delta, 6
refugees, 53, 82 (ill.), 122, 203, 221
Republic of Vietnam (RVN), 25, 136
    See also South Vietnam
Revolutionary Party for a Great Viet Nam, 165
Revolutionary Youth League of Vietnam, 134
Rhodes, Alexander de, 7-8
Rhodes, James, 109
Richards, Robert, 180
RN: The Memoirs of Richard Nixon (Nixon), 163
Roosevelt, Franklin D., 129, 139
Royal Lao, 75
Rubin, Jerry, 107
Rumsfeld, Donald, 118
Rural Electrification Administration (REA), 195
Rusk, Dean, 52 (ill.), 130
Russian Revolution, 134
RVN. *See* Republic of Vietnam (RVN)
Rwanda, 115

S

Saigon, 3
    fall of, 83, 147
    U.S. Embassy in, 51, 79, 83
    See also Ho Chi Minh City
SALT. *See* Strategic Arms Limitations Treaty (SALT)
Savage, John, 120
Savio, Mario, 101
Schell, Jonathan, 85, 96
Schlesinger, Arthur M., Jr., 29
School for Law and Administration (Hanoi, Vietnam), 154
Schulzinger, Robert D., 51
search-and-destroy missions, 45, 88, 90
segregation, 139, 197
September 11, 2001, terrorist attacks, 116
Sheen, Martin, 121 (ill.)

Shoup, David, 104
shuttle diplomacy, 145
Sihanouk, Norodom, 69
Sihanoukville, Cambodia, 69
Socialist Republic of Vietnam, 83
    See also Vietnam
Soldier Reports, A (Westmoreland), 173
Somalia, 115
South Vietnam, 31, 42, 136, 141, 156, 231
    government of, 22-23, 26, 29, 34, 86-87, 102, 131, 156-58, 183, 205, 220
    reaction to arrival of U.S. troops, 42
    See also Republic of Vietnam; Vietnam
Southeast Asia Collective Defense Treaty, 187, 188
Southern Cross, The, 236
Southwest Texas State Teachers College, 138
Soviet Union, 24, 65, 86, 101, 112, 115, 130, 144, 145, 150, 204
    diplomatic relations with United States, 74, 76, 162
    support for North Vietnam, 42, 77, 124, 135, 220, 223
Stalin, Joseph, 134
Stallone, Sylvester, 120
Stevenson, Adlai, 130
Stirm, Robert L., 80 (ill.)
Stone, Oliver, 121
Strategic Arms Limitations Treaty (SALT), 145, 162
Strickland, Hiram D. "Butch," 212-13
Student Nonviolent Coordinating Committee, position paper on Vietnam War, 197-99
Students for a Democratic Society (SDS), 101, 102-103
Summers, Harry G., Jr., 30, 89
sustained reprisal, 189-91

T

Tan Viet Cach Menh Dang, 165

Taylor, Maxwell, 171

Tears before the Rain (Tran Cong Man), 73

Tet Offensive, 3-4, 48, 49-52, 50 (ill.), 89, 105, 142, 168, 172, 200-201, 202, 205
effects of, 52-57, 59

Thanh Nien. *See* Revolutionary Youth League of Vietnam

Thich Quang Duc, 31-32, 157

Thieu, Nguyen Van. *See* Nguyen Van Thieu

Thompson, Hugh C., Jr., 215, 216, 217

Thompson, Llewellyn, 204

Thornton, Charles "Tex," 149

Tibet, 193

Ticonderoga, 36

Tonkin Gulf Resolution. *See* Gulf of Tonkin Resolution

Tonkin Province, 8

Trade Expansion Act of 1962, 130

Tran Cong Man, 73

Tran Le Xuan. *See* Nhu, Madame

Tran Van Huong, 42, 83

Trieu Da, 6

Truman, Harry S., 24, 180

Tuan Van Van, 200-201

Tucker, Spencer G., 76

U

U.S. *See also* United States

U.S. Central Intelligence Agency (CIA), 13, 26

U.S. Embassy, Saigon, 51, 79, 83

U.S. military
atrocities committed by, 88-89, 111, 116
casualties in Vietnam War, 46, 52, 68, 93
changes and reforms following Vietnam War, 116-18
fighting methods used by, 45-46, 90, 91-92
morale and performance of, 68, 92-94, 116, 118
number of troops in Vietnam, 41, 79, 141, 151, 206, 212

prisoners of war, 77, 79, 121, 231, 234-35

psychological impacts of war, 120

recollections of Vietnam War, 212-14, 215-18

views of Vietnamese, 94-96

U.S. Military Academy at West Point, 170, 171

U.S. Military Assistance Advisory Group (MAAG), 25-26

U.S. Military Assistance Command, Vietnam (MACV), 30, 71

U.S. National Security Council, 145

U.S. Office of Strategic Services (OSS), 13

U.S. Strategic Bombing Survey, 129

Uncommon Valor, 121

United Kingdom, 204

United States
Antiwar movement in, 4, 43-44, 47-48, 56, 61, 65, 69, 93, 99-112, 119, 141, 161, 197-99, 228
bombing of North Vietnam, 60, 77, 78, 110, 136-37, 141, 146, 151, 162, 189, 192, 194, 202, 203
commits ground troops to Vietnam, 41-43, 79, 90, 137, 141, 192, 212, 220
diplomatic relations with China and Soviet Union, 74, 76, 145, 162
early involvement in Vietnam, 20, 25-26
efforts to contain communism, 15, 19, 24, 30, 34, 35, 67, 86, 114, 136, 141, 144, 160, 171, 180-81
foreign policy of, 24, 132, 144, 145, 150, 152
Gulf of Tonkin Resolution, 36-38, 71, 100, 102, 141, 151, 186-88
invasion of Cambodia, 109, 146, 162, 219
legacy of Vietnam War, 114-19
reaction to Tet Offensive, 53-57, 59, 105-107
restores diplomatic relations with Vietnam, 125-26

strategy in Vietnam, 34-36, 44-46, 54-55, 59-60, 64, 65, 67, 85-87, 89-92, 131, 145-46, 171-73, 180-81, 189-91, 192-96, 219-30

support for South Vietnam, 29, 30, 81-82, 86, 102, 156, 167-68, 187, 188, 193, 209

withdraws combat troops from Vietnam, 65, 67, 68, 70, 78, 79, 109-10, 132, 152, 161, 162, 169, 219, 220, 221, 226, 227

See also U.S. military

University of California, Berkeley, 101, 148

University of Hanoi, 165

University of Michigan, 101, 102

University of Oriental Workers (Moscow), 134

V

Vann, John Paul, 76

VC. *See* Viet Cong (VC)

Versailles Peace Conference of 1919, 133

Viet Cong (VC), 28, 29, 34, 38, 39, 46, 59, 68, 89, 92, 97, 130, 136, 141, 157, 168, 182, 189, 216, 231

fighting methods used by, 45, 90, 135, 168, 172, 187, 191

Viet Minh, 28, 97, 135, 155, 166, 167, 178, 182

creation and growth of, 12-13

war against France, 14-17, 19-20

Vietnam

Declaration of Independence, 5, 13, 135, 177-79

geography, history, and culture of, 6-9

legacy of the Vietnam War, 96, 119-20

partitioned under Geneva Peace Accords, 20, 21 (ill.), 167, 182

postwar economy of, 123-25

reconciliation with United States, 125-26

reunification under Communist rule, 81-83, 121-22, 123-24, 137, 147, 163, 169, 231, 233

under French colonial rule, 5-6, 7-11, 13-14, 133, 135, 154, 155, 165-67, 177-78, 179

See also Socialist Republic of Vietnam

Vietnam Doc Lap Dong Minh Hoi. *See* Viet Minh

Vietnam Moratorium Committee, 109

Vietnam Quoc Dan Dang (VNQDD), 11

Vietnam Veterans against the War (VVAW), 110-11, 119

Vietnam Veterans Memorial, 236-37

Vietnam War

assessment of, 85-98

atrocities during, 51, 88-89, 215-18

casualties in, 46, 51-52, 68, 91, 93, 119, 141

ends in victory for North Vietnam, 81-83, 121-22, 123-24, 137, 147, 163, 169, 231, 233

film representations of, 120-21, 152

impact on United States, 113-19

media coverage of, 4, 30, 53-54, 64, 106-107, 151-52,

peace negotiations, 47, 60, 64, 67, 74, 77-80, 145, 146-47, 161, 162, 169, 203, 204, 208, 210, 222, 223, 224, 226, 231-35

race relations in, 94-96

recollections of, 200-201, 212-14, 215-18

Tet Offensive, 3-4, 48, 49-57, 50 (ill.), 59, 89, 105, 142, 168, 172, 200-201, 202, 205

U.S. ground troops committed to, 41-43, 79, 90, 137, 141, 192, 212, 220

U.S. ground troops withdrawn from, 65, 67, 68, 70, 78, 79, 109-10, 161, 162, 169, 219, 220, 221, 226, 227

U.S. strategy in, 34-36, 44-46, 54-55, 59-60, 64, 65, 67, 85-87, 89-92, 131, 145-46, 150-51, 189-91, 192-96, 219-30

See also antiwar movement

Vietnamese Communist Party, 124

Vietnamese Nationalist Party. *See* Vietnam Quoc Dan Dang (VNQDD)

Vietnamese Restoration League, 10-11

Vietnamization, 65-68, 69, 109, 146, 161, 219, 226, 227-28

VNQDD. *See* Vietnam Quoc Dan Dang (VNQDD)

Vo Nguyen Giap, 12, 13, 14, 16, 42, 48, 97 (ill.), 135
    biography, 165-69
    war strategy, 97-98

Voight, John, 120

Voorhis, Jerry, 159

Voting Rights Act of 1965, 33, 198

VVAW. *See* Vietnam Veterans against the War (VVAW)

W

Walken, Christopher, 120

Wall Street Journal, 106-107

Wallace, George, 63, 108

Wallace, Randall, 121

War Powers Act, 81

War Resisters League, 100, 102

Washington Post, 163

Watergate scandal, 65, 81, 162-63

Weiss, Stephen, 96

West Point. *See* U.S. Military Academy at West Point

Westmoreland, John Ripley, 170

Westmoreland, William C., 41, 44, 48, 53, 60, 90, 105
    biography, 170-73

Westmoreland, "Mimi" Childs, 170

Whittier College, 159

"Whiz Kids," 149

Williams, Thomas, 213

Wilson, Woodrow, 133-34, 230

Winter Soldier investigations, 111

"Wise Men," 55

Wolff, Tobias, 96

women's liberation movement, 112, 119

Woodward, Bob, 163

World Bank, 152

World War I, 133, 230

World War II, 12, 13, 116, 130, 135, 143, 148-49, 166, 170-71

Wormser, Richard L., 108

Wu-ti, 6

Y

Yippies, 62, 107

Younge, Samuel, 197

youth movement, 119

Yugoslavia, 115